IF IT'S NOT SEEN, DOES IT EXIST?

A Modern Battle Maiden's Trials In Light of Abuse, Autism, Death, Divorce

A Memoir

by

Heidi Reince Rasmussen

with

Marilyn Murray Willison

ISBN: 1515254585
ISBN 13: 978-1515254584

BOOK COVER DESIGN

My cover **concept** was to create—with **symbolic significance**—the following:

Title conveys that the trials I would face were not only unforeseen, but also not actually seen when they did occur, which made all the complicated circumstances even more challenging.

Faith presents a similar challenge, since it is in believing that seeing *then* becomes possible—not, as most of us would like to think, vice versa.

The combination of the **compass (points)** that intersect the **cross** represents direction and guidance by God, who brings **light** and **protection (shield)** from the cover's fiery backdrop reflected by the four trials—**Abuse, Autism, Death, and Divorce**—which **simultaneously confronted** me, and I would **battle** against. In my mind, this cover is a **visual** representation of my **painstaking** yet **valiant victory**.

~~ Cover Illustration Digitally Designed by My Younger Son ~~

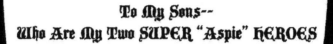

To My Sons--
Who Are My Two SUPER "Aspie" HEROES

With All My Love Always,
Your "Battle-Maiden" Mom

CONTENTS

~~ What to Expect When Your Child Has ASD ~~

~~ Early Intervention and Treatment Options ~~

~~ Notable "Breakthroughs" from Recent Studies and

Helpful Hints ~~

~~ Asperger Syndrome and Spotlight on Celebrities ~~

FOREWORD

While I was a young girl, I would often have the volume dial on my nightstand's clock/radio turned down low so that I could listen to music as I fell asleep. Perhaps that is why—as an adult—I always played soft music (like lullabies) while I rocked my baby boys before I'd put them in their cribs. Those gentle sounds always helped to lull them off to sleep.

And years later—after my divorce—I often found myself falling asleep as I listened to the *Delilah* radio broadcast. Her show has been on the air from 7 p.m. to midnight each weeknight. She takes phone calls from listeners who share their stories. Delilah then plays what she calls a "dedication," which is either appropriate music for a particular situation or a song that has been requested by the listener.

Most people tend to connect emotionally with music—perhaps (in part) because it catches their attention as they associate past experiences or memories. Since music has a unique ability to reach into our soul and move us, it can quickly bring people together. I have often found almost-eerie similarities between a caller's situation and my own. Eventually, from listening to her programs, I've even learned that Delilah had (also) been divorced, and (like me) had given birth to a son who'd later been diagnosed with an Autism Spectrum Disorder (ASD). I could definitely relate!

When I first heard Mark Schultz's song "He's My Son" on Delilah's radio show, the lyrics hit my heartstrings so strongly that I found myself in tears. I was the divorced mother of two young sons who'd both been diagnosed with high-functioning autism—a neurological disorder that is a lifelong disability. Since no cure is yet available, their future is (unfortunately) uncertain.

I had a sinking hopeless feeling after my sons were diagnosed, much like the way I'd felt when I'd learned about my Mom's unexpected late-stage cancer diagnosis. Both realities took a physical as well as an emotional toll. (Several people told me that they'd noticed a measurable weight loss as I simultaneously juggled Mom's death, my divorce, and my sons' developmental struggles.)

After my initial "numb" feeling, I eventually realized that instead of using my energy to cry, I needed to "muster up." I had to find the courage to struggle forward with the recommended treatments, and hope for good results from a well thought-out coping strategy. Needless to say, what I really needed was to stay strong, and not allow my burdened spirit to be either broken or worn down by the challenging events in my life.

So those evenings when I'd listened to Delilah before falling asleep really helped me—the music of the night almost always offered comfort and strengthened my spirit. I once heard Delilah tell her listening audience, *"Music is what feelings sound like,"* and that was exactly the validation I needed to hear at the end of a long, challenging day. Her words helped me optimistically look forward to the next tomorrow. She'd been with me for a long time—little did I know how much farther my journey would take me in the turbulent years to come...

NOTE: My sons and I relied on the healing power of music to help us cope—each in our own way—with the challenges we faced. Music can soothe the spirit, and it helped us heal from the variety of hurts that came our way. Whenever I mention a song title (and artist) that played a significant role in our lives within these pages, I highly encourage you to look up and/or listen to the actual song lyrics. Each has meant so much, and has echoed the prose of a particular chapter in this book.

INTRODUCTION

As I write this book, I am a 54 year old woman who—for the past 24 years—has been an at-home mom to my first son, who was born in 1991, and my younger son, who was born three years later. I never expected that my life would be where it is today, and—in retrospect—I often find myself feeling that my biggest flaw is the tendency to be a chronic optimist. So, when I realized that the emotional foundation of my well-ordered life was crumbling beneath my feet, I felt emotionally paralyzed with fear, indecision, and shock. That is when I remembered something that I had learned as a teenager—i.e., my name "Heidi" is German in origin, derived from Hildegard or Hilda, and its definition is "Battle Maiden!" Who would have thought that (perhaps) my actual name might be a precursor for what I would face in the years ahead?!

With the encouragement and support that I have received from friends and others—even people who may not really know me—I have managed to write my first book. The entwined elements of abuse, autism, cancer, and faith have all had a common thread in my life, and they each fit with the title for this book: *If It's Not Seen, Does It Exist?* What's more, I think that what distinguishes my story from others is the fact that I found myself confronted not only by one (or more) of these four elements *within the span of a lifetime*—which would have been challenging enough—but by *all of them (simultaneously)* during a considerably compressed period of time!

There have been times in the past when I have been told by others that I tend to be a storyteller—and now I realize that I really have a worthwhile story to tell. I truly believe that I—and my sons—have experienced unique challenges that can provide both information and inspiration to those who are in the midst of their own transforming troubles. It is never easy to bare one's soul—especially when emotional chaos lies beneath the surface of one's daily life. But if I have learned anything from what I have experienced over the last several years, it is that honesty truly does set you free.

1

If you picked up this book, you are probably wondering how divergent elements like abuse, autism, cancer, divorce, and faith can all relate to my life. Well, I have lived and been surrounded by them…and somehow managed to survive the trials that they posed. I can now truthfully say that I have experienced more real-life twists and turns than you would ever think possible.

Domestic abuse is a topic that many people prefer not to talk about because it is simply too uncomfortable. Outsiders and family members readily understand the syndrome *if* the abusive spouse or significant other is a "low-down" bum who cannot keep a job and/or has a substance abuse problem, etc. But it is not so readily acknowledged by others if (or when) that person has a high social profile or a high-ranking, high-paying job. Especially if—when in public—there are always smiles, and others (mistakenly) assume that he or she "couldn't hurt a fly." Oftentimes, in reality, that abusive person is more like a Dr. Jekyll and Mr. Hyde when it comes to appearing one way in front of others as opposed to his or her "behind-the-scenes" private behavior at home. This is truly shameful, since the very individuals these people should love—their family—are the ones who get hurt the most.

I have two sons who have both been diagnosed with Asperger Syndrome (or high-functioning autism), which is a neurological disorder that causes the brain to process information "differently." Outwardly, my boys look "normal," but in certain circumstances, their brains simply do not function like those of other "neuro-typical" males their age. And, unfortunately, this triggers behavior that other people often find abnormal, atypical and/or disruptive. In the early to mid 1990's, information about **Asperger Syndrome/Autism** was not readily available the way it is today. Getting a correct diagnosis for my sons was a challenging search, and actually became more like a "process of elimination for other disorders/disabilities," long before we realized that it was a form of high-functioning autism named Asperger Syndrome.

As a self-appointed advocate or ambassador for autism/Asperger Syndrome, I chose to make my sons' needs a priority—they required and received my regular presence in their daily lives. This helped them to make gainful developmental strides, in spite of their disorder/disability.

Therefore, the main thread of my life as their Mom has been to be my sons' primary caretaker, rather than use my college degree to establish a career.

As millions of Americans know, **cancer** can sneak up on people before they even realize they have it. And that's when, unfortunately—as in my mother's case—it becomes too late to either address the disease or look for a cure. My amazing mother was a dynamic, vibrant woman who loved living life "to the fullest." Our family's matriarch—who kept us altogether in more ways than one—could be compared to the hub of a wagon-wheel (with five spokes, i.e., her five children) that kept everyone and everything around her in balanced motion. Once she was removed from us due to her sudden and unexpected death, her children's lives came apart, which made the wheel begin to spin in a wobbly motion. Mom had always given us the strength and encouragement that we needed—and now it became necessary for us to learn how to do that for one another as siblings. This was not an easy task in light of our profound grief over the loss of the wonderful woman whom we loved, and who had loved each of us so much.

My sons were only 5 ½ and 2 ½ years old when my mom (their "Gommy") suffered her unexpected and untimely death due to cancer. I was challenged to find faith and strength (for both my sons and me) during that dark time of pain and sorrow. I—understandably—felt isolated and alone. And if that were not enough, I was soon faced with the ugliness of separation and **divorce**, due to my husband's physical abuse towards me, and then towards our older son.

My **faith** has sustained me through all the elements of abuse, autism, deaths (of loved ones due to cancer), and divorce, and has helped me to survive. It was during these most difficult times that—at first—I felt that God was farthest away when I really needed Him most. But in time (and with increased faith), I eventually found strength in the saying "Let Go, Let God," or as St. Francis of Assisi stated: "Start by doing what is necessary, then what is possible, and suddenly you are doing the impossible."

Inspired by the Spirit and encouraged by others, I was finally able to validate the worth of my experiences by writing this book. I lived

3

through a long period of emotional uncertainty, where I managed to stand by my deeply–rooted convictions. As I am sure you know, it is not always easy or convenient to do what is right. I needed to find a way (with the grace and guidance of God as my "compass") to rise above my challenges and search for my resilience. As a caring woman and mother, my character and values—i.e., the commitment to stand strong for timeless causes that I am so passionate about—helped me endure the challenges I faced. In other words, this book has become a written testament of what I believe is God's purpose for me in this life.

After you have read my story, I hope that you will be able to walk away with some insights and thoughts that will positively affect your life and touch the lives of others, as well. My purpose for compiling this book is to provide a voice for others who deserve and need to be heard (rather than just be denied and ignored).

I had to ask myself: "Why not become a better person because of your trials and tribulations, and choose to be a survivor rather than a victim?" And then I realized that when faced with challenges, it should not be about "Why me?" but instead about "What can I do with—or how can I change—a difficult situation?" It was almost as if I'd received "instructions" that told me to stand up for myself and my children. After all—I began to understand—if you don't meet challenges head on, who will?

Life has taught me that success is measured not by how much money you have (as many people would like to think), but rather by what obstacles you have overcome! In retrospect, I can now see that the focus of my story turned out to be a mother's need of fortitude—for her children, her family members, her faith, and herself. My hope is that reading this book will help you deal with life's struggles, inspire you to share hope with those who need it, and then work to help others on their own challenging journey through life. In closing, let me refer to a statement made by Oprah: "You are not your past; you are what you give to your future!"

~ ~ ~ ~ ~ ~ ~ ~ ~ ~ ~ ~

NOTE: I've written this book as a *memoir*—"a narrative composed from personal experience…based on personal knowledge…an account of something noteworthy" as defined by the Merriam-Webster Dictionary. With integrity of intention, I have recounted my recollections and reflections of the events and experiences from memory—the growth that I experienced elicited by the challenges in my life. I've chosen to use pseudonyms—fictitious names—for many of the depicted characters. I've done my very best to write about the events in my life and the lessons I've learned—with compassion and honesty—in order to both enlighten and encourage those who share the bond that so unexpectedly defined my life.

Preparing--Unknowingly--
For the Part
(My Purpose)

CHAPTER ONE

How the H--- I Got Here

When most people think of 2001, they think of 9-11. But for me, 2001 was the year when I was tested—as never before—and I was leveled to the lowest point I'd ever thought possible.

I can't erase from my memory that dismally disappointing—even depressing—day in the "dead of winter" of that year, I'd been "shell-shocked" for a second time in less than two months, and it rocked my very foundation! I'd received the Family Court Commissioner's Decision and Order Amending Judgment, which changed (I'd had the primary placement of our two sons since our divorce) to *physical placement of the minor children on a yearly basis.* The joint placement decree was designed to **alternate primary physical placement** on a **SIX MONTH basis.** What is more, I learned that my Attorney had not presented—in a timely manner—my Financial Disclosure to the Family Court Commissioner, as she'd requested at the hearing. Consequently, the child support amount was greatly skewed in my ex-husband's favor, and I wasn't given an opportunity to oppose his (and his Attorney's) financial proposal.

I really felt beat up by life—both literally and figuratively. It's difficult to stand up to one's abuser, but when the court system (particularly in custody hearings) does not want to see such unsavory facts presented—this allows a certain attorney's abuser client to "save face"—it is like suffering abuse from the court, as well. In my case, this practice put my sons in harm's way. How inane that I was able to escape from my husband through a divorce, but my sons were placed (by the court) with their father—who had abusive behavior and anger management issues! As a mother, I was unable to exhale until I knew that my children would be raised in a safe place—which up to that ruling I had already provided for them.

What is more, our two sons had struggled with developmental delays since birth, and only a few months earlier had been more accurately diagnosed with what had become known as Asperger Syndrome—a form of high-functioning autism. Autism is a spectrum disorder (from high to low functioning), and abuse could also be considered a spectrum—i.e., behaviors should be treated (in either case) rather than be overlooked just because they aren't always evident. My ex-husband and his attorney plus the family court system tried to silence me—they were all armed to shut me up and shut me down!

The fact that I had also lost my "rock" in life—my mother (who was a woman of strength)—to an unexpected and untimely death due to cancer had been undeniably overwhelming. I couldn't help but look back and wonder how my life had evolved to this point—how had I ended up in this situation?

~ ~ ~ ~ ~ ~ ~ ~ ~ ~ ~ ~

I have been told that I arrived at 2 p.m. on November 5, 1960, but my expected arrival date was October 31st, which would have been Halloween. I came into the world like a "great pumpkin" at 8 pounds, 11 ounces, and became my parents' (Helen and Jim Reince) biggest baby. My parents had suffered a late-term miscarriage of the baby who would have been the brother born between my older sister and me, so I became their fourth child/third daughter. Naturally, they had hoped for another son.

Ever since childhood, my mother had been a true theatre aficionado. My two older sisters and I, therefore, were not given common names like Mary or Jane, but—instead—theatrical monikers. I was named Heidi—after the heroine of the book/movie about the young girl in Switzerland. A few years after I was born, my parents had—once again—another daughter.

My four siblings and I shared a lengthy age span. My only brother—the oldest in our family—was sixteen years older than my youngest sister; and there was a three to five year spread in age between each of my other sisters and me. So when the youngest sister was only two-years old, my brother was already a college student.

8

Since both of my parents were Catholic, my siblings and I were baptized at the parish church that they attended. At a young age, my parents' close connection with both the Catholic Church and our neighborhood impressed upon me how important community relationships are, and how much they need to be valued.

The families in my neighborhood were close, and we enjoyed fun times during the summer when we would all be invited to our neighbors' cottages. My younger sister and I would work with the other neighborhood kids to put on regular kiddie carnivals in the neighbor's front yard—complete with games that we'd made, and prizes we'd collected. It was the "big event" of the summer for us, as well as for the other neighborhood children.

Summer days also meant time spent at my friends' houses or they would be at mine, where we would play double-solitaire or ping-pong. Sometimes we would gather friends and form teams to play a game of baseball or kickball in our backyard or at the schoolyard (which was just a house away from mine). Occasionally, we might decide to jump on the neighbor's trampoline, which they let all the neighborhood kids use.

Later, before dusk, my friends and I would gather to play a game that was similar to hide-n-seek, but we were on teams. The neighbors' yards (which were adjacent to one another) made up what was our local playing "field." My younger sister and I always seemed to be the first to be called home for the night by our dad, and we would plaintively wonder "Why?"—after all, it was not yet dark, and all the other kids were allowed to stay out and play.

At night after the ten o'clock news, Mom would tune into "Feature Theatre" (which was another name for the late night movie), while she ironed our family's clothes—including the bed sheets and underwear! She would say that late at night was the best time for her to do the ironing since we kids would be in bed, and there would be no distractions. And that's why—to this day—I remember lying in my bed at night straining to listen to "Feature Theatre" until I fell asleep.

Mom tended to be a "night owl," which would prompt my friends, (whenever I had them over at my house for a slumber party) to impatiently ask "When will your mom finally go to bed?" Remember, the point of a slumber party was to try and stay up all night while the parents were asleep. Well, my friends learned that my mom's schedule was an obvious impediment to this idea!

My dad's parents had a cottage on the bay where he had spent time as a boy and—later—where he would bring all of us so that we could spend a few days as a family with Grandma and Grandpa. Occasionally, some of my cousins from out of town would visit us there as well. As I look back now, I have to wonder: (1) "How did we all fit (much less sleep) in that small cottage?" and (2) "How did Grandma and Grandpa survive all the noise and commotion?!" When it would be time for us to go home, my siblings and I (along with my parents) would get in our car. As we drove away down the cottage road, we would see Grandma and Grandpa (who usually had one arm draped around her shoulder), stand in the yard and wave good-bye to us. They were so sweet to welcome us all, but I can (now) totally understand—after they'd had so many people all crammed together "under one roof" for several days inside their quaint little cottage on the bay—their relief as they saw us drive away!

Back at home, Grandma and Grandpa lived just around the corner from us in the neighborhood. Whenever my friends and I would visit, we would arrive at their back door and be welcomed with Grandma's homemade cookies. Soon, our golden retriever, Sandy, who had visited their home with us kids on occasion, learned the way to their back door, and would arrive there—all by herself. Of course, Grandma would immediately—and happily—give her a cookie!

~ ~ ~ ~ ~ ~ ~ ~ ~ ~ ~

My older siblings and I attended public school through First Grade since our parish school only offered Second through Eighth grades. Our parish church, convent, and school were all located practically in the backyard of my family's house. Consequently, it was easy for me to wake up for school in the morning, get dressed in my white blouse and "black-watch plaid" school uniform, and then get to school by cutting through our backyard—all in under 20 minutes!

Since I was a shy child, I preferred to blend in with the background than to stand out in the forefront. Fortunately, I received good grades as a student, which pleased my parents. The only "suggestion" that my mother ever heard at a parent-teacher conference was that I needed to participate and raise my hand more often in the classroom. Shyness and self-consciousness (which I had as I grew up) were probably due to the fact that—in every class—I was the larger-sized, almost tallest, not-so-attractive girl. So my intelligence, which helped me earn good grades, became what I was known for among my sisters. My oldest sister was "pretty," while my second-oldest sister was "funny," and my younger sister was "athletic"—and me? I was "smart." At that time and place, being a smart girl was not considered particularly advantageous. And when it came to boys' interest in girls, it not only seemed less attractive, but perhaps even "threatening" because—back then—males were automatically assumed to be more intelligent than girls!

This flawed idea was even at play within my parents' marriage relationship. My father had graduated from Marquette University, my mother from Mount Mary College, and they married in 1947. The next year, with the arrival of my brother, they started a family. Mom was a stay-at-home mother (like most wives of that era), while Dad had a successful career at IBM. My mother, whose college degree had been in Education, started taking part-time substitute teaching jobs, which ultimately led to a position as a part-time English teacher at the all-girl Catholic high school in our city. She taught English classes that were scheduled in the afternoons, and—like the other teachers—she would have to stay a half hour after classes had been dismissed for the day in order to be available to students who needed extra help.

Since my younger sister and I would get out of school earlier than Mom did, we became "latch-key kids" (unlike most other kids in our neighborhood, whose moms stayed at home and did not work outside the home). I had been given the house key so that I could unlock the door for my younger sister and myself when we arrived home from school each afternoon. After we'd changed out of our school uniforms into our "play clothes," she and I would make ourselves a snack, and then watch some TV until Mom came home an hour or so later. When my father arrived home for dinner after his day of work at IBM, he would occasionally complain that his wife—our mother—worked outside the home. His mother had stayed home each day to raise him and his siblings while his father went to work each day, and he preferred that type of "traditional" old-fashioned family structure.

My grade school years seemed to pass by "without a hitch," except for the Seventh grade. In January of that year, I came down with a bad bout of the flu that kept me in bed for over a week. When I finally felt somewhat better, I returned to school, but in just a couple days I had a relapse—which put me back in bed again. Ultimately, I was forced to stay home from school—to recuperate from the flu—for nearly a month. Consequently, I had lost over ten pounds, and when I returned back to school, my school uniform hung on me—it was way too big. From that day forward, I felt light physically as well as psychologically—my flu-induced weight loss had erased my self-conscious feelings about my size. I'd "turned the corner" just in time to enter my pre-teen years!

CHAPTER TWO

Stepping Up and Out—of Shyness

Due to my parents' high regard for Catholic education, I attended (as did my sisters) our city's all-girl Catholic high school—where my mom taught Junior English. (My brother attended one of the two local all-boy Catholic high schools.)

As high school freshmen, my best friend and I both campaigned among our classmates to be elected as Student Council Representatives. She was elected, but I was not. When I came home from school that day, my mom suggested, "Why don't you campaign for Class Officer?" I replied, "Are you kidding?! I have already lost the Student Council election!" Whenever we were faced with a difficult situation, Mom would say, "Pick yourself up by your bootstraps (and get back on the horse)." She had enjoyed horseback riding as a girl, and this was her way to get her optimistic point across: "Don't give up...you'll never know the outcome unless you try again!"

With this in mind, I decided on my campaign slogan and ran for Freshman Class Officer. I received the largest number of votes, and, consequently, was elected Freshman Class President. It was now my duty to stand up and speak in order to represent our Freshman Class; and that meant I had to overcome my lifelong shyness, which I eventually managed to do. When I became a sophomore, I had enough courage to run—and then be elected as—Student Council Representative. I had found my place within my high school's student government, and finally felt a bit more confident about being (and speaking) in front of people.

During my Junior year I took a leap of faith...or perhaps it was fate! One of the two all-boy Catholic high schools was putting on the musical play *Oliver*, and in study hall one day, a classmate mentioned that she planned to attend the play try-outs that were scheduled for that night. She asked me if I would try out. I'd enjoyed musical theatre for years because while I'd grown up, I'd heard my mom either (a) listen to record albums of Broadway musicals while she did her housework, (b) play her favorite Broadway tunes on our piano at home whenever she took a break from doing housework, or (c) take us to summer music theatre shows at the nearby college. Sometimes she would even take part in these productions. When I mentioned to her that my friend wanted me to accompany her that evening and try out for the play, Mom enthusiastically encouraged me to go. She sat down and played the piano while I stood, looked over her shoulder, and sang the lyrics on the sheet music. I practiced singing a few different musical tunes for the audition, and ultimately I chose "Matchmaker, Matchmaker" from the Broadway musical *Fiddler on the Roof.*

Just a few hours later, I was called by name to take the stage and sing in front of a small audience scattered in the public high school auditorium. The pianist—who was the choral director at this high school—played a few notes on the piano, gave me his cue, and I then started to sing. I was relieved when I'd finished, and could take my seat again to continue watching the other students' auditions.

Days later, I was informed that I had a solo in the show's biggest musical number "Who Will Buy?" During our ensemble practice, which included all the cast members, I learned that my role as the "woman street vendor selling roses" was to not only start out the song as a solo, but to also sing the first verse *a cappella,* i.e., without any musical accompaniment. And this was to be done while I walked from the back of the auditorium all the way down the center aisle—among the audience—until I reached the stage! Each night before the curtain went up, I had "butterflies in my stomach," but had to overcome this feeling. My job was to go from backstage up the stairs, and quietly walk across the top of the auditorium in order to make my entrance from the back door. There was no time to worry about how I felt, since—before I knew it—I had to take my cue, and start to sing my solo! When the curtain came down for the last time on closing night, I felt a huge sense of accomplishment. This theater venture really stretched me musically, physically, and psychologically—my shyness was replaced with the comfort of becoming more socially outgoing and secure within myself.

Junior year in high school brought me another surprise...my classmates elected me to be on Junior Prom Court. At an all-girl high school, Prom meant that we would have to ask a boy to be our date for our Junior Prom, which was scheduled for late April. During spring break, in March of that year, it was my turn (just as my older siblings had done at this age) to fly with my mom to Southeastern Florida to spend time with my maternal grandmother at her condo. While there, my mom and grandmother took me shopping for the floor-length dress I would wear when—just weeks later—I would stand as part of Prom Court. My best friend and I decided to ask guys who were also good friends, so that we could double-date to this momentous high school event.

My mother had been one of the Junior English teachers at the high school where my sisters and I attended, and fortunately for me—she was liked by most of the students. My mom and I decided (just as my sisters had done) that we would "pretend" that she was just another teacher (instead of our mother) during school hours. Still, I remember that—once the bell rang to dismiss the last class of the day—she might hear the voice of one of us (her daughters) calling out to her in the school hallway, "Hey, Mom, can I drive your car home? And can you get a ride with one of the other teachers?!"

Senior year was also significant because it meant that I would attend what was known as the Charity Ball. It was a formal event that offered parents and graduating seniors the opportunity to enjoy an elegant evening together. It also acknowledged the volunteer services their mothers had contributed toward the needs of the children in our county through this women's organization. Given this long-time tradition—and my mom's involvement—it was my turn (as my sisters had done before me) to be "presented." As required, I wore a white floor-length formal, and was escorted by my father (who was dressed in a black tux), while my name was announced. My mother's name was also called in honor of her volunteer contributions during her term in past years. Since my best friend's mom had also voluntarily served with this women's organization, we again (just as we'd done for our Junior Prom) asked boys who were friends with one another (not the same ones we'd taken to Junior Prom!) It gave us another chance to double-date.

Our parents and adult family members attended this special event and viewed each of the senior girls who were announced individually, and then presented on her father's arm. The Charity Ball evening was truly a memorable experience—I'd felt elegant, and finally realized that I'd become a young woman!

CHAPTER THREE

College Bound

When it came time to decide which college to attend, I knew that my parents had two provisions: First, the college or university needed to be located within, or just beyond, our state borders (Wisconsin) so that the driving distance would take no more than a single day. And the other requirement was that the school be private—i.e., Catholic. Ultimately, choices were narrowed down to two—the College of St. Thomas (now the University of St. Thomas), located in St. Paul, Minnesota, or Marquette University, in Milwaukee, Wisconsin. But after I'd attended an all-girl high school for four years, one of *my* criteria was that the school be co-educational! A weekend visit to each campus for a tour was also a parental prerequisite, and tours were scheduled during my senior year of high school. Both my father and my brother had attended and graduated from MU, while some of my cousins (on both sides of my parents' families) were CST alumnae. Since time (i.e., my senior year) had nearly run out, and I'd been accepted by both undergraduate schools, I finally decided to attend the College of St. Thomas.

I took the freshman year course load, and one class that stood out for me that year was taught by a faculty member who was also a Catholic priest. Since he'd had some experience from work that he'd done with one of the local broadcasting stations, his class lectures were of interest and inspired me, particularly because of their relevance to the working world beyond our college campus.

Throughout my first year away at college, I only traveled home for Thanksgiving, Christmas/Semester Break, and Easter. To drive home after my classes were over on Friday afternoons meant that I would arrive shortly before midnight, and then be back on the road again by noon on Sunday in order to arrive back at CST that night. I did well academically, but as the year progressed I began to feel—in my freshman year—that I had already outgrown CST. I had second thoughts, and approached my parents to discuss my desire to transfer from the

17

smaller college to the larger university (Marquette), which I had also visited the year before. When I was informed that my freshman grades at CST were transferable, I ended my first year of college at CST, and made plans for a bigger adventure on a much larger campus.

Similar to what had first happened at CST, that fall I arrived at my assigned dorm room at MU before my new roommate. I nervously waited for "her" to arrive, and remember—as I unpacked my things in the dorm room—I heard my R.A. say (from out in the hallway) that my roommate had arrived. We were introduced, and before we knew it, we had clicked and decided to go out for a beer. We were both "transfer" students to MU, and across the hall from our dorm room were two other "transfer" students, who had also been placed together as roommates.

One day, as I walked down the dorm hallway to the girls' community bathroom on our floor, one of those two other "transfer" students noted that I was wearing a "CST" T-shirt. She stopped and asked, "Might CST stand for College of St. Thomas?" I replied, "Yes, it does." She then told me that her brother had attended and graduated from CST, and she mentioned a few of his college friends' names. It was beyond belief for us to learn that one of my cousins, who had also attended and graduated from CST, was her brother's best friend! From then on, we also became (and stayed) best friends! A couple of months later, we learned that we had been born just one day apart in the same year—so each year at MU we celebrated together from my birthday all the way through the following day, which was hers! We also carried on the tradition that her brother and my cousin had started during their college years, which was to perform like Diana Ross and The Supremes when we heard Motown songs such as "Stop! In The Name of Love" or my favorite "Ain't No Mountain High Enough." We had so much fun together!

~ ~ ~ ~ ~ ~ ~ ~ ~ ~ ~

With each day that passed, I felt that MU was a great fit for me—academically as well as socially. Spring of my sophomore year, I'd briefly dated a guy on campus who planned to graduate from MU at the end of the semester. Thanks to his referral, I landed a summer job (as his replacement) with a local insurance company in downtown Milwaukee.

My roommate told me that she planned to study abroad during our upcoming junior year, and hoped to rent an apartment, which she would sublet to me over the summer. With this arrangement—and my newfound ability to make some money of my own—I convinced my parents to allow me to live in Milwaukee during the summer. It was my first time to take a break and not go home for the summer.

Occasionally, while I'd been away at college, one of my roommates would tell me that my younger sister was on the phone, and really wanted to talk to me. Over the years, our parents had slowly grown apart, and their increasingly unhappy marriage caused them (and their children) a lot of stress. When my college roommates and friends told me that they found that sad information hard to believe (because my parents seemed like "such nice people"), I answered that they were right—my parents were wonderful people as individuals, but not when they were together.

My senior year, my parents finally allowed me to live on MU's campus in an apartment—rather than in a dorm room. Since it was my last year of college, most of my classes were in Marketing—the specialization I'd chosen within the College of Business Administration. With my grades at an all-time high, I took on a part-time job as a Sales Associate at The Limited in the Grand Avenue Mall in downtown Milwaukee. This position gave me experience with the retail world, and I soon learned how to make sales (and earn commission) while I worked on my feet and wore heels—which led to sore, tired feet at the end of the day. I also learned (groan) how—in the retail world—holidays were spent at work. Since I was scheduled to work the day of Christmas Eve, my mom drove two hours in winter weather to pick me up at work—only to drive us both back home to Green Bay in time for the Christmas Eve celebration with my family. (I wrapped my presents for the family at the last minute, only to have them be opened by others in a matter of minutes!)

My senior year at MU was my most successful, both academically and socially. My friends and I enjoyed fun times together with a couple of beers at the campus bars, and we occasionally attended MU's basketball games. Only a few years earlier in 1977 (under Coach

19

Al McGuire), the NCAA Champions were the MU—then-named—"Warriors." In other words, someone who (a) fights in battle, (b) is known for having courage and skill, or (c) is engaged with some struggle or conflict. Of similar significance (if not coincidence), there stood—in the middle of MU's campus—a small stone chapel from medieval France that had been reconstructed and dedicated to St. Joan of Arc, whose lifetime showed magnificent courage as she stood for justice with God as her compass—even as she faced death when "burned at the stake." (In retrospect, it seems to resonate with the recurrent "Battle Maiden" theme of my later adult life. Perhaps, my transfer to the Jesuit college of Marquette University—also home of the "Warriors" and the reconstructed medieval chapel named for St. Joan of Arc—subconsciously, if not consciously, was a fit for me much more than I'd realized at the time, especially in light of what was to come.)

I graduated from Marquette University in May of 1983 with a Bachelor of Science degree in Business Administration with a Marketing specialization. Due to the size of our graduating class, the ceremony was held in a large building in downtown Milwaukee that had arena-type seating. Immediately after our class commencement ceremony, each of MU's colleges then held its own assembly at various facilities located on or around the campus. As graduates of the College of Business Administration, we were called by name, and handed our diploma as we crossed the stage. My younger sister was there, as were my parents who—in previous years—had watched my brother (as well as my dad himself) take part in this same ceremony. I was the third in my family to become proud alumnae of Marquette University.

~ ~ ~ ~ ~ ~ ~ ~ ~ ~ ~ ~

NOTE: At one of the events during our college class's graduation week, the song "Steppin' Out"—released as a single in August 1982 by Joe Jackson (about the anticipation and excitement of a night on the town)—was played. Perhaps, it was meant to be a theme song to send off our 1983 college class into the real world. It was a perfect musical choice for me. Since I'd stepped up and out of shyness during my teenage years, now had my B.S. college degree in hand, and was full of anticipation and excitement about what I might face personally (as well as professionally)

20

in my post-grad world—at that time, the word "autism" hadn't even crossed mind. And little did I know that it would later shadow my early years as a new mother with children who would be (ultimately) diagnosed with a high-functioning Autism Spectrum Disorder (ASD) named Asperger Syndrome.

CHAPTER FOUR

"Stumbling" Into Adulthood

I'd worked in retail during my senior year of college, and it became evident that the dressy shoes I'd been required to wear had aggravated the flat feet I'd had since birth. (As a Sales Associate at The Limited, I was required to wear women's "corporate" business suits and high heels, which was the fashion trend at that time.) Literally, as well as figuratively, I was "stumbling" into adulthood!

Throughout my childhood years, whenever Mom would take me to shop for new shoes, my choice was limited to only the ones that had shoelaces. Why? Because only they provided enough much-needed support for the fallen arches on both of my feet. Additionally, I often couldn't even take my newly purchased shoes home because before I could wear them, they needed to be "built up" with an additional artificial arch. As a little girl who grew up in the 1960's, I was disappointed that (like my friends) I could neither have nor wear penny loafers. Sadly, it was either tennis shoes or flats with shoelaces for me!

When I became a teenager, arch support orthotic supports were custom-made for me to place inside my shoes. Let's face it—I really would have preferred to wear high heels like my teenage friends—but this was not what my orthopedic doctor recommended. Since I rarely dressed up, on those few occasions, I managed to wear high heels.

But my painful foot issues escalated during my senior year of college when I had to wear heels (along with a fashionable women's business suit) each day when I worked at The Limited. After work, I would literally limp my way from the bus stop to where I lived. My orthopedic doctor—who had told me since childhood that I had one of the worst cases of flat feet he had ever seen for a girl—informed my parents that he could perform surgery to help improve, but not cure, my flat feet. He recommended that my left foot (which was worse than my right) be surgically reconstructed. This operation was scheduled for just after Labor Day weekend the year I graduated from college.

During that summer I also learned that my nose required surgery because it had a deviated septum, which at times adversely affected my breathing. With this news—and my feeling that my nose (especially when seen in profile) was too large—I asked my parents for permission to get a "nose job." Logic told me that since I would be laid up for a couple of months due to my reconstructive foot surgery, I could use the same time to recuperate from reconstructive nose surgery as well! The nose procedure was scheduled for approximately two weeks after my foot surgery.

The day after Labor Day weekend, I was admitted to the hospital, and when I woke up in the recovery room after the operation, I realized that I had a white plaster cast from just below my left knee all the way down to my toes. My parents took me home, and I was laid up in bed for a few days before I learned how to correctly use the crutches I'd need in order to walk during the weeks ahead.

Two weeks later, on the night before I was to be admitted to the hospital (again) for my rhinoplasty, my parents and I sat at the kitchen table. They—with concerned faces—asked me if I was still serious about going through with my nose surgery the next morning. I replied, "Yes, it's something that I really want done, and I'm more than willing to go through whatever it takes."

When I arrived at the hospital the next morning, I received a few double-takes before I was prepped for my surgery. After all, only two weeks before, I'd been admitted for major surgery on my left foot, which was now in a leg cast. In a previous appointment with my surgeon, I had been told that I would not be totally "put under" for the nose surgery. There would be enough anesthesia for me to avoid feeling any pain, but I would still be awake during the procedure.

My doctor talked me through the steps he would take as he proceeded with the surgery. I remember the moment when he said "Now, I'm going to tap on your nose," just as I saw a hammer-like instrument flash before my eyes! He then tapped on my nose, and I heard the cracking sound that was necessary for him to be able to reconstruct my nostril and correct its deviated septum. When the surgery was almost finished, I heard my doctor say to the nearby anesthesiologist that I looked like a "Miss America!" I knew—with the bandages and gauze on my nose, as well as the black and blue areas that were now around my eyes since my nose had been broken during the surgical procedure—that he was teasing. In my mind, however, I realized that the worst was over, and within weeks I would have a more attractive face with a "new, improved" nose!

I was quite a sight as the nurses wheeled me out of the hospital after this, my second major *elective* surgery in just two weeks. When my brother, who lived out of town, came home to visit my parents the following weekend, he walked into the bedroom where I lay in my bed with my left leg (in a cast) propped up on pillows. He saw my bruised eyes, which could be seen through the bandages across my nose, and exclaimed, "You look like you've been run over by a Mack truck!" It really wasn't what I wanted to hear—but then again, what else would a brother say in that situation?! I replied, "I know…but it's worth it! In a few weeks I will have a brand new nose, and I'll no longer limp!"

A few weeks later, I met with my ENT doctor to have the bandages on my face over my nose removed for the big reveal. The reconstructive nose surgery had not dramatically changed my appearance, but *I felt* greatly different and at peace with a distinctive improvement in the way my face looked.

By early November I had celebrated my 23rd birthday, my two surgeries had been successful, I'd recuperated from both, and it was now time (complete with my "new features") to find a job and use the college degree I'd received a few months earlier. Since employment opportunities were slim in 1983, I decided to venture out to a more favorable job market for the Business Administration-Marketing degree I'd recently earned. Dallas, Texas, seemed promising, and since my brother, his wife, and family lived there, I was able to move in with them temporarily until I was able to get on my "own two feet," with a job, apartment, etc.

~ ~ ~ ~ ~ ~ ~ ~ ~ ~ ~

In mid-December, my mom and I left home in Green Bay, Wisconsin—once again with all my belongings (just as when I went off

24

to college in our family car)—to drive down to Dallas, Texas. She loved any opportunity to travel, and although we were tightly packed in the car with all my belongings as well as Christmas presents for my brother's family, Mom was enthusiastic to make this road trip with me. After we celebrated the Christmas holidays at my brother and sister-in-law's house with their children, Mom flew back to Green Bay, and I "hit" the classified listings to look for available job openings in the Dallas area.

I interviewed with large corporations as well as small businesses. But with the low employment rate, it seemed just as hard to land a job in this market as back home—especially for a recent college graduate. I was finally hired by a small graphic design firm that developed illustrated maps—as advertising tools—of businesses in the Dallas area. The company phased out as I did—the area just seemed to be more transient than I was comfortable with. I sincerely appreciated that my brother and his wife had let me stay with them, but at that time, my "small-town girl" side was calling me back home.

On my return from Texas, I'd learned a few valuable life lessons: (1) take a chance—taking the leap of faith always helps you learn something, and (2) going home doesn't necessarily close a door; it can actually open a big door, and there's no shame connected to the undeniable, magnetic call of home.

Once I was back home in Wisconsin, I "pounded the pavement" (as my mom would say) and searched for employment in what was still a dismally weak job market. Occasionally, I would spend time at my oldest sister's home with her husband and their family (as I'd often done in the past), which was less than 40 minutes from Green Bay. During one of my visits, I was invited to interview for a job at a company owned by one of their friends, and was soon accepted for a Front Desk position at one of the company's hotel properties. For the first few months, I learned the operational end of the hotel business, and then—when my training period was over—I was promoted to the Convention Sales Department. As a Telemarketing Representative, I supported the three Sales Representatives who had the hotel's established client accounts. Additionally, I became the Group Tour Consultant, and my responsibility was to further expand this market for the hotel. I enjoyed my work each day because I was at hotels where—for business or pleasure—people almost always enjoyed themselves.

The company I worked for was a family-owned business, run primarily by two brothers who instilled the importance of good customer service in their employees. Fortunately, I learned from their example, and group tour clients often mentioned my name specifically when—during their stay—they completed the hotel's comment cards and/or rebooked a future group tour.

As time passed, I approached the hotel's management and asked to be considered as a Convention Sales Representative. I'd researched and proposed a viable market that was untouched and had not been targeted by the three other Convention Sales Representatives, who had the hotel's established client accounts. This newly created position put me "on the road" nearly four days a week. As I promoted and obtained new convention/meeting group business for each of the company's four hotel properties that I represented, it was the beginning of my Business Development career.

~ ~ ~ ~ ~ ~ ~ ~ ~ ~ ~

NOTE: "Stumbling" into adulthood gave me an appreciation for those with disabilities. I'd had fallen arches since birth, so I'd been unable to do many things that my peers could. They remarked about how I "hobbled" when I could no longer endure a long walk or roller-skate great distances with them. I also became self-conscious about my (to me) unattractive big nose, which I blamed on my hearty (Belgian) ancestors. My motivation behind both surgeries was an attempt to correct and improve these physical features as much as was realistically possible. I thought that they would empower (and improve) me. Little did I know that these qualities—as well as those I'd gained early in my business development career—i.e., compassion for clients and a willingness to search and provide creative solutions to meet their needs, would later play a huge role in my life as a mother with special needs children.

26

CHAPTER FIVE

MEETING THE MAN WHO WOULD FOREVER CHANGE MY LIFE

My marketing development/sales efforts for the four hotels I represented meant weekly travel among the cities of Chicago, Madison, and Milwaukee. I soon learned that so much out-of-town travel was detrimental to my dating life. Unlike my two older sisters—who had been engaged and married while still in their early 20's—I had reached 25, but was still single. Even my little sister had managed to meet a young man and became engaged during her last year of college.

During that same year, my parents' divorce became final— something that was pretty inevitable given their increasingly regular arguments. It was stressful for them as well as for their children— especially for my younger sister and me, who still lived at home during those acrimonious years. In light of their Catholic morals, upbringing, and values, my parents believed that they should "stick it out" together until their youngest child—my little sister—had nearly completed college. As much as children might hope that their parents will stay together and not get divorced, we no longer wanted to see our parents argue and fight with one another. It was obvious that they'd fallen out of love with each other during their 38 years of marriage. Despite my parents' divorce, they each loved us children, and made a disciplined effort to get together to celebrate the holidays (with us and with their grandchildren) as a family.

My younger sister, her fiancé, and I were all in town for a few days to celebrate Christmas that year, and—although recently divorced—my parents took the three of us out to dinner. My sister and her fiancé asked me to join them later that night to meet up with friends at one of the area nightclubs. I thanked them for their invitation, but since I travelled so much for work, a nice quiet night at home felt more appealing. They would not accept my decision, however, so the engaged couple literally—physically—put me in the backseat of their car. Whether I liked it or not, they had "hijacked" me to accompany them to

27

the nightclub as a "third wheel!" I knew that they had good intentions, and really did want me to go out and have a good time with them—no matter how tired I'd said I was!

When we arrived at the nightclub, we discovered that the place was "packed" with people. Fortunately, we found an empty table on the upper level that overlooked the dance floor. While we sat there, my sister made her way through the crowd to find a recently engaged childhood friend who was also there with her fiancé, and then she brought them back to our table. The groom-to-be had brought along two of his friends, who were introduced to us. I sat against the wall at the end of the table between the two newly-engaged couples while they talked across the table to each another. Soon, one of the two friends tried to talk to me above the couples' conversation, and invited me to dance. I declined, however, because I realized that it would disrupt the couples' conversation if I got up from where I was seated. He persisted (and the couples finally realized that he'd invited me to dance), so they all stood up to let me pass through—and they also encouraged us to dance and have fun.

Like the nightclub, the dance floor was packed with people. We didn't have much room to move, and it was so noisy that it was hard to hear one another when we spoke. The next song was a slow dance, so we were then able to talk—and actually hear—one another. I mentioned that I lived out of town, but had grown up in Green Bay, and had been there that weekend to attend my childhood best friend's sister's wedding. When I mentioned their names, he said that he was also good friends with my best friend's brother and brother-in-law. My initial thoughts were that he was teasing me with this information, which seemed somewhat far-fetched. He suggested that I should ask his best friend (who would be at the wedding I would attend that weekend) about how they were connected. The song then ended, the lights went up to signal that it was "bar time," and the place was about to close for the night. The crowd of people that moved toward the coat check separated both of us, so we never had the chance to say "Goodnight."

After the weekend in Green Bay, I headed to Milwaukee and Chicago for that week's scheduled sales appointments. When I returned from my typical work week of three or four days on the road, I stepped inside my apartment to the sound of my (land-line) telephone ringing. I quickly dropped my briefcase, purse, and suitcase to pick up the phone, and heard a male voice greet me. Since I didn't recognize who this was, I tried to solve the mystery and asked several inconspicuous questions, but did so without much success. Finally, I came directly to the point, and asked him where we had met. He then told me about the night we'd been introduced through my sister and her friends—who happened to be his friends, as well. It all became clear—it was Jay!—and during that initial phone conversation we scheduled our first date.

Since Jay lived in Green Bay, I stayed at my mom's house so he could pick me up there for each of our first few dates we scheduled on the weekends. In conversation, Mom learned that my date had been recruited out of college to work as a mechanical engineer at one of our hometown's large local paper plants, and she told him that her father had been the founder of the paper-converting machine company in our hometown. When he mentioned that his brother worked at one of the subsidiaries of my maternal grandfather's company, it was the beginning of our understanding of what a small world it was. With each passing day, my boyfriend and I learned more and more about (and from) one another. The string of coincidences to find out that (1) one of my co-workers at the hotel's Convention Sales Department was his first cousin—she'd even spoken about her favorite aunt and uncle (no name ever came up) who were his parents, (2) I could have met Jay five years earlier at my best friend's sister's wedding when he'd been a groomsman paired with my best friend, who was a bridesmaid—since he was five years older and I'd finished high school just as he'd recently graduated from college—we obviously weren't yet meant to meet at that time, and (3) each of us were friends with members of my best friend's family who lived across the street from my family as we had grown up. Fate can have so much to do with time and place—to fulfill God's purpose for us in life!

We had known each other for over a month when Jay was scheduled to travel overseas—primarily for business, but he had also arranged to include some additional destinations for pleasure. Since we had only dated for a short amount of time, I teased him that he would probably meet some alluring woman while abroad, and never return to revisit either me or Green Bay! But he followed through on my request to send me a postcard from each place he visited, and the one he mailed from the last place on his itinerary asked me to meet him at the airport when he returned to Green Bay.

On my way to the airport, I stopped to pick up a bottle of wine so we could celebrate his homecoming. There was a dusting of snow on the roads, and as I tried to make it to the airport on time, I found myself stuck behind a slow-moving car driven by an older couple. Later, when I saw Jay at the arrival gate, I learned that this cautious-driving couple had been his parents—who were also there to meet him.

We all then went to his house, where his parents had hung a "Welcome Home" banner. He'd brought gifts back for them and his brother, as well as for me—mine was a hand-stitched blouse from Switzerland that was styled like the ones worn by "Heidi" of the Alps! Naturally, I was delighted.

~ ~ ~ ~ ~ ~ ~ ~ ~ ~ ~ ~

While Jay had been abroad, I came to realize how very much I'd missed him—an intense feeling I hadn't had before. Beside the string of coincidences and the favorable impression which each of us had made with one another's family, I believed that fate had brought us together. Our dates in Green Bay included socializing with his friends, many of whom played on a fast-pitch baseball team. Jay was the team's manager who kept games stats using his proficient engineering skills, and also planned the team's annual banquet. Because of his fast-pitch game schedule, I would frequently drive two hours from Milwaukee (where I worked during the day) to Green Bay—nearly 100 miles—in order to attend his evening game. (I knew I was at the right baseball field because when I drove up and got out of my car, I could hear Jay's loud voice—it was distinct and carried clearly in the distance.) Then I would return to Milwaukee for appointments that had been scheduled for the next day! In hindsight, I realized that—in order for me to have made that roundtrip journey so often—I must have really fallen in love with Jay.

I soon began to sense that he felt the same way toward me. On a Saturday when a fast-pitch baseball game was scheduled near where I lived, we began to look at engagement rings together. We looked over the rings in the jewelry cases, and one in particular caught my eye. Since Jay liked it as well, he purchased it, and the plan was for him to formally propose to me the following weekend. As we left the jewelry store and walked down the Avenue together, I suddenly grew short of breath during our conversation. Perhaps it was the excitement of the moment— I realized that I would soon be engaged and be married. I'd found a wonderful man who wanted to spend the rest of his life with me as my husband, and the reality of what that meant overwhelmed me a bit emotionally. I realized that every single aspect of my life was about to change.

Although it may not have been "love at first sight" when we'd first met, I believe that we—instead—shared a "meeting of the minds" type of courtship. We were both college graduates who'd had a few years to settle into our careers and, consequently, we were mature enough—as we'd grown in love with one another—to "know" that we were meant to be a couple. We shared similar interests in movies and music, plus we both enjoyed tennis, waterskiing, etc. Jay told me that he really liked the fact that I was an avid Green Bay Packer fan, and enjoyed watching football—as well as basketball—games with me. We often watched the Packer games on Sunday afternoons together on the couch or we would go to the stadium when we were offered tickets. I liked that he enjoyed the opportunity to dress up for a formal event as much as he liked "dressing down" for a casual outing. We had similar outlooks on the future goals we had as couple. His attentive pursuit "won me over," and I realized that I wanted to spend every day I could with Jay. And, fortunately, he felt that way about me, too!

The following weekend, Jay picked me up, we drove to the one of the upscale hotels where I worked as a convention sales rep, and were seated in a dining room booth that overlooked the water. After wine with our dinner, Jay stepped out of the booth, got down on one knee to propose to me, and then slipped on the ring—which we had previously picked out together—on the third finger of my left hand. It was a perfect night.

Excited to share our news, we then drove to my mom's house to surprise her. She was scheduled to leave the next day on a group tour with friends, and when we walked in the kitchen, she was on the phone talking to one of my sisters. When I held up my left hand to show off my ring, she dropped the phone, and happily hugged both of us.

The next day was the 4th of July, so we drove to Jay's parents' cottage on the lake. In the past, they'd warned us about the local wood ticks, and I'd asked what one would look like. Since his father had compared it to the large brown freckle I have on the back of my left hand, we decided to use a creative way to share our news with them. When we arrived and went inside the cottage to greet them, I exclaimed that I was worried that a wood tick was on my left hand. The minute they began their "inspection," they noticed my beautiful diamond engagement ring; we all hugged, and toasted our future together with a couple of old-fashioneds.

After we celebrated both the holiday and our engagement that weekend at his parents' cottage, we then drove to my dad's house to share our good news with him.

CHAPTER SIX

PLANNING A WEDDING AND BUILDING A HOUSE

After our celebratory July 4th weekend, I went into work that week and approached my manager, who was the Director of Sales for the hotel enterprises. When I told her that I'd accepted my boyfriend's proposal over the weekend, she said that she wasn't too surprised—was it obvious that she'd seen it in my eyes, my smile, the spring in my step, etc.? As required, I gave her my notice, and was later given a good referral to the Green Bay Area Visitor & Convention Bureau, where I was then hired as a Convention Sales Representative. I moved back to Green Bay and into my mom's house because it would help with the planning process for our upcoming wedding, which would take place in Green Bay, where we'd both grown up and had family.

Since Jay had been raised Lutheran and I'd been raised Catholic, we decided that ours would be a "mixed marriage," neither of us would ask the other to convert or change religions. After all, we'd become who we were in the faith that we'd each practiced up to this point in our lives, and the two religions were relatively similar in overall beliefs. It was important to my parents that we would be married—just like my sisters had been—at the same Catholic Church with an evening wedding ceremony. And we agreed to adhere to this family wedding tradition.

We first met with the priest (who'd been at my family's Parish while I grew up and had become friends with my family), and then with Jay's pastor (who'd come to know my parents through my childhood best friend's parents over the years). They knew each other well, which we felt could only enhance the celebration of our marriage. While we married in the Catholic Church, "my" priest would preside over the wedding ceremony, and "Jay's" pastor would also stand on the church altar—both to respectively, take part. We'd felt it was important to convey that our wedding ceremony was truly about two people who—despite our different religions—would become one both in the eyes of God, and of those who attended. Jay and I would receive Communion together—as we became joined as husband and wife! (Jay had been married before—he told me that his first wife had been responsible for the divorce, and this information had been echoed by his family and friends. I was told that he and his then-sweetheart had dated for a few years—many of his friends had become married, so Jay proposed to her. They were married around the first of May, and by fall of that same year they were divorced. He had been in his mid-twenties at the time, and when he met me, Jay was thirty.) Jay went through the process to get his first marriage annulled (which was granted), so that he and I could be married in the Catholic Church.

Since I'd moved back to Green Bay, I'd become a member of the Catholic Parish, which was in the neighborhood where Jay's house was located. Jay informed me that the house had become his when the last of his roommates married and moved out. When Jay had married his first wife, she'd moved into his house with him, but after their divorce, she moved out and he stayed. It was a two-story home with four bedrooms and 2 ½ baths, and since it was located in a nice residential neighborhood, we agreed that I would move in after the wedding.

Those plans changed unexpectedly when Jay and I—for the fun of it—spent an afternoon at the Showcase of Homes, and we both fell in love with one of the houses. Its curb appeal had such charm—it was a two-story home that had an outside upper porch off of the upstairs master bedroom suite—it was unique with its contemporary Victorian style. We hadn't planned to be "in the market," but this house had certainly caught our eye! With his proficient engineering/mathematical skills, Jay decided that he would create a spreadsheet which listed the cost estimates from various local homebuilders (to whom he'd given the blueprint of this particular house's floor plan).

The next step for us was to look at local vacant lots (not too far from Jay's house) that were for sale, but there weren't very many since this area had been built up over the years. We'd heard that there had been a recent land sub-development created where a farmer's old barn had once stood. As a young girl, I'd often ridden my bike in this neighborhood, and seen that old barn—an eyesore—as it stood all alone among the houses that had been built up around it over the years.

When we'd driven into this new sub-development, we found a lot that appealed to us in what would become a "J-shaped" cul-de-sac of about twenty homes. After he'd again put his math skills in motion, Jay told me that if he could sell his home, we would be able to afford and build the house that we'd fallen in love with on this particular lot. When I heard what he'd said, I once again felt that anticipatory shortness of breath—could this really be happening?! Within just a matter of months, I'd become engaged, moved back to Green Bay, taken a new job, started to plan for our upcoming wedding, and finally—WOW—I'd learned that we would be able to build our "dream" house?! I felt the need to pinch myself to wake up—I'd felt so fortunate to think this would become a reality for Jay and me! Since we would have a new life as I became his new wife, we would also have a new start in what would become *our* new home! The memories Jay might have had with his first wife in his current house could be laid to rest in the past as he put "their" house up for sale.

From then on, we scheduled our dates to shop for cabinetry, flooring, light fixtures, wall textures, etc., etc., etc. We had been told that sometimes marriages can be stressed or even broken up when a couple builds a house together—due to all the timely decisions that needed to be made. But Jay and I, evidently, were the exception—at least according to the builder's family, who commented on how well we worked together—(perhaps) because we built a home *while we planned* to get married?!

~ ~ ~ ~ ~ ~ ~ ~ ~ ~ ~

NOTE: As I dealt with all the plans for a wedding and building a house—at the same time, much less—I never thought that those multi-tasking skills would later prepare me as a "case manager" mom for my sons who needed to be "juggled" between various service providers. I quickly evolved into a "battle-maiden" mom. When, in later years, I had to untangle layers of doctor and therapy appointments for my boys, I thought back to my pre-wedding days. Silly me to have thought that bridal issues and home-building plans were super stressful!

CHAPTER SEVEN

WEDDING DAY CEREMONY: PRELUDE TO MARRIED LIFE

Spring was in the air when April arrived and our wedding plans became finalized. The wedding rehearsal had been scheduled for the evening before our wedding day. Jay and I met up at the church with the priest and pastor, our parents, and immediate family, who had all become a part of our wedding party in some way. We went through all the motions, and made a "dry-run" of how our wedding would play out the next day. My younger sister was my Maid of Honor, while Jay's only sibling (his brother) became his Best Man. My two older sisters both stood up with their respective husbands; and although my brother and sister-in-law had recently divorced, they stood up together as well. My childhood "bestest" friend stood up with her brother-in-law, who'd also been Jay's best friend. My youngest sister's fiancé and a good friend of Jay's were ushers, while my two young nieces were to hand out our wedding programs to guests. My mom was escorted to her seat in the first pew by two of my young nephews just before the processional began.

We asked each of my two close college friends to deliver the First Reading and Responsorial Psalm that we'd selected, respectively. A couple words were stumbled across in the First Reading Genesis (2: 18-24); where the last line stated, "That is why a man leaves his father and mother"—she then looked up from the podium at the audience and continued to say "and clings to his *mother*" (when the line read *wife*), "and the two of them become one body." (As I write this book, I look back and wonder if this might have been a foreshadowing of what I would face later in my life!) Later, I told my friend not to worry—after all, that was the purpose of the rehearsal, and I knew that she would have no problems with this reading at our wedding. I felt that Jay and I had been truly blessed to have *all* of our family not only present, but also as participants in our wedding.

When we'd finished with the rehearsal, we all gathered at what was known then as the Towne & Country Supper Club for dinner, which was hosted by Jay's parents. After we had all enjoyed a delicious meal, my friends, Jay and I went to a favorite local bar for after-dinner drinks. Although we learned later that a few of our friends had stayed until "bar time," Jay and I left early so that we would be rested for "our big (wedding) day." Before he dropped me off at my mom's house, we exchanged our wedding gifts with each other—he'd given me a pair of diamond earrings that I was to wear with my wedding dress, and I gave him a gold pocket watch, engraved with his monogram.

Whenever we'd gone dancing, his hand movements looked as if he was swinging a pocket watch on a chain at his side. I'd teased him that he'd created his own signature dance move—and he'd seemed to like that thought! As I gave him the gift, I'd told Jay that I hoped it would become an heirloom that he would hand down someday, if we ever had a son. After he'd walked me to the front door of my mom's house, we kissed each other goodnight—our last kiss as Mr. and Miss!

~ ~ ~ ~ ~ ~ ~ ~ ~ ~ ~ ~

When I awakened the next morning, it dawned on me that by the end of that day, I would be Jay's wife! Mom's house was full of energy and excitement as my three sisters, sister-in-law and I dressed, and soon the wedding photographer showed up to shoot home "pre-wedding" photos.

Once all the photos had been taken, the limousine escorted my father and me from the house—it felt so special to have this moment alone with Dad. As the two of us rode off to the church, I realized that it would be my last ride with him as one of his "red-squirrels"—as he teased us—since I would soon be married and no longer be called by my maiden name. The church wasn't all that far away from home, and when we'd arrived, Dad gave me his hand to help me step out of the limo. My bridesmaids and Mom, who had already arrived at the church, helped me as they gathered up the long train of my wedding dress, and I then slipped into what was known as the "Bride's" room at the back of the church.

I soon heard the church organ play as the male and female vocalists—friends of Jay and mine, respectively—started to sing. I began to feel a bit nervous and had "butterflies in my stomach," just like when I'd had to walk down that center aisle among the high school musical's audience who'd been watching me?! The processional music began and each of my bridesmaids took her turn up the aisle to where she joined her groomsman, and then they walked up on the altar as a couple.

The cue came then for me—my dad took my arm as we began our walk down the center aisle of the church among our invited guests. With each step I took, I tried to remind myself to walk slowly—the long train on my wedding dress certainly helped with that! I smiled as I looked from one side of the aisle to the other, and saw our guests' happy faces. They'd all arrived to celebrate this happy, momentous occasion with us! When we were almost at the altar, I saw Jay—dressed in his tux and tails as he looked at me with a big smile on his face—and I felt just like Cinderella. It was almost as if—just like in the fairytale—I'd made my grand entrance as the "belle of the ball," and caught the eye and attention of the Prince! After my dad shook hands with Jay and said a few words to him, he then kissed me and placed my hand in Jay's. I took his arm as we stepped up on the altar—together as the wedding couple.

The church had the layout of a theatre "in the round" where nearly everyone in the pews could see the activity on the altar. Two kneelers had been placed next to each other in the center for us, while the rest of the bridesmaids were on kneelers to my left while the groomsmen were on kneelers to the right of Jay. When it came time for the First Reading, my college friend looked over at me as she read the lines correctly during the ceremony, and I winked back at her.

Our ceremony was concelebrated with "my" priest and "Jay's" pastor. After the petitions had been read by Jay's pastor, he asked for a moment of silence—during this quiet pause, a woman had come through a door, on the far left of the church, and as she'd walked up the aisle toward the altar, she chanted and ranted. Our two ushers reacted quickly and took her away out of the church. Needless to say, this part of the ceremony hadn't been planned, and people didn't know what to make of this woman's disruptive entrance. Since we were on the altar up in front of everyone, I'd subtly looked at Jay out of the corner of my eye to see his reaction to what had just happened in church. (My first thought was that perhaps this woman could have been Jay's former mother-in-law, since he'd said that—even after their divorce—his first wife's parents, sister, and brother had still liked him.)   But his face looked as dumbfounded as mine and those of others. Consequently, I told myself that this woman must have been a total stranger.

As soon as she'd been ushered out, the ceremony resumed with the exchange of vows and wedding rings, and then—since it was a Mass—Communion was distributed, which we *both* received on this special day as we became a newlywed couple united in marriage.

As the wedding ceremony came to a close, we were given our blessing by both priest and pastor, and then presented as the married couple by name. After our kiss, we walked back down the center aisle, arm in arm, and left the church with our bridal party behind us. Jay and I were then quickly escorted into the waiting limousine. Our plan had been that we would make a special stop—from the time after the church ceremony until the time we would arrive at the hotel lobby for the reception line before the dinner and dance. The limo drove us by the lot where the cement foundation for our new home had been laid just the week before our wedding. We had a glass of champagne as we sat in the backseat of the limo, and after we rolled down the limo window, we toasted to our new foundation—and a new life as husband and wife as well as to our new home!

We then arrived at the hotel to meet and greet our guests in the reception line. We'd selected this hotel for the wedding reception, in part, because of its elegant large white, winding staircase in the lobby, where the bridal party and group pictures would be taken. In the banquet hall, Jay and I sat at the head table with our bridal party, while our parents, family, and friends and other guests were seated at round tables throughout the room.

A live band had been hired to play until midnight. As the wedding couple, Jay and I danced the traditional slow first dance but when the music had been turned up, Jay pulled out his pocket watch to perform his signature dance move. We had a great time as we celebrated

39

with our family and friends, so we decided, as the wedding couple, to stay until the last dance of the night. We thanked our parents, family, friends and guests before we left—still dressed in our formal attire—and drove to an undisclosed hotel out of town, where we'd spend our first night together as husband and wife.

CHAPTER EIGHT

Our First Years as Mr. & Mrs.

The day after our wedding, we arrived back at my mom's house to open our gifts with family. The next day, we were scheduled to leave and drive to Chicago, where early Tuesday morning we would fly to spend our honeymoon in Cancun, Mexico. We'd decided to spend our honeymoon at Cancun because we were both water lovers.

Within a couple weeks after our return to Green Bay, Jay was able to sell his house. Since our new home was under construction until mid-August (and we'd needed to move out of Jay's house over Memorial Day weekend), my mom offered us the use of her cottage on the bay—only a twenty-minute drive north from Green Bay.

We commuted from the cottage daily to our jobs in Green Bay. And each day after work, we either stopped by our new house to view the construction progress or we'd spent time with sub-contractors to finalize our choices of cabinetry, flooring, light fixtures, wallpaper, etc. Early one morning, we received a call at the cottage from one of the subcontractors, who asked us what texture we wanted for the walls in each of the rooms in our new house. And on another morning we were asked how we wanted the front sidewalk cement poured—from the front porch toward the driveway on the side of the house (we had a corner lot) or toward the front curb? Should it be straight, or did we want it to have some curve? Many times we made these decisions during our twenty-minute commute. As much as we'd felt fortunate to have Mom's cottage over the summer months, we rarely had a chance to enjoy either the bay or the water, since we left early in the morning only to often return after dark. We both loved to water-ski, but that summer meant work (on the house), rather than play (on the water).

We were able to spend our first night in our newly-built home in mid-August. It was a hot summer night, and we were so thankful that we'd added a ceiling fan for the upstairs master suite in the building plans!   Within just a few days, we were totally moved in and comfortably settled.

Surrounded by an older, established neighborhood, our new sub-development had been built within a span of almost three years before it was completed. Since all the houses had been newly built, it meant that we—and all of our neighbors—were "in the same boat at the same time" regarding our desire to get to know each other. Whenever we watered or mowed the lawn, our cul-de-sac gave us the opportunity to strike up a conversation while we worked in our yards. Sometimes those talks led to what we referred to as "time for curb beer"—when one of the neighbors would bring out enough cold beers to share with all of us.

Most of the neighbors were in the same age range—I was the youngest—and   we all became good friends through the planned neighborhood holiday parties, couples' golf outings, or neighborhood family picnics at a local park. One of the neighbors and I planned a "Ladies' Get-Away Escape to Chicago for the Day," which included shopping at Water Tower Place, lunch at the Hard-Rock Café, and then "curtain time" for *Steel Magnolias* staged at one of the downtown area theatres. Initially, we'd thought it would be an overnight trip, but many of the neighbors had young children who would be in their fathers' care for more than a day—consequently, it became a daytrip. Since it was an eight-hour drive roundtrip and it would be just for the day, we added the special touch—to be driven in a limousine. The ladies' interest caught on quickly—we'd already booked two limos, and I needed to arrange for an additional limo from another company.

It was quite a sight to see three limos—one of which was a stretch—drive up in our cul-de-sac early on that Saturday morning! Once on the road to Chicago, we enjoyed "continental" breakfast served in our continental limousines. When we arrived in downtown Chicago, people seemed to watch (curiously) to see who would step out of our motorcade of three limousines. Perhaps to their dismay, it wasn't anyone famous—just a group of suburban friends who'd travelled to enjoy a leisurely lunch, shop, and take in a stage show for the day! It was early evening when we came out of the show and were whisked off in the limousine motorcade to ride back to Green Bay. While we'd all sat back and relaxed, we enjoyed wine and cheese all the way home. A thick fog

42

had set in that night—you could hardly see beyond the front hood of the limousine—so we all felt fortunate that we'd left the driving to the professionals!

As a newlywed couple, Jay and I decided to have a couple of years alone together before we started our family, which was something we'd both ultimately wanted. We'd even chosen the lot for our new home, in part, because it was within walking distance of both the parish grade school and the public elementary school. The nearby schools made for a family-oriented neighborhood. At that time, forty young children lived on our cul-de-sac, and before too long we decided that we wanted to join in and add to our neighborhood's children "stats."

~ ~ ~ ~ ~ ~ ~ ~ ~ ~ ~ ~

NOTE: Jay and I felt fortunate to have our own families as well as good neighbors who would provide the perfect "backdrop" when, and if, we became parents. But life would soon teach us that things aren't always what they seem…

CHAPTER NINE

Mrs., Miscarriage, and Longing to Be a Mom

At first, it was difficult for me to conceive, but because we both badly wanted to have children of our own, we decided to get tested. Due to a fertility concern, we put every effort into each method that was suggested to us.

In the fall of 1989, I'd found out that—at last—I was pregnant. We'd been invited by my brother and his girlfriend to meet them in Las Vegas for a weekend, and I had mixed emotions. We hadn't been there before, so I was excited, but something—my gut feeling—didn't seem right. Consequently, we declined the invitation. During what would have been our weekend spent in Las Vegas, I began to hemorrhage, and ultimately miscarried.

We were disappointed—to say the least—but with all our previous efforts and then the miscarriage, we began to wonder if perhaps we weren't meant to have children. It was November, and I'd turned 29 that year. With my maternal instincts in high gear—or perhaps because of the hormonal changes due to my recent miscarriage—I asked Jay to go with me to see a litter of Sheltie puppies, which had been listed in the newspaper classified ads. Jay was a bit hesitant, but I told him that we were "just going to look." Once we arrived at the breeder's home on a farm, however, only one puppy had been left in the litter. We'd noticed that it played well with the breeder's little boys, and (needless to say), we drove back to Green Bay with the sable Sheltie puppy in my lap. Since it was a last-minute decision, we had to make a stop to pick up puppy supplies, so Jay stayed in the car with the Sheltie while I went inside the store. By the time I came back to the car with dog food, toys, and a large dog crate in tow, Jay had bonded with our new puppy. We named her "Bailey" because the color of her sable fur coat reminded us of "Bailey's Irish Cream."

Although that year didn't bring us a child to join the neighborhood children, at least we had a puppy. The local children often came to our door, and asked us if Bailey could come out and play with them in our backyard.

We didn't give up on our efforts to become pregnant. My doctor suggested that I take my temperature each morning (before I got out of bed) with a Basal Body thermometer, which would indicate whether or not I was ovulating. It certainly wasn't convenient for me, but I knew it was worthwhile if it meant that I could become pregnant.

Over the Memorial Day weekend we were invited to join Jay's parents and his brother attend the Indy 500. Jay had told me that one of his life goals was to try to attend every major sporting event he could during his lifetime. So we travelled by motorcoach to Indianapolis, and attended the event with a group tour. When we arrived, I'd felt tired so I told Jay and his family that I would lie down for a nap before I would meet them for dinner. The next day, we attended the Indy 500 race and, as we sat in the stands, watched the cars "whiz by" on the track. Our weekend had let Jay check the Indy 500 off his "bucket list," but when we returned home, I felt fatigued.

A few weeks later, I realized why I'd been so tired—I was pregnant! Since I'd miscarried during my first pregnancy, we decided to keep quiet about our news until I was well beyond the first trimester. I was nauseated on a daily basis throughout my first six months, and ate graham crackers to help fight off the waves of nausea that arrived throughout the day. Even when I'd reached the third trimester, I was still somewhat concerned about having another miscarriage.

Throughout my pregnancy I truly looked like I had a baby "bump." It became quite large and hung somewhat low, i.e., it was really apparent that I was pregnant from both the front and the side. But from my back, I didn't look pregnant at all. My due date was February 9, 1991, and I worried that I would go into labor during a big snowstorm—typical weather for February in wintry Wisconsin. If so, would we be able to make it to the hospital in time for the baby's delivery?

When February 2ⁿᵈ arrived, I teased about our baby being like the Groundhog on that day—ready to come out into the world from its cozy burrow in my belly! We went out for pizza with Jay's parents that evening, and when the waitress asked when I was due, I replied "Anytime now." Her unsettled reaction reflected her silent wish that we would eat quickly and leave before I delivered at the Pizza Hut!

I woke up in the middle of that night—as I had regularly of late—and as soon as I got out of bed, "my water broke." I ran to the bathroom, stood in the shower, and yelled to Jay, who was still sleeping in bed, "Get up! My water broke—it's time to go to the hospital!" He helped me into the car, and quickly drove us to the same hospital where I'd been born. It was around 3 a.m., and as we drove by the dark houses that lined the main street—where so many people were asleep—I thought to myself that I'd like to yell and say, *"Wake up! We're on our way to have our baby!"* I'd also noticed that my earlier severe weather worries had been pointless—it was mild and even rained that night.

~ ~ ~ ~ ~ ~ ~ ~ ~ ~ ~

At the hospital, I was helped into a wheelchair and brought to one of the new birthing suites. This was the trend at that time—while you awaited the delivery of your baby, you could go through labor as if in the comfort of your own home! The only non-residential décor component exception was the bed, which had the traditional medical-look of a hospital room. After I'd dressed in a hospital gown, I sat in the suite's recliner and listened to the classical music that Jay had recorded to help me relax, (as suggested from our Lamaze instructor). The doctor stopped by around 7 a.m. He mentioned that he thought it would take some more time, and told us that he would check back after he'd completed "his rounds."

Within minutes after he'd left the room, I felt that things were definitely about to change due to the strength and frequency of my contractions, so asked Jay to help me get into the bed. After I lay down, I felt a lot of pressure and frantically said to Jay, "Get the nurse in here, NOWWW!" I could hear her—out in the hall—tell Jay that it probably wasn't time. But when she entered the room, and took one look at me, she shouted, "Get the doctor back here, NOW!" I'd dilated from five to ten centimeters in what seemed like no time! The doctor rushed in, and since there wasn't any time for Jay to change into a sterile hospital gown, the nurse threw one over the front of him.

At 9:08 a.m. on February 3, 1991, I heard our baby's first cry as the doctor said, "You have a boy!" From what I could see, our son was a redhead—I'd never thought about having a red-haired child because Jay was blonde, and my hair was brown. (We found out later that one of Jay's grandmothers had red hair, as had some of my mom's aunts.) We'd already picked out the name—"Blake" (I'd always liked that name, and it went well with our long last name) "James" (after my Dad). After an uncomplicated pregnancy and a rapid delivery, Blake's Apgar scores were both 9's, he weighed 8 pounds, 13 ounces, and was 22 inches long.

Our first visitors included "Gommy" (my mother) as well as Grandma and Grandpa (Jay's parents), who were welcomed in the birthing suite within just a few hours of Blake's birth. They talked among themselves in astonishment as they compared the current homey trend of giving birth to "back in their day"—when the father wasn't present and family members only saw the baby through the window of the baby nursery. They (and I) watched in awe while "Dad" gave Blake—as he lay under a warming lamp on a cart that had been wheeled into the suite—his first (sponge) bath with step-by-step instructions from the neonatal nurse. Jay bathed Blake from head-to-toe and I'd heard him say quietly, "Good boy, Blake. Good boy." He especially related—given Jay's interest in football—to the nurse's instructions to hold Blake in a "football hold" next to the side of his body in one hand and use his other hand to wash Blake's head of red hair.

As new parents, the hospital served us a celebratory meal during our stay. As we held our champagne glasses, Jay made a toast to both Blake and me as he said, "I love you very much. I am a proud Dad." He'd brought me flowers and had handed out cigars of blue bubble-gum (as well as chocolates) that said "It's a Boy!"

Blake and I were discharged on the second day of our hospital stay. When we drove up to our home, we were welcomed with a sign that Jay had made and hung from our upper porch. It said "It's a Boy...Blake

James." He had also arranged for a large cut-out stork with a blue bundle hanging from his beak (which stated Blake's name, birth date, and birth weight). It had been placed in our front yard to share with our neighbors—and the world—the news of our new baby!

As new parents, we'd realized the importance of our first "baby"—our dog Bailey—not being jealous of the new baby Blake. Consequently, Jay and I both gave lots of attention to Bailey as we entered the house, while my mom happily held Blake. We then gave Bailey the chance to check out—i.e., sniff—Blake to slowly become acquainted. That day we all settled in at home—all four of us—Dad, Mom, Blake and Bailey.

I'd felt so fortunate and blessed back then. Before I would fall asleep each night, I prayed to God in thanksgiving for our happy marriage and the blessings of new parenthood, and asked that we would continue to be as happy as we were—both as a couple and, now, as a new family!

~ ~ ~ ~ ~ ~ ~ ~ ~ ~ ~ ~

We'd arranged for Blake to be baptized within three months of his birth. Jay and I'd agreed that ours would be a "mixed marriage," but it wasn't quite as clear-cut when it came to decide in which religion our son would be baptized. As much as Catholic and Protestant religions were similar, only one of these two faiths could be chosen for the baptism of our son—how would we decide? Jay wanted our baby to be baptized Lutheran in his church just as much as I wanted our son baptized Catholic in my church. Our discussion progressed from what we each wanted to what was practical.

Our other major decision as a married couple had been that— since Jay had the better-paying, stable career—I would work part-time once we had children. We felt that it would allow one of us—me—to provide stability for our child(ren). This was significant, and became a deciding factor—since I would be at home with the child(ren), available to follow through with them regarding their education, it would thereby be practical that they be baptized Catholic—as I had been. It would make no sense for me to follow my faith while at the same time learn

Jay's faith—additionally—for the child(ren). So he and I agreed to baptize our child(ren) Catholic with the idea that—since our religions were so similar—we would be open to our child(ren) learning about both. Once they became adults, they could decide for themselves. The realistic and functional decision we arrived at was that our child(ren) be baptized Catholic—with (again) both "Jay's" pastor and "my" priest (who'd married us) present. Consequently, the baptism was held after Sunday Mass, which gave us a private family setting.

While we got ready the morning of Blake's baptism, Jay told me that he hadn't shared with his parents our feelings/decision about the baptism. This reality check brought me to tears—as much as he and I were a married couple and parents who had come to a decision together, he seemed to feel that he'd let his parents down. I tried to use makeup to cover up the puffy red eyes I had from crying, and I put a smile on my face—after all, it was Blake's baptismal day! Our immediate families were present for this eventful day as Blake was baptized into God's family. When I stood before the baptismal font while I held Blake and Jay was by my side, I noticed that the banner on the altar said "Alleluia!"—it was the same one that had been used four years earlier at our wedding. Ironically, but perhaps meaningfully, both our wedding and Blake's baptism date were in spring—a time for new beginnings!

~ ~ ~ ~ ~ ~ ~ ~ ~ ~ ~ ~

NOTE: In light of my faith, I learned (1) not to take life for granted, (2) although not confirmed, my "gut" feeling was that the baby I'd miscarried was a girl, and (3) any baby that we could conceive and bring to term would be a blessing.

CHAPTER TEN

FIRSTS FOR BABY AND PARENTS

Like other married couples, between the two of us we'd figured which household responsibilities were whose. He didn't like to mow the lawn or pull weeds, but I didn't mind this chore because I felt it gave me the chance to get some physical exercise and stay in shape. But when Jay came outside and criticized the way I'd mowed the lawn, I took his words to heart (they also hurt my heart), but followed his suggestion anyway. As time passed, a couple of the neighborhood men teased me and made the comment that perhaps they should get their wives to follow my example. I had mixed feelings about those chance remarks, but chose to accept it all with humor.

Since Jay liked to cook and I didn't (much like my mom and most of my sisters), he made dinner for the two of us, and I would then clean up the kitchen afterwards (which he didn't like to do). This arrangement also gave him some after-dinner one-on-one time with Blake, since Jay had been at work all day while I'd taken care of our baby. Our kitchen opened up to the family room, so one night while I cleaned up the kitchen after dinner, I'd watched Jay lie on the couch as he held Blake, who was then four months old. He laughed and talked to our baby while Blake blew bubbles and made noises back at his Dad. Our dog, Bailey, wanted to be a part of this action, so she'd brought her ball into the room, and dropped it by them as if to say, "Don't forget about me!" As I'd watched this sweet domestic scene unfold, I inwardly celebrated how fortunate and blessed we were as a family.

Bailey became protective of Blake—which was typical of Shetland Sheepdogs, a.k.a. Shelties. Whether Blake was in his playpen or on a blanket laid out on the family room floor (while he batted his hands at the overhead Sesame Street characters on his baby "gym set"), she was almost always nearby. Bailey soon learned—to avoid getting smacked—that she needed to stay clear of Blake as he swung back and forth in his indoor baby swing. Like most babies, Blake loved the swinging motion, and would kick his feet in excitement as I would say to him, "You're such a cute boy!"

One weekend that summer, we'd packed up Blake and Bailey (as well as my mom/Gommy) and drove up to Grandma and Grandpa's cottage on the lake in northern Wisconsin. Grandma had held Blake while she and Gommy swung on the double-swing in the yard. Since it overlooked the lake, they'd watched as Jay and I each water-skied behind the boat that Grandpa navigated. We'd all enjoyed ourselves, and celebrated Jay's first birthday as a Dad.

As first-time parents we marked many of Blake's milestones:

5 ½ months—spoon-fed first meal (baby cereal), 6 months—he got up on knees to rock his body back and forth, 8 months—he sat unsupported, and 9 months—he started to crawl.

For Blake's first Halloween—he was our "little pumpkin"—we dressed him in a little orange pumpkin costume that matched his red hair. We took him to trick-or-treat at Gommy's house, as well as at Grandma and Grandpa's house, where he showed off his recently developed skill of crawling. By his first Christmas, Blake was able to stand alone.

That year we started our own family Christmas traditions. We celebrated at our home on Christmas morning—Blake's awe and excitement as he tried to unwrap each of his Christmas presents (that had been placed under the tree) was priceless! Bailey had learned (in previous years) that there was sure to be a wrapped box of milk bones among the presents. After she'd sniffed out its location, we then had Blake rip off the wrapping paper for her. After we'd opened our gifts at home, we then bundled up and drove through the wintry weather to Grandma and Grandpa's house. We celebrated with them, Jay's brother, his wife, and their son—who was five months younger than Blake and also a redhead. By late afternoon, we'd bundled up again and travelled to my oldest sister and her husband's house—where we socialized with their family, my other siblings and their spouses, as well as my mom and dad. Although they were divorced, our family holiday celebrations remained (fortunately for all of us) a priority for both of them.

51

With the New Year, Blake grew to enjoy "peek-a-boo" with us. He loved the "sights and sounds" fire engine, which sounded its siren and flashed its red lights. Blake would hold the white "ladder" handle to push it while he crawled on his knees, and it became one of his favorite toys. At that time, he was teething; when I gave him his first baby teething biscuit, he looked at it with curiosity, and then passed it back and forth in his hands. When he finally put it in his mouth, he gagged—as if he'd wanted to swallow rather than teethe—on the baby biscuit. I immediately took it out of his mouth since he'd nearly choked on it.

We celebrated Blake's first birthday "in style"—Jay had recently won a certificate for a free limo ride, and when it arrived in front of our house, the driver set up the car seat for Blake while Gommy, Jay and I climbed in to get buckled up—and we were off! We then picked up Great-Grandma (Gommy's mom), as well as Grandma and Grandpa. Once we'd arrived at the Country Club, we all walked in the Dining Room as piano music played and we were seated. While Blake was seated in a highchair, Dad and Great-Grandma stayed at the table while the rest of us walked over to the buffet. Dad had videotaped this event (as with other momentous occasions since Blake's birth) from the time we'd left the house until we'd been seated in the Country Club's Dining Room. Unbeknown to us at that time, the video camera and its audio had been left on.

Blake was heard giggling—which sounded like a belly-laugh—and Jay started a game with Blake as he put his finger in Blake's mouth. Blake had been teething—Jay would say to Blake, "Good boy." But as the game continued, a couple minutes later he said, "Blake is biting my finger hard—it hurts." Jay continued the conversation and then was heard to tell my Grandma that we "wanted a baby so badly—we feel very lucky."

~~ When People Say "Autism," What Do They Mean? ~~

When I had first heard from medical professionals that the diagnosis—for not just one, but both of our young sons—was autism, I initially reacted with denial and disbelief. I was relatively ignorant about the disorder, and at that time—the only knowledge I had of autism was from the 1988 movie *Rain Man* (just three years before the birth of our first son).

I gradually adopted the mindset of any mother who might have received news that her child had been diagnosed with a life-changing condition, i.e., diabetes, etc. She, obviously, would need to become knowledgeable in order to cope and care for her child, and I realized that I needed to learn how to do the same. I didn't want to be like some of the other parents I'd observed who wore "blinders" to make their life with a health-challenged child more tolerable—or so they thought. Instead, I felt the need to take off my emotional "blinders" and accept that my world (and that of my sons) would never be the same. Their own "true colors" (imagine the colors of a rainbow) would reveal where they each fell on the spectrum of autism.

After that realization, I began to read and learn about autism (more recently referred to as Autism Spectrum Disorder, ASD), which is the "umbrella" term that also includes Asperger Syndrome. When I read Claudia Wallis's article "Inside the Autistic Brain" in the May 15, 2006, issue of TIME Magazine, I learned that, "Autism is almost certainly like cancer, many diseases with many distinct causes. It's well known that there's a wide range in the severity of symptoms—from profound disability to milder forms like Asperger syndrome, in which intellectual ability is generally high but social awareness is low." She also added, "Roughly 1 in 166 American children born today will fall somewhere on the autistic spectrum. That's more than three times the number with juvenile diabetes." The changes/ramifications in research/treatment have grown since the time my boys were diagnosed in the mid-late 1990's—back then the statistics were said to be 1 in 250. Today, that number is 1 in <u>68</u>. Autism also now affects 1 in every 34 parents and 1 in every 17 grandparents according to Autism Speaks.

Unfortunately, at that time resources were limited, but I did learn about the Autism Society. It was the oldest organization within the autism community, and was founded in 1965 by Bernard Rimland, Ph.D. In 1968, Ruth Sullivan, Ph.D., became the organization's first elected president, and it has since then grown from a handful of parents to a network of members and supporters. These include parents and professionals who have formed a collective voice on behalf of the autism community. In 1987, the organization was renamed to what we know today as the Autism Society of America (ASA).

Its nationwide affiliates work to (a) provide information and education, (b) support research, and (c) advocate for programs/services that the autism community needs. It continues to provide public awareness of daily challenges/concerns faced by individuals with autism and their families, as well as by the professionals who support them. In 1999, the Autism Awareness Ribbon was created to acknowledge its cause: "the puzzle pattern reflects the mystery and complexity of the autism spectrum, while the different colors and shapes represent the diversity of the people and the families who live with the condition. The brightness of the ribbon signals hope—that with increased awareness of autism, early intervention and appropriate treatments, people with autism will lead fuller, more complete lives."

I decided to contact and connect with our local ASA affiliate— the "chapter" was known as ASNEW (Autism Society of NorthEast Wisconsin). I longed for information, referrals, and meetings for parents. Through my search I even found and attended a couple workshops as well as their annual state conference. They provided me with an "arsenal" to become a better-equipped mom and "benevolent battle maiden" to advocate for and guide my boys through their autism/Asperger Syndrome challenges. The ASA was my "go to" resource back then, and it continues to be so today even though my sons are now in their early twenties.

NOTE: The information that you find in this (and the two similar subsequent sections of this book) were obtained through the Autism Society and its website www.autism-society.org to provide a glimpse into the combination of what I (1) learned, (2) wished I'd known back then, and (3) would like to share with you—especially any parent whose child may have received the diagnosis of an Autism Spectrum Disorder. I sincerely want to help others know and understand—perhaps even take away the fear and mystery of ASD—and ultimately cope and deal with a child who has been diagnosed.

A Not So Perfect
Family

CHAPTER ELEVEN

Outward Signs from Our Son—and My In-laws

Back at home, we celebrated with birthday cake, and Blake put his fingers into it but only played with the cake in his hands. Someone commented, "He doesn't put his fingers in his mouth" (i.e., to lick the frosting as most other kids would). Blake had more fun as he kicked his feet—which made noise—while he was seated in his highchair. One of the birthday gifts was a toddler-sized Fisher-Price Rocking Horse. I'd helped him get seated in its saddle, and slowly rocked it back and forth as we sang "Pony Boy" to him. Someone noticed that Blake didn't hold onto the handles of the rocking horse, and a comment was then made that, "He doesn't seem to like to hold on to things right away."

Grandpa, who had cut his own sons' hair for their entire lives—both as boys and men—offered to give Blake his first haircut. He'd grown curls at the ends of his hair and some people even thought he was a girl. As his grandson sat in the highchair, Grandpa attempted to cut his hair—but Blake didn't like it at all; he cried and moved his head away from Grandpa's hand that held the scissors. Grandma said to Blake, "You can't cry on your first haircut!" Blake continued to dread haircuts—as did we, his parents. I would have to hold Blake on my lap (with my arms around his) while Jay tried to distract or entertain Blake, so the hairstylist could try to cut his hair. We often left exhausted and frustrated—all of us—and settled for even the smallest bit of hair-trimming success the stylist could achieve.

By the time he turned one year old, Blake had learned to climb *up* stairs, and by the following month he'd begun to walk. He continued to enjoy it when I would play games with him like "Peek-a-Boo. I see you" and "Patty-Cake." He would do the motions, but not say the words. Blake and I continued to "work on his words" while we "played" with his toys during our days spent together.

After dinner, while I cleaned up the kitchen, I began to notice that Jay would go in our family room to sit down and read the paper while the TV was on. Occasionally, I would encourage him to take Blake outside in the backyard to play while I continued to clean. Since Jay worked all day during the week, I thought that it would give the two of them some valuable one-on-one time together as father and son. While I stood and rinsed off the dinner dishes at the kitchen sink, I looked out the window to watch their interaction in the backyard, but what I'd noticed was that Jay tended to stand in one place while Blake randomly ran around in the backyard.

Since Wisconsin winters can sometimes endure for months on end, Jay and I decided to take Blake with us for a weekend get-away to a hotel with a swimming pool—it was only 40 minutes away. It was enough for us to just have a change of atmosphere as our antidote for our "cabin fever." After we'd checked in at the hotel, we all changed into our swimsuits so we could then introduce Blake to the pleasures of the swimming pool. But whether we brought him in the pool with us or just sat together poolside, Blake would either scream or stubbornly resist being with us at the indoor pool. We'd hoped that it would be an enjoyable experience for Blake, but his reaction was far from that. Our last morning at the hotel, we decided to take a late check-out. Since many guests had already checked out—and there wasn't anyone in the hotel's swimming pool—we attempted to give Blake another try at getting into the water with us. He was a bit hesitant, but did not scream or resist as he had before—and he actually looked like he enjoyed the pool!

When spring arrived, I took Blake for a ride in his stroller, and noticed that he had his arms stretched forward with all ten fingers spread out. And when we had warmer weather, I would carry Blake outside to play in our backyard, and then set him down to stand barefoot in the grass. I tried to encourage him to walk toward me, but he would not move from the spot where I'd placed him in the grass. Blake held his hands in the air with his fingers spread, and then—as he stood barefoot on the grass—he'd made noises as if he were in pain. I'd thought this would be an enjoyable experience for Blake, but he showed me that he wanted no part of walking barefoot on the grass!

58

One summer weekend, Jay, Blake, Bailey, and I went up to Grandma and Grandpa's cottage. Since Blake was active on his feet, Grandpa played with him in the yard while Grandma, Jay, and I visited together in their screened-in tent, which overlooked the lake. At one point, the conversation turned into a discussion about Blake's inability to talk like others his age—Jay's mom directed the comment at me that she thought he would talk "if you (meaning me) would only talk to him (meaning Blake) more!" I was taken aback by her comment, so I looked over at Jay—who also looked surprised by his mom's attempt to blame me. He then told her that I (meaning me) talked to Blake a lot, and was a good mom. Upset by his comments, she got up, and walked away out of the screened tent.

I looked at my husband and asked, "What just happened?" He seemed as shocked and confused as I was, so I suggested that perhaps we should leave and go home. Jay went up to the cottage, and returned to say that his parents really wanted us to stay for dinner. It felt as if—in light of his mom's earlier outburst—that was the last thing she would want. We did stay for dinner, but it was understandingly uncomfortable. Afterwards, on our drive home, I was still dumbfounded and hurt by my mother-in-law's comments, so I asked Jay for his thoughts about what had happened. His response was passive, and he seemed resigned to act as if it hadn't happened—he'd "put his head in the sand."

A few days later when I saw my mom, I told her what had happened up at the cottage and about Jay's mother's outburst toward me. Mom was as shocked and surprised as I had been. She had raised her daughters to try their best to get along with their mothers-in-law, and I'd always felt that Jay's Mom and I had a good relationship. But that visit made me wonder if I'd maybe been naïve.

~ ~ ~ ~ ~ ~ ~ ~ ~ ~ ~ ~

NOTE: In retrospect, I can now see how revealing this critical and hurtful statement made by my mother-in-law would come to be.

CHAPTER TWELVE

DEVELOPMENTAL DELAYS—AND FAMILY FEELINGS—EMERGE

That fall, some of my friends, who also had children Blake's age, had enrolled their kids in "Mother's Day Out"—a program that gave children (as well as their moms) a couple of "out" hours each week. Moms could use this window of time to catch up on housework, pay bills, run errands, grab a cup of coffee with a friend, etc. It also gave our children an introduction to peers of their own developmental age in a safe, social playtime setting. Jay and I decided to sign Blake up to give him this social opportunity, which might benefit him. Especially since—at nearly 20 months of age—he still wasn't talking. All he could do was make grunts and guttural sounds with his throat. Blake's first day at the program was a "big event," so his Dad videotaped him as I put on his jacket, handed him his lunchbox, and then helped him get in the car to drive away to Mother's Day Out. This was our toddler's first day of "school."

When we talked to *him*, Blake seemed to understand our words and meaning, but he seemed to have difficulty when he tried to talk to *us* and/or others. My mom had attempted to soothe our concern regarding Blake, and she told us that it wasn't unusual for boys to be "late-talkers." I responded that while I appreciated her support and encouragement, "my gut feeling" (as his mom) was that it wasn't so much that Blake *wouldn't* talk—rather he *couldn't* talk! I told her that when we talked to him, he responded with hand gestures, and made sounds in an attempt to respond to us.

At that time, Blake could only say four to five words, which included "uh-oh" and "owl." He could respond to the following questions:

What does the horse say?—"Neigh"

What does the ghost say?—"Booooo"

What does the duck say?—"Quack, Quack"

For his second Halloween, we decided to have him wear a costume of either a ghost or a duck since he had a tiny vocabulary. Blake had seen Donald Duck on TV cartoons and in Disney animated movies, and I was able to find a Donald Duck costume that he liked and could relate to. Just like the year before, we took him to trick-or-treat at Gommy's house, as well as Grandma and Grandpa's home. When they asked what Donald Duck says, Blake responded with "Quack, Quack," which sounded almost exactly the way Donald Duck "spittingly" said it! Wrestling was on TV at Grandma and Grandpa's house, so Grandpa got down on the floor to wrestle with Blake—he would giggle as he tried to get out of Grandpa's strong-hold hugs!

Blake openly showed us that he loved music and rhythm, both when the radio was on, and especially when we watched animated Disney movies at home. He would stand up and dance around as the music played—especially during *Aladdin*, an animated movie in which Robin Williams voiced the "Genie" character. When the Genie sang "You Never Had a Friend Like Me," Blake would enthusiastically dance (as if he were high-stepping) and wave his arms. He would keep in tempo with the music, stop when it slowed, and then start to dance again as soon as the music started to play once more. Blake was so cute as he performed along with the Disney animated movies that played on our family room TV/VCR.

At his two-year-old "baby well check-up," his pediatrician recommended that Blake have a speech evaluation at our local hospital. The evaluation—not surprisingly—revealed that he had a speech delay, so Blake then started speech therapy at the hospital as an outpatient. It was also noted that he'd had difficulty transitioning from smooth baby foods to textured table foods, which would make him gag to the point that made his eyes water. During one of the initial speech therapy sessions, an occupational therapist (without Blake's knowledge) observed his movements, and recommended that Blake have an occupational therapy evaluation. Afterwards, we were told that our son has what is known as sensory defensiveness (auditory, oral, and tactile), as well as some fine motor-skill delay. Additionally, we were informed that Blake's special needs *were not* due to *behavioral* concerns, *but rather sensory defensiveness*—what he had was *neurologically* based. In other words, the motor planning/processing part of his brain functioned differently as it received information from his body when it sensed stimuli. Although Blake was found to have special needs, medical experts went on to say that "at this time," he had a "non-specific" diagnosis.

Naturally, this news "hit us like a ton of bricks." How could we have a son with special needs for both Speech AND Occupational Therapies, but have a NON-SPECIFIC diagnosis?! Up to this point in Blake's life, there hadn't been any known event or thing that could have seemed to cause a situation for which he would now need therapy services for an "indefinite" amount of time. The doctor told us that as much as they didn't know the cause(s) for Blake to have "special needs," what was more important was for us to treat him in ways (speech and occupational therapies) that could help him as he continued to develop and grow. In other words, we were told that our son had "developmental delays"—for lack of a more specific diagnosis at that time. Consequently, Blake was one month past his second birthday when he began to take both speech and occupational therapies at our local hospital. He was scheduled for two outpatient visits each week, and one therapy sequentially followed the other.

~ ~ ~ ~ ~ ~ ~ ~ ~ ~ ~ ~

That same month was Grandpa's birthday. Blake, Jay, and I were invited—as well as Jay's brother, his wife, and their son (who was five months younger than Blake)—to celebrate the occasion with Grandpa and Grandma at their house. We were all seated at the diningroom table and Grandpa was about ready to blow out the candles on his birthday cake, but then he started a game with two-year-old Blake and his younger cousin. Each boy was to try to blow out the flame on Grandpa's long-stemmed lighter, which he'd used to light the cake candles. Blake sat—with the palms of his hands on the table while he kept his fingers from touching the table's surface—as he blew out the lighter's flame and laughed, which showed that he enjoyed the game. Then it was his cousin's turn. When the game had ended, we all—with the exception of the two boys—sang "Happy Birthday" to Grandpa, and Blake moved his body in time with the tune.

Grandma then insisted that each of the boys say "Happy Birthday" to Grandpa, and suggested that the birthday cake be moved closer to Blake's cousin so he would say it. She repeatedly said to him, "Sing *Happy Birthday to You*…sing to Grandpa, and Grandma will take your picture." Blake's cousin responded with words that included "Grandpa, cake, cool off," etc. Meanwhile, Grandpa had noticed that Blake looked around and seemed somewhat confused. So he brought everyone's attention back to Blake, and asked him to help Grandpa blow out the candles on the cake. With Grandpa's smile and encouragement, Blake blew on the candles and made a guttural-sound of "oooooo…mmmm" in excitement. His cousin was then asked to blow on the candles, and after he did, Grandma again asked him, "Say Happy Birthday to Grandpa." She herself then sang, "Happy Birthday, Grandpa (she'd used his first name)." Blake's cousin responded with "Happy Birthday," but Grandma was persistent and insisted that he said it as she had. Then she added, "He's been saying it all day, but now he's not talking!?"

Grandpa—like the rest of us—understood that Blake wasn't capable of following the act of his younger cousin, so he turned and asked Blake to once more blow out the candles, which he did, and then he clapped his hands together in excitement. Grandma turned her focus on Blake and said, "Say Happy Birthday to Grandpa." Blake looked around, seemingly confused, and then got up from his chair and ran out of the dining room. I understood just how much he needed to get away from the pressure of being asked to do something that he was not yet able to do. He couldn't do what his younger cousin (who was smaller in size, but developmentally ahead of Blake with his speech) could do.

I went in to the living room to look after Blake and, gradually, the others joined us. While Blake knelt on the livingroom floor, his cousin put one of the empty Cool Whip plastic bowls on top of Blake's head, and then hit the bowl with his hand while it was on Blake's head. The cousin's parents told their son, "Be nice," and he then kissed Blake on the head. Grandma remarked, "Awww, he's throwing kisses."

63

Blake's younger cousin could say many words, and Grandma responded to each with a laugh and said to him, "That's right." She wanted to take a picture of the boys and said to our son, "Blake, get your hands away from your face." With the directives that Grandma gave her two grandsons that evening, it seemed to me as if she wanted the boys to compete with one another. She obviously played favorites (as she'd done with her own two sons), which was something I didn't—and don't—understand. A mother/parent's heart—if blessed with more than one child—does not need to pick and choose. Instead, it should expand and open up with more love in order to enjoy each one of his/her children for whom that child is—and not for what the parent wants that child to be.

~ ~ ~ ~ ~ ~ ~ ~ ~ ~ ~ ~

NOTE: The life lesson I learned was that despite the developmental delays (or whatever the diagnosis could someday be), I needed to accept my son Blake as he was—a blessing and gift from God. I know that he has his own purpose in life—and what it is—only time will tell. Consequently, it's not up to me to decide and tell him who or what to be.

CHAPTER THIRTEEN

Break Down of Barriers and Let Down by In-Laws

We were encouraged to keep Blake enrolled in the Mother's Day Out program, since—potentially—it might assist his special needs if he could learn from modeled behavior of the other children his age. When I'd talked to the MDO staff about the news we'd recently received about Blake, they were wonderful. They wanted to keep him in the program despite his special needs, and they also felt that the role-modeling from his peers might help. I'd explained that although Blake had special needs, we didn't expect special treatment. Consequently, we agreed that if Blake presented a difficulty for them (i.e., anything that was more than what was "typical" of other children his age), I would be contacted to consider his withdrawal.

WOW. I felt that if this was the start of things to come (Blake would be raised as a boy "with special needs"), then, as his mom, I would additionally become his advocate. I began to realize how extremely important my role was—and would continue to be—in my son's life. I needed to become informed as well as actively seek recognition for—and then help meet—my son's needs. I needed to learn how to become assertive—who else would be as concerned or better equipped to understand him (not to mention more motivated) than I? As a caring parent, I would have to learn how to ask questions and then insist on getting answers. I would have to seek out appropriate resources whoever or wherever they might be—hospitals, insurance companies, schools, community resources, etc.—in order to get the needed help for my son. I knew—almost immediately—that this was would not be an easy task, but it was the job that had to be done for Blake's future well-being. I would have to use whatever knowledge I could gain in order to maximize the future for my son and our family.

With this in mind, Jay and I concluded that since these needed services, which could benefit Blake, were scheduled for a few days each week, it—indefinitely—wouldn't be realistic for me to have a job outside the home. So I put my career on hold because I had more important things to accomplish in my stay-at-home career. From that time until today I became a "battle-maiden" mom, who would immerse herself—as he grew up—as an advocate for her son with special needs.

Blake's occupational therapist explained to us that he had "sensory integration dysfunction"—a disorder in which children have difficulty processing stimuli from the outside, consequently become overloaded very easily, and can have trouble calming themselves down...(perhaps) can even trigger them to throw a tantrum. We were told that this condition can respond well to a form of occupational therapy called Sensory Integration (SI) therapy—which helps children interpret outside stimuli. Since they often lack body awareness and social skills, this is not a *choice* for them but rather an *inability* to organize sensory information as they take it in. They learn improvement of hand-eye coordination and how to join in playground games, both of which can increase their ability to focus and tolerate being in a social group.

She suggested that I take him on a regular basis to Discovery Zone, where they had giant-sized ball bins that kids could climb in, play in, and slide into. The therapeutic idea behind this recommendation was that since Blake had some motor skill delays and tactile sensory defensiveness, it would offer him the opportunity to improve his motor-processing/planning. Theoretically, his brain would receive information from his body as it sensed the stimuli that the ball bin provided. It was just a big indoor playground to the "typical" adult's eye, but I came to realize what it provided for my developmentally delayed son!

At home, Blake and I would "play"—for speech purposes—with his Fisher-Price Farm (animal sounds), Mr. Potato Head (facial features), or make puzzles (he would put in each puzzle piece I'd asked for). He showed a real strength as he put puzzle pieces together in a short amount of time. Similarly, he could complete mazes—from "Start" to "Finish" without taking his colored marker off the page—in coloring books, and he enjoyed objects that fit together ("Transformer" toys). Blake liked to dance along with TV's "Barney" (the purple dinosaur), whose songs were appropriate for and popular with children his age. Blake and I would "blow bubbles" from a bubble wand because the blowing action from his mouth and his hands clapped together to pop the bubbles achieved occupational therapy goals. He and I would also take turns to roll the "Busy Ball" down its plastic "chutes and ladders"—he especially loved—which created auditory stimuli and fine-tuned his small motor skills. Each time I took Blake to his speech and occupational therapy sessions, I was placed behind a one-way mirror so that I could secretly watch Blake with each of the therapists, and learn their strategies as they worked with him in the hospital's therapy room.

~ ~ ~ ~ ~ ~ ~ ~ ~ ~ ~ ~

On our way home from Blake's therapies at the hospital, he and I'd stopped in to visit Grandma and Grandpa at their house. While we stood in their kitchen, I shared with them what I'd learned from the therapists that Jay and I could carry over at home with Blake. When I'd mentioned this to them, Grandma's response discounted what I'd said. They wanted to believe that nothing was wrong with Blake—and questioned his need for therapies, as did Jay. I'd hoped for support but, instead, they wanted to look the other way rather than deal with the reality. I wondered if Jay felt that way, too.

On a Sunday morning, while Jay and I started out our day, I shared with him the conversation that I'd had with his parents. Jay became so upset that he walked out our bedroom, left the house, and drove off—with Blake. Jay was angry when he left, which scared me—for his and Blake's safety. Consequently, I called my mom—who was up at her cottage at the time—and told her what had just happened, and how concerned I was. She told me not to worry—she would drive into town and come over right away. Since I hadn't taken my shower yet that morning, Mom's drive from the cottage would take about twenty minutes, and I had no idea where Jay had taken Blake, I decided to take my shower—and wait. When I stepped out of the shower, I heard the doorbell ring. I threw on a shirt with a pair of pants, and quickly walked downstairs to answer the front door. When I opened the door—Jay carried Blake, Grandma was with Grandpa, and lastly, Mom—all silently walked into the house. While they made their way to the family room, my mom pulled me aside at the front door and quietly said, "Jay's parents told me that they rang the doorbell, but you wouldn't come and answer the door for them." I couldn't believe what I'd just heard, and replied in shock, "I was up in the shower...it was when I'd just stepped out that I'd heard the doorbell ring, so I threw on these clothes and came down immediately to answer the door...as you see me now!" Mom quietly responded, "Alright, but you need to explain that to them."

She and I then walked into the family room and found Jay (he'd put Blake in his room to play) and his parents, who were seated on our couch. I opened up the conversation to explain (as I just had to Mom) why I hadn't been able to answer the front door sooner—nothing was meant to be taken intentionally. I asked Jay where he and Blake had gone when he'd left so angrily earlier. He said that the two of them went to his parents' house, and then decided that all four of them would come back to our house. At that point, I felt the need to ask Jay's parents—directly—what had happened to bring such misunderstanding and distance from them, especially with regard to Jay's and my decisions as a married couple and Blake's parents. They both were passive, and did not respond. I then turned to Jay, who sat—somewhat hunched over—on the brick hearth of our family room fireplace, and heard what seemed to be sobs. Was he crying? His mother got up immediately from where she'd been seated on the couch, went over to Jay, and put her hand on his shoulder to comfort him.

I then walked up to Jay's Dad, who was seated on our couch. I knelt down before him, looked directly into his eyes, and asked, "What is it? Is it something I've done? Jay and I are a married couple and are Blake's parents, and we've tried to make the best—which may not agree with your—decisions for our family. Can't that please be understood?" I'd felt as if I'd spilled my guts out, yet Jay's Dad did not respond, and even looked away. He then got up from the couch to make his way out of our family room. My mother, who had stood in the background, then came forward and asked Jay's Dad, "Please, answer Heidi...she asks you from her heart." I then looked over at Jay—I'd never seen him cry before—but what didn't seem quite right was that when Jay looked up (although he'd sounded as if he'd been crying), there weren't any tears!? What was this all about?

Mom then stepped up and told Jay's parents that she, like them (she'd hoped), wanted the best for us as a couple and parents of Blake. She added, "We know that our kids are trying again for another baby—stresses and tensions aren't good for them…" Jay's Dad was passive, told his wife to follow him, and they then walked out; Jay followed them out of the house as well. Mom and I looked at each other with shock and surprise over what had just happened.

When Jay stepped back into the house, Mom tried to give us assurance that—with time and understanding—things would work out. Jay dismissed the day as if it hadn't happen. My mother told me later that while she'd (urgently) driven from her cottage to arrive at our house, she'd nearly been in a car accident—a driver tried to pass in her lane and nearly hit her car head on.

Blake was just under three years old when Christmas neared that year. While I put Christmas decorations out—specifically, hung the garland and placed bows on the railings of the upstairs—Blake sat on the stairs in his onesies feet-pajamas and drank from his sippy cup while Jay videotaped. As I decorated, I talked to Blake, who rather than answer my questions, repeated singular words—especially the last word I'd said. He waved at his Dad (who held the video camera) and said, "Hi Dad! Ab thilk"—he meant "Hi Dad! I'm drinking my milk."

And though that year had put our family on a totally different path than we'd planned, we were even more surprised to learn that we would expect another baby—I was pregnant, again!

CHAPTER FOURTEEN

Arrival of Our Second Son

Winter weather can really be a drag in Wisconsin, especially when—according to the calendar—spring should have already arrived. It had become our (Blake and mine) regular routine to visit our local hospital for his Speech and Occupational Therapies, which were scheduled consecutively—and regularly—a few times per week.

One morning, Blake wasn't very cooperative, and by the time we arrived, he'd had a "melt-down" in the lobby. Although I tried to encourage him to come with me (as we'd always done before), that morning he resisted and lay down right in the middle of the lobby floor. Then Blake made loud noises and refused to come with me. Since I had become big and pregnant, I sat down on a nearby lobby bench, which was where I continued to try and coax Blake to go with me to see his therapists—we were already late. As this disruptive and embarrassing scene continued in the lobby, two older women walked by, and one remarked to me, "Looks like some little boy needs to be picked up and held by his mommy!" Feeling uncomfortable, I responded, "I can't lift him up—I'm (big and) pregnant!" Once the women had passed by, I continued to ask Blake to come over by me and take my hand so we could make our way to the hospital floor where his therapists waited for us. When we finally met up with Blake's therapists, I explained to them why we were late and what had happened—I assumed that they had probably even heard Blake because their floor overlooked the atrium of the hospital lobby. They told me that they totally understood, but I wished I could grasp what had triggered Blake's "melt-down."

Spring had finally arrived, and on the first week of May I had a regular prenatal visit. That's when my doctor told me that—even though my due date wasn't until June 9th—I was already dilated one centimeter. As the month of May progressed, I'd become more uncomfortable because the baby had "dropped." I'd already been admitted (three different times) to the hospital for labor and delivery when the contractions had increased more regularly; but then the contractions would stop, and I would be sent back home. The plan was that when I would go into labor, we would then drop Blake off at Mom's house. But each time (needless to say) Blake, Mom and her friend John were let down—as we were. On May 23rd I was told that I was dilated two centimeters, effaced at 60%, and at second station; I really felt this baby was about to come at any moment. On Memorial Day weekend, I became really uncomfortable with the pressure of the baby's head—it even affected my legs so that I could hardly walk. As I lay in bed, I looked out the windows and could hear the sounds of summer. It was a gorgeous sunny day, but I felt miserable. When I'd talked to the physician who was "on call" that holiday weekend, I was told that since I was in my 38th week of the pregnancy term, I should contact my doctor the next morning (after the holiday) to induce labor.

I was admitted to the hospital at 8:50 a.m. on Tuesday, May 31, 1994. Once again Jay and I settled into one of the birthing suites—it looked like the same one we'd had when Blake was born. My doctor soon showed up to induce labor—he punctured the membrane so that my "bag of waters would break." After that procedure, my labor contractions continued naturally. At 12:15 p.m., I was told that I was dilated to four centimeters, and then at 2:38 p.m. (after only three pushes) our second son was born! He was 22 inches long and weighed nine pounds, ten ounces—almost a pound larger than Blake had been at birth—no wonder I'd been so uncomfortable during my last month of pregnancy! We were told that our second son's Apgar scores were 8 and 9—due to his blueness because of the rapid delivery—but otherwise he was healthy, and the monitor showed a good heart rate. Our second son wasn't named until an hour after his birth—Jay and I took that time to discuss and ultimately decide to name him Daniel Michael.

Once again, Jay was in the position to give the first bath to our second son (since he'd been instructed by the neonatal nurse), and Gommy—our first visitor—videotaped this momentous event. When Daniel cried during his bath, Jay said, "Exercise your lungs…do you like to sing like your mom, dad, and your brother Blake?" Once Daniel was placed on his tummy, he seemed to settle down as his father washed his back and said, "Good Boy…Looks like you have darker brown hair than your brother, Blake."

After Jay gave Daniel his first bath, I—as his mom—gave him his first bottle. He was all wrapped up in a receiving blanket in my arms—his face and his hands were all that showed—someone noticed that (like me) he had long fingers. When Grandma and Grandpa arrived later, they each took turns as they held Daniel—their third grandson. Gommy later returned to the hospital room we'd been moved to, and brought Blake to meet his newborn brother, Daniel. As I lay in the hospital bed (and Daniel was wheeled in from the newborn nursery in a clear-sided newborn cart), Gommy pointed out his new baby brother to Blake. The attempt to bond as brothers for the first time was a precious, memorable moment that I will never forget!

We later learned that since I'd delivered Blake, the hospital policy had changed. The new rule was that Mother and Baby would be discharged after 24 hours; before we'd been given two days. Given the condition I'd been in before Daniel's delivery (plus the fact that I'd delivered rapidly), I was worn out. To go home within 24 hours would hardly allow me to get strong enough to care for a newborn plus an active three-year-old who had "special needs!" We'd attempted to contact our medical insurance provider to see if we could be granted an "exception," but—unfortunately—they decided that we didn't qualify. We even looked into what the cost would be if I stayed the second day, but it would have been an outrageous amount. Mom then suggested that when the 24 hours had passed, and Daniel and I were discharged from the hospital, she would stay at our house for my first night back home. She saw how exhausted I was, and told me—as a mother would to her child—"You go straight to bed and regain your strength while Jay and I take care of Blake and Daniel." And that is exactly what happened.

~ ~ ~ ~ ~ ~ ~ ~ ~ ~ ~ ~

I was moved and touched when I later saw the video footage that Jay had taken, and could watch our two sons spend their first night at home as brothers. Gommy had Blake sit on the family room couch and then showed him how to carefully hold his baby brother, Daniel, who was all wrapped up in a receiving blanket. Later, Gommy asked Blake to

72

sit next to her on the family room couch and showed Blake how to hold the bottle and help feed Daniel while she held the baby. As Gommy held our infant son over her shoulder–after he'd finished his bottle—she encouraged Blake to gently pat Daniel on his back to help burp him. While Jay videotaped from behind the camera he said, "Good job, Blake."

As Jay had done for Blake, he'd made and hung a sign from our upper porch that said "It's a Boy…Daniel Michael." He'd also arranged for a large stork cut-out that had a blue bundle hanging from its beak (which stated Daniel's name, birth date, and birth weight). It was placed prominently in our front yard to (again) share the news about our second son with our neighbors—and the world!

We'd arranged to have Daniel baptized when he was three months old. As we'd done with Blake, we had the ceremony after Sunday Mass, which gave us a private family setting. Daniel's baptism was performed before our immediate families, and "Jay's" pastor gave him the father's blessing while I received the mother's blessing from "my" parish priest.

With each day that passed, Blake and Daniel grew closer as brothers. Blake tried to make his little brother laugh when he'd said to him, "Goo-Ga-Ga-Ga." And Daniel would respond and reach out his arms to his big brother while he giggled, made noises and blew bubbles with his mouth. There were other times when Jay asked Blake to make Daniel laugh while he videotaped our boys. When Daniel was seated in his highchair, Blake would hold his legs and move them to the music; and sometimes, he would hold Daniel's hands to clap them together and play "Patty-cake."

As that year came to a close, Blake had his first Christmas Concert at his pre-school. Jay had planned to videotape this momentous event, so I sat with my mother in the audience. I'd mentioned to her that I felt nervous for Blake—as any parent might feel regarding their child's performance—but more for him because his sensory defensiveness might cause him to have a "melt-down." Fortunately, his pre-school teacher and her assistant understood both Blake's developmental delays and his sensory defensiveness. His teacher held Blake's hand as she and he led the other children onto the stage area, and then she placed him on the end—where he watched the others and moved his arms as they did—in order to look like candles that "flickered" with the lyrics of the song. Consequently, his pre-school teacher and her assistant made it possible for Blake to succeed as he performed the *Flicker, Flicker Flame* song along with his pre-school peers. I offered a warm, heartfelt thanks to both of them—and (silently) to God—for the gifts we'd received that Christmas (Blake's performance with appropriate stage presence) as well as earlier that year (the birth of our beautiful second son, Daniel)!

CHAPTER FIFTEEN

ADAPTIVE TECHNIQUES TO COPE

After he completed the "Birth to Three" program (which offered Speech and Occupational Therapies) at the hospital, Blake then transitioned to the Public School's "Early Childhood" program. Initially he received services for Speech & Language, but by the end of that year, he qualified for Occupational Therapy services that the "Early Childhood" program provided as well. Occupational Therapist evaluations showed Blake to have:

1) Inadequate processing of sensory information—*can have significant impact on his social relationships in the educational setting.*

2) Increased sensitivity to sound—*can affect his willingness to participate in classroom fieldtrips or go to school pending fear of unexpected fire drills, loud noises, etc. His increased perception of sound can make it difficult to concentrate and tune out distracting noises such as the building's heating system, classroom whispering, etc.*

3) Mixed perceptions of touch (increased sensitivity in the mouth and decreased sensitivity to pain)—*sensitivities to textures in the mouth are also felt to impact speech development due to the different oral patterns needed to eat a variety of foods (i.e., chewing increases proprioceptive input which can provide better sensory awareness in the mouth, sucking increases stability, etc.). Blake's apparent decreased sensitivity to pain may be partial explanation for perceived physical "aggression" due to his low responsiveness to pain and his need for deep pressure input, i.e., at times he would pound his hand on his chest while vocalizing "aaaaah."*

4) Low muscle tone that results in increased range of motion at the joints and fine motor skills are below age level—*indicate that Blake has decreased proximal stability at the joints, particularly*

at the shoulder and wrist, which are foundational skills necessary for the development of fine motor skills and precision.

In other words, Blake had sensory processing problems. More formally called Dysfunction of Sensory Integration (DSI)—a neurological disability in which the brain is not able to accurately process information coming in from his senses— further defined by Terri Mauro at the internet link: http://specialchildren.about.com/od/gettingadiagnosis/g/DSI.htm "Individuals may be *oversensitive* to some sensations, wildly overreacting to touch or movement or loss of balance; *undersensitive* to some sensations, needing crashing or banging or sharp sounds and flavors to register anything; or a combination of both. Sensory integration problems can affect the five traditional senses—particularly touch and hearing, but also taste, sight and smell—as well as two additional senses: the *vestibular* sense, which tells us where our body is in space, and the *proprioceptive* sense, which tells us what position our body is in. Children with Dysfunction of Sensory Integration may appear hyperactive, oppositional, obsessive-compulsive, or detachment disordered, when in fact they are just reacting to and compensating for their unreliable and unpredictable view of the world."

According to the Occupational Therapist, Blake's nervous system difficulties (i.e., processing sensory information adequately) had contributed to his difficulty to plan new motor tasks. This may also have been partial explanation for some types of inappropriate behavioral and social interactions. To address Blake's increased sensitivity to sounds, (i.e., he showed to be uncomfortable in a gym setting where loud buzzers were utilized and go off unexpectedly, which was why he wanted to avoid indoor sport games), she discussed with me the following "adaptive" techniques such as:

- Avoid settings with known increased auditory input.
Jay and I found this out when we attended the circus and Blake wanted to spend time with us on the mezzanine, rather than watch the circus from the seats

we'd bought in the arena stands.
- Have Blake wear headphones/earplugs to reduce sound. *We provided these to him when he attended indoor sports played in gymnasiums.*
- Use verbal pre-warning prior to known "loud" sounds, etc. *His teachers used this technique during school fire drills, i.e., they would walk beside Blake during the fire drill, and reassure him while they guided him out of the school with his classmates.*

She informed us that with Sensory Integration Therapy she performed with Blake, attempts would be made to eliminate—if not help cope with—these problems. I was instructed to bring Blake to the designated Public School that had a "sensory integration" gym for his occupational therapy sessions. She discussed with me the techniques she planned to use with Blake in his OT sessions to address his increased sensitivity—"reduce sensory sensitivity in the auditory channel through sensory input to other sensory channels, such as vestibular (movement) and proprioceptive (pressure to the muscles and joints)."

Before she'd started the OT session, she explained that the sensory "brushing" technique was used for those—like Blake—with sensory defensiveness. These children seek deep pressure for calming and/or before focus attention was required. She raked a small, soft plastic (sterile surgical) brush across the skin on Blake's arms, legs, and feet to get the nerve endings stimulated so that they could send sensory information to his brain. Then the OT would take Blake's upper arm in one of her hands, his lower arm in her other hand, and then gently make back and forth movements toward the elbow (joint)—so to stimulate his joints and muscles to send sensory information to his brain. As she demonstrated, this technique would also be used for his other joints, i.e., his wrists and knees.

As Blake "worked" with his OT—he swung across the gym to drop himself into a big ball bin, or sometimes he would lie on his tummy on top of what looked like a large, square "skate board" with roller wheels while he used his arms and hands to propel his body across the gym floor—I would watch. I sat on a school chair that had been set up against a wall of the gym next to Daniel, who would sit in his "bucket" (the trendy transportable carseat with an adjustable handle, which made it look like a bucket).

At times, his OT would have Blake participate in an activity with her, which would include a tactile component—such as "work" as he would dig to uncover objects that she had hidden in the sand in the sand table OR play with modeling clay. He had shown sensory defensiveness whenever he touched substances that were gooey and sticky, (i.e., glue, modeling clay, etc.) or coarse (sand). After one of these sessions—as I held Daniel in my arms while I guided Blake through steps to wash his hands at the sink on the side of the school gym—I heard Blake's OT say to me, "You have such a way with Blake." Her comment took me by surprise—I visibly had my hands full as I'd held Daniel while I attempted to get Blake through the motions to wash his hands—and I sincerely thanked her for the comment, which I took as a compliment. After another day's OT session for Blake, I told her that while I brought Blake to Speech and Occupational Therapy sessions—with baby Daniel in tote—I continued to hold hope that things would get better. I added, "Someday, when Blake's all grown up, I will never forget where he started—with simultaneous needs for Speech and Occupational Therapies."

Blake's OT also recommended that he take a martial arts class because it would address concerns with his vestibular and proprioceptive senses. We signed him up for karate classes. He seemed to enjoy them since (to him) he felt that he was taught movements, which the "Power Rangers" used when he watched them on his favorite TV show. He had no idea that karate could help him with his developmental delays.

~ ~ ~ ~ ~ ~ ~ ~ ~ ~ ~

We celebrated Daniel's first birthday on the last day of May that year—he hadn't been able to crawl yet. He'd learned to roll over at 9 ½ months, but when he tried to sit up he would "tripod"—as the pediatrician said. At fourteen months, Daniel was not yet able to walk alone, and still didn't talk. Consequently, concerns emerged, and at his "baby well" check-up, his pediatrician referred him for evaluations at our local hospital. Evaluations showed that Daniel needed Physical Therapy (gross motor delays), Speech (significant developmental delay in language), and Occupational Therapy (low muscle tone and sensory integration dysfunction).

When I drove into our driveway at home, I saw our neighbor (who was a neonatal doctor) outside, and felt the urge to share the news that we'd been given regarding Daniel's need for Speech, Occupational, and Physical Therapies. We had two sons out of two children who were shown to have these special needs. His response was that Jay and I had better stop (having children) "in our tracks" and be tested! It was a big blow to us—how could this be when we weren't known to be "at risk" for children with special needs? I'd had two uncomplicated pregnancies, and two healthy newborns!

Consequently, our two children—our two sons—were then referred to our local hospital's Genetics Department. They forwarded our boys to be evaluated by a notable Clinical Genetics Center (located elsewhere in our state) in July 1995. The Clinical Geneticist performed physical examinations of Blake and Daniel to tell us that neither of our sons "is strongly reminiscent of any recognizable syndrome." Recommendations included that the chromosomes of both boys be evaluated—as decided to be done on Blake first—to rule out Fragile X Syndrome as well as any other chromosomally related diagnosis. They would let us know the results of their tests as soon as they would be available—if blood needed to be drawn, it could be done prior to Blake's surgery on August 11th (when he would have his tonsils and adenoids removed).

We'd found that Blake suffered from sleep apnea, so he was scheduled to have surgery performed at our local hospital. Jay's parents said that they would babysit Daniel at our house while we took Blake for his outpatient procedure. As Blake, Jay, and I got seated in our car, Jay's Dad said to us, "Glad I'm not you!" How (un)reassuring was this for us to hear as parents—especially in front of our son who was scheduled for surgery!

When we arrived at the hospital, the nurse told us to get Blake dressed into a hospital gown, and when she'd arrived back at the room, she told us that she would walk Blake down to the operating room. There we stood in the doorway as we watched our "big" boy—dressed in an oversized hospital gown that nearly hung to the floor—hold the nurse's hand while they walked down the hospital's hallway. He looked back and waved to us—as if he wanted to assure us that he would be okay! Jay and I waited together in the hospital room until we were told that we could see Blake after his surgery. We walked into the room to find him lay in a "groggy" state—while he recovered from the anesthesia—in a large crib with its sides pulled up. We were so proud of Blake—he acted like such a brave boy—that we surprised him back at home with a new Power Rangers playset that he'd wanted. A few weeks later, we'd noted—as did Blake—that he breathed easier and slept better at night. It also seemed like his appetite was better. I couldn't help but wonder if the enlarged adenoids and tonsil had been in the way when he'd tried to chew and swallow??

Before the summer ended, Blake, Daniel, Jay, and I went up to Jay's parents' cottage on the lake. Jay videotaped Blake as he would run to the end of the dock, stop, and then jump into the arms of Grandpa—who stood in the water as he waited for him. Also "caught on camera" was an intensely involved Grandpa who helped Blake swim and played with him—while Jay just stood nearby in the water. Jay showed less interaction with his own son—instead he was a "bystander" just as he'd been when I'd seen him "play" in the backyard with Blake back at home.

Up at the cottage, we also noticed that whenever we called Daniel by his name, he did not respond.

CHAPTER SIXTEEN

TESTING AND TREATMENT FOR BOTH BOYS

Daniel had quite a few ear infections that year, and they had been treated with Amoxicillin. We'd also noticed—as had his Physical Therapist with the "Birth to Three" program—that he had little or no recognition of danger. He was active—he loved to walk and was somewhat distractible. This became quite a challenge—particularly, when I took the boys to shop with me. If I didn't hold Daniel's hand, he would wander off. Even worse, he didn't respond when we called him by name. One time, when I was in the check-out line and had to use both my hands to write a check from my checkbook, he'd—in just those couple of moments—wandered off past the lines of registers and back down the grocery aisles. I had to tell the cashier to please wait as I ran from the line to catch up with Daniel, and take him by the hand back to where I'd been at the check-out line. I learned that grocery shopping would be something I would have to do alone. And the boys would simply have to stay at home with their Dad.

In October of 1995, we received a phone call from our local hospital's Genetics Department, which had received the report regarding the blood work on Blake and both tests showed negative: (1) for any missing/added chromosome (46 chromosomes were shown to be present and the XY chromosome was present) and (2) for Fragile X Syndrome (the X chromosome was shown to be normal). Consequently, it was suggested that we follow up next year—especially if shown more evidence of more significant needs, i.e., Daniel.

Blake had an appointment with his pediatrician that same month, so I discussed with him these test results that we'd received from Blake's blood work. Our pediatrician also recommended that no further medical testing be done at the time and then suggested that—although there was no known genetic reason for both Blake and Daniel's delays—there seemed to be an "apparent" risk if we were to have more children (even though the risk couldn't be calculated).

A neonatologist reinforced our pediatrician's recommendations; he also felt that further medical testing seemed to be pointless at that time, and we should accept those results. Only with time and Daniel's development, should we (perhaps) pursue any further medical testing. Although genetic testing results eliminated chromosomal abnormalities for Blake—since there was no known reason for the developmental delays, etc.—we were advised to focus our attention on an appropriate education for Blake when he entered school.

We were also told to think about the possibility of holding Blake back a year before he enrolled in Kindergarten. We were told that regular education (rather than private education, which was our preference) might be a more appropriate option for Blake. I found a Progress Report, which stated that (at four years/seven months) in some ways Blake displayed the developmental level of an early four-year-old. It would therefore be appropriate to hold him back a year, since this developmental level would fit with most of the children's ages in that class behind him. The other consideration was—would his intellectual level then be as challenged? The trade-off/compromise would seem to be cognitive ability level versus common-sense ability.

A few weeks before Christmas that year, Blake's teacher—at the parish pre-school he attended—decided that her class would put on the story of the Nativity for the school's Christmas Concert. She had each student pick a slip of paper from a container that had a Nativity character role written on it. Guess which slip Blake happened to pick? Joseph! We were told that he was to sing "Away in a Manger" as a duet with "Mary." Even though he received treatment for a speech delay, Blake's pre-school teacher assured us that he would do fine with her direction. The day that the character roles were picked, two girls had been absent. When they'd returned to school, the girl who then picked the slip with "Mary" written on it was a sweet girl, and—given her nurturing nature—could not have been a better fit for Blake.

The school's Christmas Concert took place at the parish church where I'd attended grade school. It was so sweet to see Blake dressed as "Joseph" as he held a stick for a staff and walked—alongside the girl who was dressed up as "Mary"—down the main aisle to the front of the church. He followed "Mary" to where she sat down on one side of the manger, and then he was directed to sit on the other side of the manger. Like a gentleman, he saw to it that "Mary" was seated before he sat down on the other side of the manger. "Mary's" mom and I had become friends, and thought up that her daughter and Blake made a "cute couple"—perhaps the foreshadowing for them both since they each went on to perform in major musical roles during their high school years.

That year, Jay and I decided to invite both sides of our families to celebrate Christmas Day at our home. Since we'd travelled to Jay's parents' house in past years (as well as to my sister and her husband's family home), we felt that we would finally like to host Christmas at our house. Jay's parents didn't care for this idea, but when they realized that my side of the family went along with the idea, they agreed. After all, it was a better option than to not celebrate Christmas with their son Jay and his family.

Our living room was packed with all of our immediate family members as we exchanged Christmas presents from under the tree with one another. It brought a warm feeling—literally (since there were a number of us in a relatively small room) as well as figuratively (both sides of our immediate family were brought together to celebrate the reason for the season)—to host this Christmas holiday at our home. After the gifts had been opened, we all relaxed downstairs in our newly professionally-finished basement rec room. While we visited with one another, Daniel picked up one of his presents—a "Bumble Ball," which was a plastic ball that had stubby-ended "spikes" so that when it was turned on, the ball would move along by itself when placed on the floor. Once the ball's motion would seem to stop, Daniel would bend over to pick it up off the floor with his hands. As soon as the music and the motion started again with the "Bumble Ball," it would shake in Daniel's hands. Then he would drop it on the floor, where it would continue to move and play music. Daniel would giggle and squeal with excitement each time he repeated these actions, which seemed to provide the sensory input (in the OT sense) that he liked. Daniel was entertained as much as we were entertained by his enjoyment!

~ ~ ~ ~ ~ ~ ~ ~ ~ ~ ~

In July 1996, we took the boys to revisit—as had been requested one year earlier—the Clinical Geneticist at a notable Clinical Genetics Center (located elsewhere in our state). I'd shared in our discussion that the situation with our two sons could be compared to an occupation in which a machine that one is responsible for simply wasn't able to work. Its dysfunction triggers the need to either search for a better understanding of the problem or attempt to repair it. Similarly, we have two children—two sons—with obvious needs for services with Speech, Occupational, and Physical Therapists, yet both the cause and diagnosis remained unknown. It baffled us to think that our boys' (and our) lives had become significantly altered, yet the "why" and the "what it is" remained obscure. This became a major "stumbling block" when we sought support groups/resources.

The Clinical Geneticist conducted another physical exam on each of our boys, whose impressions included: *(1) Both boys have a similar problem, and (2) Both resemble one another and have a somewhat distinctive phenotype, which is characterized by (a) Mildly square-shaped head, (b) Characteristic facial features, (c) Developmental delays, and (d) Large for age size.* Since DNA analysis ruled out chromosomal abnormality as well as Fragile X Syndrome in Blake, a referral by the Clinical Geneticist was made for the boys to be scheduled/seen by a Pediatric Neurologist (August 1996), as well as a referral for metabolic tests scheduled/performed by Biochemical Genetics Program (Fall 1996)

Amidst the testing and treatment, Blake, Daniel, Jay and I took our annual summer trip to Door County—a resort area often considered the "Cape Cod of the Midwest" due to its quaint little villages and towns along the shoreline of Wisconsin's peninsula. Like the year before, we took the boys to "The Farm" to feed, pet, and spend some time among the animals, as well as to an amusement park called "Thumb Fun." I pushed Daniel in his stroller—I wasn't one much for rides—and videotaped Blake as he and Jay drove in a "go-kart" around the track, and rode together on the merry-go-round; Blake waved to me each time they passed by. By then, Daniel had become restless and needed his nap. We said one last "Good-bye" to the merry-go-round, and then we all headed back to our hotel.

Before summer came to its close, we took the two boys (as scheduled) for their comprehensive neurological evaluations through the Child Neurology Outreach Clinic at our local hospital. The Pediatric Neurologist reports (dated August 22, 1996) that we received—although an independent evaluation—stated much of the same findings/information, as the previous medical evaluations and developmental history for each of our sons.

The Pediatric Neurologist included in his "Formulation" for Blake the following: *"This was a nearly two-hour comprehensive, neurologic evaluation that involved history taking, evaluation, and extensive discussion upon the nature of sensory integrative dysfunctions as non-specific common denominators of a number of developmental disorders. I did not, of course, in the absence of a significant disorder, feel a diagnosis of an autistic spectrum disorder at this point in time would be appropriate, but did point out some of the aspects of Blake's uneven development that he shares with children who appropriately are designated as such...I suggested that he get evaluated neuro-psychologically within the next six months...I strongly suggested that he continue to receive occupational and speech therapy and suggested that I have the opportunity to meet with him...in about one year's time."*

In the Pediatric Neurologist's "Formulation" for Daniel, the following was included: *"Daniel is a two year old with significant language delay and sensory dysfunction, has low muscle tone as well as motor delays, needs much repetition to master tasks as is the case with his sibling...I suggested to Daniel's parents that I have the opportunity to revisit him when he is three years old...we talked at length about potential significance of sensory dysfunctions and some of the aspects of his development that he shares with children with autism and other developmental disorders without committing ourselves to a specific diagnosis at this time."*

~ ~ ~ ~ ~ ~ ~ ~ ~ ~ ~

NOTE: An Occupational Therapist—who had treated both of our sons—had told me that they were somewhat opposites regarding the "spectrum" of sensory dysfunction. Our older son, Blake, could be considered more *hyper-sensitive* since he could become overwhelmed in an environment where there was an overload of stimuli. These could include visual and auditory distractions, i.e., several conversations in the same room, buzzing sounds of fluorescent lights and/or fans, many people moving around. Tactile stimuli, i.e., skin pressure when wearing certain types of clothing could also cause an over-reaction.

Our younger son Daniel could be considered more *hypo-sensitive* since as a defense, he would focus on one thing at a time, ignore certain stimuli in his environment, or even shut it out and retreat into a world of his own, unaffected by all that goes on around him. Consequently, he could need extra stimulation through his senses that don't get enough information from the environment.

Although both sons are high-functioning, they each seem to have a different sensory threshold to interpret and tolerate stimuli in their environment. The challenge lay in understanding *each* of our son's difficulties as they *each* experience the world—which can affect their *own* functioning—and then find effective strategies for *each* to help them *each* cope and live a productive life at home, in school, as well as in the community.

CHAPTER SEVENTEEN

Seeking Support

Many of the medical tests that were performed on Blake and Daniel needed to receive a preauthorization through Jay's policy with his employer's insurance company. This meant that calls would need to be made through the doctor/hospital/insurance channels to gain coverage for the procedures.

One day, when Jay came home from work, I explained to him how difficult it was for me to contact—much less connect with—the insurance company. I'd been repeatedly passed along their system (i.e., transferred) as I struggled to get through to the appropriate contact that could assist me. Then, once connected, I'd been told that I would receive a callback with the necessary information—unfortunately, that could happen at any time (or, worse), during a window of time when I would be unable to take their call. If they called while I was at therapy sessions for each boy or as I did their therapies at home—there would be no way for me to effortlessly drop everything to take the awaited callback! My time was consumed as I kept up with the day-to-day motions of caring for two very young special needs children—and tried to be prepared for what might happen next. Would that be the important phone call, the next "melt down" from the boys (due to their sensory defensiveness issues or frustration with their developmental delays), or would it be something totally unexpected? Sometimes I would have to make a follow-up call when the insurance company hadn't returned my call as I'd been promised. Given my frustration, I turned to Jay and asked if he would make the needed calls—after all, under his employer's plan he was the "insured" (and I wondered if—perhaps as a man—he might have more success and get through to obtain the answers we needed). I'd explained to him how time was of the essence for us to get the necessary insurance approval "in place" by the time the boys were scheduled for their metabolic lab tests.

Jay said that he would make the calls the next day, but when I followed up with him regarding what he had found out, he was slow to say that he hadn't yet made the call(s). He told me that he hadn't had time. I couldn't help but think—"No time even when you took your break or lunch, which was often undivided time?"

In the months that followed, I tried to process the genetic results that we'd been given to date and "accept" the situation that both of our boys had a non-specific diagnosis of developmental delays. It just didn't make sense—but then I'd realized that there are things in life that don't make sense—at least not at the time. I learned that I needed to juggle Blake's schedule between morning pre-school classes and his afternoon therapy sessions at the public school—all while I slotted Daniel into his sessions of three different therapies within openings of Blake's schedule (or vice versa). Consequently, many of the "playdate" invitations that my boys and I received (from their friends or mine), had to—unfortunately—be turned down.

When I'd shared the confusing information regarding our boys with my family, a couple of my sisters commented that the concerns I'd expressed regarding the boys would only make doctors feel that they *had* to come up with something wrong with our children. Those statements hurt my feelings because it seemed like they weren't really concerned or interested—or sympathetic. I'd hoped that they would be, especially when I'd taken interest and spent time with them and their family—for years I'd frequently babysat my nieces and nephews. I assumed that I would receive a friendly shoulder. It would have been nice—if only we could have talked one-on-one—but instead, both families didn't seem to want to recognize our sons' condition and behaved like "ostriches with their heads in the sand." Perhaps it was a matter of misplaced pride and/or fear…

I was introduced to the MUMS (Mothers United for Moral Support) group, which was led by a woman who—I later found out—lived only blocks away from our house. MUMS was "A national Parent-to-Parent (volunteer) organization for parents or care providers with *any* disability, disorder, chromosomal abnormality or health condition. MUMS' main purpose is to provide support to parents in the form of a networking system that matches them with other parents whose children have the same or similar condition…Parents can then exchange valuable medical information, as well as the names of doctors, clinics, medical resources or research programs. Families provide each other with emotional support and they don't have to feel so alone when they have each other to reach out to in the time of need…The *Matchmaker* newsletters allow families to share and speak out about issues affecting their lives…"

I liked the idea that *Matchmaker* newsletters would give parents like me an opportunity to be matched with someone—almost like a "pen pal"—on the basis of the similar conditions of their children. This would allow us to correspond, and perhaps learn from one another in order to potentially better help our special needs children. Not long after I'd started to receive the *Matchmaker* there was a "match" posted that seemed to very much mirror the situation with our son Blake: *"UNDIAGNOSED My son is four years old. He does not have an official diagnosis, however, he exhibits sensory integrative disorder…He has speech delays…I would really like to hear from someone who also may have a child with the same issues…He has been through all the genetic tests as well as neurological and everything comes out normal…Does anyone relate?"* MUMS newsletter helped parents connect in many ways—medical support information as well as emotional support with pages titled *"My biggest problem with having a child with a special need is…"* and conversely, *"THE GREATED GIFT THIS CHILD HAS BROUGHT TO OUR LIVES IS…"* I found these topic pages interesting in that, although their child may have a different diagnosis, disorder, etc., the parents could similarly relate and respond. The poem *It Matters to This One* (which can be found in Appendix A) touched my heart as a mom. It reinforced my "battle-maiden Mom" mindset.

I called a friend, who was also an OB-GYN, and explained the news that we'd recently received regarding our two boys. The response I received was that during his or her last eight years in local practice, he or she hadn't seen a single situation where two out of two children had a condition—as our sons did. Consequently, I was told—as a friend—that it would be best to not take a chance to become pregnant since it *seemed* that there was a chance that our next child could also have the condition—given these two out of two odds—and the condition didn't *seem* to be diagnosed. It was suggested that if we wanted a third child, we should get *both* donated egg and sperm (from contacts that could be provided) in order to avoid any possible genetic information of our own to be involved. This suggestion was made even though we didn't yet know if our egg and sperm contained any of the genetic information that had caused the condition for both of our boys. Obviously, Jay and I could not even be tested until we knew what the boys had.

~ ~ ~ ~ ~ ~ ~ ~ ~ ~ ~

Since the boys were still babies, I put each of them to bed with a nightly routine—I would hold them in my lap as we rocked in the rocking chair to music that played softly. Our favorite became "Rock-A-Bye Lullabies" because each song's tempo gradually became slower, which gave them (and me) time together to wind down from our busy day before they fell asleep. After I'd put the boys to bed, I would go downstairs, and often find Jay seated on our couch in the family room as he read the paper and/or watched TV. I would usually then join him, ask about his day, and then I would tell him about the day I'd had as well as the boys' day. More recently, I'd found that when I talked to Jay about the boys (i.e., the information that we had received about their developmental concerns, etc.), he didn't seem very responsive. In fact, I often felt that I had the conversation with myself since he seemed disinterested and distracted by the paper, TV—anything to avoid a conversation along this line.

One evening when I'd asked him, "Why did you marry me?" he'd somewhat blown me off at first. So I'd asked again, "No, seriously, I would really like to know the reason you married me." He finally responded, "Because you're smart, you take good care of me, the boys, the house, etc."

Although we had both become parents to Blake and Daniel, Jay seemed to only want to share the good times, the good moments. As long as "things" were taken care of, he was happy. But when it came time to help me take care of "things,"—especially if they were difficult—more often than not, it was left up to me to do those "things" alone. As we sat on the couch one night, I felt somewhat overwhelmed

91

due to the situation of our boys' special needs and the search for answers. When I'd tried to talk to Jay about it, however, he didn't seem to really listen. Consequently, I expressed interest in seeing a counselor and asked him what he thought. He didn't seem resistant about it, but also wasn't overly supportive—as usual, it more or less was up to me.

Within a few days, I was scheduled to meet with a family counselor for the first of our insurance plan's ten approved appointments. When I'd neared the limit of visits, she told me to ask Jay to attend the next session with me. She stated that much of the counseling we'd had was regarding our sons, but since Jay was the other parent, she felt that we should both be in on this issue together. When I'd arrived home, I asked Jay (as the counselor had requested). His response was lukewarm, but he said he would go along with me. I'd asked my Mom if she would babysit the boys for us while we both attended this appointment—only she knew that Jay and I were in counseling at that time. On our way to our appointment with the counselor, I'd asked Jay how he was feeling. He told me that he'd done this before with his first wife, and didn't see much use in it.

The counselor welcomed both Jay and me into her office, and we were seated in separate chairs that faced each other diagonally—both sat toward the chair where the counselor sat. She directed questions to Jay as well as to me. I answered one of her questions, which had to do with Jay's parents, and before I knew what had happened—Jay slapped me across the face. The counselor's eyes widened and her mouth literally dropped open in shock. I heard her tell Jay that she would have to ask him to leave the room, and then she escorted him from her office down the hallway and into another room.

When the counselor returned to the room, she asked me if I was okay. Still in shock with what had just happened to me, I was hesitant to even respond. She then asked me two questions: (1) had it ever happened to me before, and (2) did I feel safe to leave her office with my husband. She went on to explain to me that if/or when Jay hit me again, I should immediately call 9-1-1; they would then send the police to arrest him. She also added that I should continue to come to the couple of remaining counseling sessions—but I should do so without Jay.

Jay and I drove home together in silence, but my emotions were a tangled web of chaos, disbelief, hurt, and pain. I was shocked that not only had he hit me—for the first time ever—but that he'd behaved in such a hostile way in front of a third party. My thoughts boomeranged from dismay that he had so little respect for me to humiliation that I'd been treated that way in front of someone else to quiet whispered fear that the disrespect his parents had recently shown me was now mirrored in my husband's behavior as well. Instead of an attempt to discuss any of this with him, I did what far too many wives have done in the past, and worked overtime to convince myself that something outside our relationship—his boss? the economy? his unspoken anxiety about our sons?—had prompted this aggressive outburst.

Once the last of my insurance company allotted sessions with her was finished, we were referred further and a new approach was recommended. From that point forward, Jay would have a male counselor, I would have a female one, and the four of us would meet together—as directed by the two counselors—in the fall of 1996.

~~ What to Expect When Your Child Has ASD ~~

<u>FACTS AND STATS</u>: Did you know that Autism is the fastest growing developmental disability? On March 27, 2014, The Centers for Disease Control and Prevention (CDC) announced that they now estimate 1 in 68 children (or 14.7 per 1,000 eight year olds) in multiple communities in the United States has been identified with autism spectrum disorder (ASD). This new estimate is roughly 30 percent higher than previous estimates reported in 2012 of 1 in 88 children (11.3 per 1,000 eight year olds) being identified with an autism spectrum disorder...The data continue to show that ASD is almost five times more common among boys than girls: 1 in 42 boys versus 1 in 189 girls. White children are more likely to be identified as having ASD than are black or Hispanic youngsters. This study also found that almost half of children identified with ASD have average or above-average intellectual ability (i.e., an IQ above 85) compared to a third of children a decade ago. The report also showed most children with ASD are diagnosed after age four, even though ASD can be identified as early as age two. "More needs to be done to identify children with autism sooner," said Coleen Boyle, Ph.D., M.S. hyg., director of CDC's National Center on Birth Defects and Developmental Disabilities. "Early identification is the most powerful tool we have right now to make a difference in the lives of children with autism."

<u>EARLY IDENTIFICATION</u>: Characteristic behaviors of Autism Spectrum Disorder may appear in infancy (18 months to 24 months), but usually become clearer during early childhood (24 months to 6 years). As part of a well-baby or well-child visit, your child's doctor should perform a "developmental screening" by asking about your baby's progress. Five behaviors that warrant further evaluation include: 1) does not babble or coo by 12 months, 2) does not gesture (point, wave, grasp) by 12 months, 3) does not say single words by 16 months, 4) does not say two-word phrases on his or her own by 24 months, or 5) exhibits any loss of language or social skill at any age. Any of these "red flags" does not necessarily mean that your child has autism. But **because the disorder's symptoms vary so widely, a child showing these**

94

behaviors should be evaluated by a multidisciplinary team that is **knowledgeable** about autism.

INFANTS AND TODDLERS: Just as we have height and weight parameters for children that can help determine if a child has a developmental delay, such as ASD, we also have milestones that parents should watch for.   As parents observe their children, they should both trust their instinct and use their newfound knowledge to identify any concerns. Here are some behaviors common to ASD:

- Has trouble relating to others or no interest in other people

  at all

- Avoids eye contact

- Prefers not to be held or cuddled

- Has trouble expressing needs by using typical words or

  motions

- Has extreme trouble adapting when a routine changes

- Has unusual reactions to the way things feel, look, smell,

  sound or taste

- Does not smile (on his or her own) by 5 months or laugh by 6

  months

- Shows no interest in games of peek-a-boo by 8 months

- Repeats or echoes words or phrases said to him or her, or

  repeats words or phrases in place of normal language

  (echolalia)

- Has other language delays, such as not saying "mama" or

"dada"

- Does not play imaginary games, such as pretending to feed a

  doll, by 24 months

- Does not look at objects when another person points at

  them by 12 months

- Does not point at objects to show interest by 24 months

Other common signs include:

- Apparent insensitivity of pain

- Unprovoked and repeated tantrums

- Extreme distress for no apparent reason

- Acting deaf

- Showing no fear of real danger

It's important to remember that any of these signs by themselves can be typical; however, a pattern of unusual behaviors, constant use of certain behaviors over time, or problems with either communication or social skills are cause for concern. Talk with your doctor about your concerns, and ask for an assessment by your local early intervention program. Early identification of an ASD is critical because it means that helpful services can begin right away, which can make a huge impact on a child's behavior, functioning, and future well-being.

DIAGNOSIS: A brief observation in a single setting cannot present a true picture of someone's abilities and behaviors. Developmental history and input from caregivers, parents, and/or teachers are important components of an accurate diagnosis. A *medical diagnosis* of ASD is most frequently made by a physician, and based on a specific number of symptoms stated in the Diagnostic and Statistical Manual

(DSM-5, released 2013) of the American Psychological Association. An *educational determination* is made by a multi-disciplinary evaluation team of various school professionals. The evaluation results are then reviewed by a team of qualified professionals and the parents in order to determine whether a student qualifies for special education and related services under the Individuals with Disabilities Education Act (IDEA) (Hawkins, 2009).

(Source: http://www.autism-society.org)

My Mother--
My Rock

CHAPTER EIGHTEEN

SUPER BOWL

Our hometown NFL football team—the Green Bay Packers—had won the NFC Championship, and would play the New England Patriots in Super Bowl XXXI, which was scheduled for January 26, 1997. It had been a long time since our team had been to the Super Bowl—i.e., have the chance to bring the "Lombardi Trophy" back to "Titletown, USA" (as the city was nicknamed)—so we all were truly excited! Like many Packer fans, Jay and I decided to make arrangements to fly to New Orleans in order to attend the Super Bowl. The media really played up the game, and took every chance to promote our Green Bay Packers. After all, they would make a long overdue Super Bowl return appearance; they'd won the first (1967) and second (1968) Super Bowl games.

A few days before the big game would be nationally televised, my mother was out for lunch with her friends at a downtown restaurant when a local television reporter approached their table. Since she and her friends were old enough to remember the Super Bowl I and II games (which the Packers had won), the reporter asked if they had any stories to tell. Mom spoke up and explained that she and the Packer's Head Coach Vince Lombardi shared the same June 11th birthday. Years ago, when she and her family had been at the Country Club to celebrate her birthday, Coach Lombardi was also there to celebrate his. When they realized that they had the same birth date, he gave her an unexpected "birthday kiss" on her cheek! Mom then confessed—humorously—that (for days afterward) she hadn't washed her face!!

At approximately 3:40 a.m. on January 22, 1997—four days before the big game—Jay and I were awakened by a phone call from my new stepfather, John. He said that Mom was experiencing chest pains and, consequently, had been taken by ambulance to the hospital. As I hung up the phone and sat on the edge of our bed, I realized that I was awake—this was not a dream—and my life, as well as my mother's, was about to take a big turn for the worse. Mom and John had married only a month before, on December 23, 1996, and they had planned to take a belated honeymoon. Their packed luggage was already in the car, ready to leave that morning to begin their drive down to Florida. Instead, my Mom had now been taken to the hospital in an ambulance!

I called my older sister, who lived nearby, to tell her that I would pick her up so we could drive to the hospital together. When we arrived, we saw that our other two sisters were already there. The four of us were allowed to enter the Emergency Room, where Mom sat up on the hospital gurney with her hair perfectly done (she had gone to her hairdresser the day before, since she and John were to leave for their trip), and she looked—outwardly—like she was fine.

Since her father had died from a heart attack, Mom assumed that she experienced a "cardiac episode." But after more tests were conducted by the Emergency Room Doctors, they discovered that the chest pains Mom had experienced weren't due to her heart. Instead, the doctors were concerned about Mom's liver because her enzyme levels were elevated, which was not a good thing.

Another symptom Mom had experienced in the past four months was lower back pain. It had slowed her down at times, which was so unlike the active, dynamic 71-year-old woman we knew. She'd had her annual physical exam the previous month, and was told that her back pain was probably due to arthritis. She thought that perhaps she had "pulled a muscle" in her back when she'd lifted her large suitcase during a tour group trip to Spain a few months earlier. Travel was a passion for Mom—she could pack a suitcase in just a matter of minutes if she knew there was an opportunity to travel to an interesting destination—particularly European ones. As a high school English teacher who taught Shakespearean literature, Mom had travelled to England a few times.

(One of those trips to the U.K.—only a few years earlier—had included a personal tour she'd arranged with top management at the English PCMC—Paper Converting Machine Company facility. Since her father and her grandfather had been the original founders of the company—which had started in Green Bay, and was officially incorporated as PCMC in 1923—this opportunity was very meaningful for her.)

Once it was determined that Mom's liver was the problematic cause of her chest pain, she was scheduled for surgery early that afternoon. Her four daughters and her newlywed husband gathered around Mom's hospital gurney as she waited for her surgery. Outwardly, she looked okay, but I could see concern in her eyes. She kept her fear to herself in order to protect us from worry about what might lie ahead...for her...for John...her children...everyone!!

After the surgery, the doctors told her four daughters and son (who had arrived at the hospital after he'd flown in from Texas), that she had a large (nine centimeter) aggressive cancerous tumor. It was medically termed "cholangiocarcinoma" (cancer of the bile duct), and was very rare. Later, when the surgeons told her what they'd found, Mom informed us that she would fight this cancer. After all, she wanted to enjoy her new life, which she had just begun a month earlier when she'd married John.

With this news regarding Mom's serious health condition, I realized that I simply could not leave for the Super Bowl in New Orleans with Jay the next day as we'd planned. I told him that I would never forgive myself if I didn't stay with my mother while she underwent treatments. I added, "You won't forgive yourself if you don't take this opportunity to make your dream (to attend each of the major sporting events in your lifetime) come true. I, as well as Mom, want you to go." The only thing I asked of Jay was that he talk to his parents, who had previously said that they would take care of Blake and Daniel while the two of us were in New Orleans. We still needed their help. Only now I would be spending time each day beside my Mom in the hospital.

~ ~ ~ ~ ~ ~ ~ ~ ~ ~ ~

After I asked Jay to offer my ticket to his father to attend the Super Bowl with him, Jay told me that his father had said, "No." I then thought of my godson, whose father and older brother already had tickets—this would give him an opportunity to attend as well. I talked to my godson's mother—my oldest sister—and found out that it would

101

work. The plan was that Jay would fly out of Green Bay with my godson, whose father and brother would meet up with them in New Orleans.

Jay had walked upstairs to pack the last of his things to leave for the airport when he told me that his parents had arrived to watch Blake and Daniel. He then told me that his parents said that they had been "only kidding" when his Dad had said that he wasn't interested in the other Super Bowl ticket. We were both confused by his Dad's change of heart—especially since it came within just minutes of when Jay would leave for the airport with my godson.

When Jay's Dad returned back after he'd dropped off Jay and my godson at the airport, I was folding clothes in the laundry room, and he said to me (with a chuckle in his voice), "Yah, I was only kidding Jay about my not being interested in going to the Super Bowl...in fact, maybe a friend of mine and I would have taken those (our two) tickets!" I was confused by his remark and thought to myself how sad it was that Jay's Dad would lay a guilt trip on his son just as he was about to leave for this dream "bucket list" trip. After I'd put the clean folded clothes away, I kissed my sons "good-bye." They would stay with Grandma and Grandpa while I went to the hospital to check on Mom.

Jay's parents had agreed to babysit for a few hours each day while he was at the Super Bowl over the weekend, so I made my way to the hospital on Saturday—the day before the game, and our youngest sister's birthday. A birthday cake was brought into the hospital room where we all celebrated the occasion. In spite of Mom's dire physical condition, we hoped it might provide some emotional relief.

In light of the situation, we asked her doctor whether or not it would be a good idea to have Mom's 96-year-old Mother fly in from Florida. In more recent years, the two of them usually stayed together in Florida during the harsh winter months. The doctor's response was along the lines of "better to have her come home than not." This statement let us know that Mom's cancer was terminal, and it was just a matter of time before it would take her life. We decided among ourselves to ask her doctor(s) to not tell Mom how serious her condition was. We reasoned that she had often said, "Nothing is going to break my spirit!" So we wanted her to have every opportunity to fight the cancer if she could/would. She had also—at different times in her life—told us that she hoped (when it came time for her death) that it would be fast. In other words, she did not want to linger in her physical body, especially if she could no longer communicate (i.e., Alzheimer's).

The next morning was Super Bowl Sunday, and Jay's Dad arrived mid-morning—but without Jay's Mom. This was odd because they were almost always together, so I asked where she was…was she outside? Jay's Dad responded, "She's not here, and she won't be coming. Her sister's husband (whom I'd been previously told had struggled with health problems for most of his life) is in the hospital."

I said, "I'm so sorry to hear that," but Jay's Dad interrupted me to say, "And as soon as you can get someone over here to babysit, I'm out of here!" His comment really shocked me. I quickly thought to get on the phone and tried to call babysitters, but THIS WAS SUPER BOWL SUNDAY! Most people had already made plans weeks earlier to get together socially to watch the game, so my efforts to get a babysitter at the last minute were more than difficult. One of our regular babysitters offered to call a friend of hers who, in the end, was available—but could not arrive until noon. It was already mid-morning, and since this was all I could come up with through my phone-calling efforts, I told Jay's Dad that a new babysitter—who had never even met our boys—could come over at noon. He and Jay's Mom had committed to Jay for whatever time would be needed each day while he would be away at the Super Bowl. But now—when I needed them most—they had suddenly changed their minds. I then asked him if they would keep me informed about her sister's husband's condition, but Jay's Dad only responded, "As soon as the babysitter arrives, I'm out of here!" His tone of voice hurt me, but I knew that I had to put this remark behind me and turn my attention to Mom, who was terminally ill.

When I returned home from the hospital, the (new) babysitter told me that my father-in-law had left as soon as she'd arrived. I thanked her for the assistance she'd provided at a last minute's notice, paid her, and then hugged both of my boys. After the turbulent events of that day,

103

I really needed to hold them. Unfortunately, more stressful developments were to come!

That evening the Green Bay Packers became Super Bowl Champions, once again! I had mixed emotions about their victory—since as much as that day would become football history—it paled when compared to the fact that soon my wonderful Mom's life would also "become history."

The next morning was Monday, and Jay would return that evening. Neither of his parents showed up that day to care for our sons—I didn't even receive a call from them. Fortunately, one of my neighbors (who, like others, had begun to hear the news regarding my mother's serious condition) offered to babysit Blake and Daniel. I'd always known that I had nice neighbors, but I now realized that they were real friends who truly cared for me and my family. (During this sad time, they helped take care of our boys, brought over prepared dinners, or made a friendly call just to see how I was doing on a daily basis, etc.)

Monday evening, Jay called to tell me that air traffic was backed up, and that he probably wouldn't arrive back in town until early Tuesday morning. I was exhausted, and decided to wait until Jay arrived home to tell him about his parents' strange behavior. In the morning I would bring him up to date on all the unpleasant happenings—both at home and at the hospital.

CHAPTER NINETEEN

Days Following Diagnosis

When I awoke the next morning, I saw that Jay had returned home. After he shared all the happenings during his Super Bowl trip with me, I then told him what I'd experienced while he was away. Particularly, how his parents had walked out on the boys and me halfway through the weekend, and hadn't fulfilled their commitment to babysit for a few hours each day while he was gone. Then I told him about his uncle's hospitalization due to an ongoing health condition, as well as the sad news that my mother had terminal cancer and had only a few weeks left to live. When Jay heard all the things that had happened while he was away, he said, "Go ahead...I'll take a day off work so you can be with your mom." I really appreciated his offer, thanked him, and then got ready to leave for the hospital amid goodbye kisses and hugs from Blake and Daniel.

Later that day, when I'd stepped out and then returned to Mom's hospital room, I saw Jay there. With surprise, I asked, "Jay, what are you doing here? Where are the boys?" He answered, "My parents are watching them. My cousin is in town because her father (my uncle) is in the hospital, and I'm on my way to see them right now." I thought it was ironic that his parents jumped in to babysit so that he could visit his cousin and uncle in the hospital, when they had so recently reneged on their commitment to babysit for me. I also thought back to just a month earlier when Mom had invited his parents (plus Jay, Blake, Daniel, and me) up to her condominium over the Christmas holiday week. Is this how much they thought about my mother (much less, of me) especially in the midst of her unexpected and devastating cancer diagnosis?? It hurt me to even think such thoughts!

I asked Jay if he would step out into the hallway with me for a moment to talk while Mom lay in her hospital room bed. Jay then told me that he wanted to walk next door to the hospital where his uncle had been admitted so he could visit with his uncle's daughter, who'd flown in to Green Bay. I asked him if he would meet me back outside Mom's hospital room at 6 p.m.—at that time we could decide whether we would stay a while longer at the hospital, or return home to the boys.

Soon it was 6 p.m.…and then almost 6:45 p.m., but there was no sign of Jay. I thought that perhaps he'd forgotten and had just gone straight home, so I made a call to our house. When his Dad answered the phone, I asked him if Jay had returned home, but was told "No?!" I then explained that we had planned to meet at 6 p.m. at the hospital, and Jay had not yet shown up. His Mom then picked up the phone, and I asked her if she could please look in the refrigerator and fix something to hold the boys over until Jay and I could get home—as soon as he met me at the hospital as planned. To my surprise, she passively responded, "I don't know." Confused and unable to get anywhere, I then (finally) saw Jay. So I told his parents not to worry—Jay had just arrived. Relieved, I hung up the phone.

I asked him, "Jay, where were you?! We'd agreed that we would meet back here at 6 p.m., and now it's almost 7 p.m.!" He said, "My cousin's father is in the hospital, and she needed a shoulder to cry on." So much had transpired in the last few days that I just said, "Since you asked your parents to come over to take care of the boys, you can relieve them of their babysitting and go home ahead of me. I will pick up some pizzas on the way home, which by then should be 9 p.m. Please make sure your parents leave our house by the time I get home. I can't deal with them right now in light of my priorities, what little time is left due to Mom's terminal cancer, and how they behaved." So, Jay then left for home in his car, and I left in mine to pick up the pizzas as I'd promised.

But when I turned into our driveway after 9 p.m., I saw that his parents' car was still parked in front of our house. And as I parked my car in our garage, I saw that Jay's car was there, too. I walked into our house with the frozen pizzas in my arms. Just then, the three of them started to walk down from upstairs, so I glanced at them but walked straight into the kitchen—to avoid any conversation. Blake was still awake, walked up to me, and discovered that I had carried in the type of pizza that he loved! I then heard Jay's Mom say (as she walked into the kitchen with her husband and Jay behind her), "Do you want a hug?!" I replied, "Are you talking to Blake?" She responded, "No." I then told her—as well as her husband and Jay—that it would be hard to accept a hug in light of the way that I'd been treated by them the last couple of days. I added that on top of all that, I'd just learned that Mom would soon die from cancer. Jay's Mom then remarked about her high blood pressure and that she didn't need to hear what I'd said!?

At that point, I was so upset that I felt the need to interrupt her. With tears in my eyes, I said, "Well, at least you still have a blood pressure, whereas my mother will soon have no blood pressure at all to keep her alive! She was so good to all of you, yet when she needs you to be there for her daughter and grandchildren to support them through this difficult time as she lays dying, you just walk away?!? What's more, your actions have been hurtful, yet you act as if nothing happened?!?" With nothing left to say, Jay's parents walked out of our house, and he followed behind them to their car. He then came back in the house, had pizza with Blake and me, but nothing more was said about his parents' behavior—or mine.

~~~~~~~~~~~~

Once, when I'd gone along with my new stepfather, John, to wait with Mom for one of her sessions of radiation and/or chemotherapy, I noticed that as she lay on the hospital gurney, he stood by her side. To me, he literally resembled her "knight in shining armor." She'd teasingly said—long before her illness—that he played that role in her life, and Mom referred to him (kiddingly, yet lovingly) as "Sir John."

As she lay in her hospital bed, Mom awakened to see her 96-year-old mother, who had flown home from Florida, sitting by her bedside. I'd watched as Mom slowly opened her eyes, turned her head to see her mother, and then exclaimed, "Mumma, you're here!" Grandma was healthy with the exception of her eyes—she had become legally blind over the past years due to macular degeneration. Perhaps it was God's way to spare her from the sight of her daughter's decline from cancer. Through their mother and daughter bond, they shared tears and held each other's hands while each tried to be strong for the other during this heartbreaking reunion.

107

When Jay and I met with our counselors and shared with them Mom's diagnosis of terminal cancer, they suggested that we put our joint sessions "on the back burner" for awhile. In their opinion, our need to deal with and grieve my mother's inevitable death in the upcoming weeks was more urgent.

Mom requested that she not have any visitors beyond the immediate family and her best friend. She wanted people to remember her as the active, dynamic woman that she had been—rather than see the effects of cancer, which would alter everything about her. For this reason, she didn't see her youngest grandsons—my son Blake (nearly six) and Daniel (age two and a half) after her diagnosis. At various times, I'd asked Mom if she would like to have the boys visit with her in the hospital—Daniel had speech/occupational/physical therapies a few days a week on the second floor in the hospital's Birth-to-Three Program, while Gommy was on the 9th floor oncology unit at the same hospital. I brought pictures that Blake and Daniel had drawn to put up on the walls in Mom's hospital room as a way for her to—at least—feel connected emotionally.

~ ~ ~ ~ ~ ~ ~ ~ ~ ~ ~ ~

It was decided that Mom would leave the hospital and have hospice come in and take care of her at home. Blake and Daniel were scheduled to meet and be evaluated by a notable Neuropsychologist (they'd been referred by their Pediatric Neurologist), who was located in Madison, Wisconsin. So, on the Sunday before Valentine's Day, Jay and I had to drive to Madison with our boys. We had checked into a hotel, and the plan was for my college friend, her husband, and their kids to all join us at the hotel's pool. Jay and our boys went on ahead to the pool, and as I got ready to join them, my friend came up to meet me in the hotel room. She told me that Jay suggested that she come up and talk to me, which gave me an opportunity to tell her the tragic news about my mom.

On the drive down to Madison, I had been somewhat quiet in the car—it gave me time to process the difficult situation regarding my mom's serious condition. And now, as I shared my sad news, I found myself able to break down in tears. As always, my friend was there for me "through thick and thin," and kindly provided the shoulder I needed to cry on. After I dried my tears, she and I then joined our families at the pool—and I tried to let our time together serve as the (temporary) distraction I needed.

The next morning, Jay and I took our boys in for their scheduled appointment with the Neuropsychologist. In addition to test administration and interpretation, the evaluation included interviews with Blake, Daniel, Jay and me, interpretation of behavior rating data from both home and school, and a review of school records—which had also been provided. In a nutshell we learned:

- *Blake's developmental history was consistent with a very mild autistic spectrum disorder—perhaps the origin of his delays, his continued difficulties with expressive language and auditory processing, his continued mild social anxiety, and his continued need for social skills and pragmatic language training.*

- *He has exceptional educational needs that are secondary to autism.*

- *In addition to the speech/language and occupational therapies, there will be continued need for the foreseeable future for significant adaptation of instructional methods in the classroom to address his language and social skills issues—he'll only make progress in these areas to the degree that his therapy can occur in small groups and in the classroom.*

- *He will need direct instruction in social communication, play skills, and considerable assistance in benefitting from his social experiences.*

- *His concept formation ability will need to be closely monitored in coming years.*

In closing, the Neuropsychologist signed off with saying, *"I am very optimistic about his future progress."*

When we returned home, we were told that Mom had enjoyed her best day since she'd been back home from the hospital. She'd even felt well enough to sit upright in one of the wing-backed fireside chairs in her living room. Jay and I, my siblings, as well as my stepfather, John, were all there at the house when Mom told everyone that her wish for John was to live at the house for a good year to figure out if he would want to stay there in Green Bay. Only a couple of months earlier, he'd sold his family home in Indiana in order to move to Green Bay.

After we heard about her good day on Sunday, which we'd missed, I walked back to the bedroom where she rested. Mom asked how the boys were, and how the doctor's appointment in Madison had gone. I noticed that she was in physical pain and tried to get in a comfortable position—so I decided to not "dump the diagnosis" on her about the heavy news that we'd received about Blake and Daniel. I could only say, "They seem to feel that they've figured out what's going on with the boys." I never did tell Mom about our boys' actual diagnosis. It was neither the right place, nor the right (oh-so-limited) time.

CHAPTER TWENTY

Gone Long Before Her Time

Mom's condition declined, so she was checked back into the hospital—it almost seemed as if she knew, and preferred to be there so the doctors and nurses could administer to her needs in the days that remained. Ultimately, there would be only seven weeks between Mom's diagnosis and her death, and the entire process was unbearably painful.

When Mom felt that she could no longer win her battle with cancer, she asked for her family (i.e., newlywed husband John, her five children, as well as her brother and sister) to gather around her hospital bed before morphine was administered to dull the unbearable pain. As we all stood by Mom's bedside, tears and sniffles could be heard as her brother told her, "Turn it over to God, Helen Claire" (as he called her). Mom then said, "Don't feel that I've left you...look for me in small places!" As the morphine was administered, she seemed to drift in and out of consciousness, and at times we heard her call out "Daddy." (She'd been very close to her father, who had died years earlier from a sudden heart attack.) At other times, Mom had said, "I'll help the children across...I'll help the children across..."

As Mom slipped more and more into a coma, our family sat in the room that adjoined her hospital room. My brother and oldest sister (as designated executors of Mom's will) began to read through the notes that she had written regarding her "death requests." One of them was that the infant son she'd had—who'd died at birth, and had been placed in the baby section of the cemetery—be moved to the cemetery plot where Mom would be buried. Initially, this request wasn't taken seriously by my oldest brother and oldest sister, but I told them that as co-executors of her will, they should at least attempt to fulfill Mom's request. I also brought another detail to their attention. Just months before (as the two of us drove on the lower road by the cemetery), Mom had told me that the dress she had bought to wear for her and John's wedding, she wanted to be buried in as well. She then added "Should anything happen to me…" It was quite odd to hear at that time since she seemed fine—who would have thought then that she would soon be gone?

Mom lingered in a coma nearly two weeks longer than the doctors and nurses had predicted. In fact, the family was asked if there might be some "unfinished business" that she was holding on for.

On Thursday, March 13, 1997, a snowstorm hit the city. As I drove into the hospital's parking ramp with Daniel, I saw my oldest sister get into her car. I asked, "Are you going to your class down in the Valley? I hear that the roads are terrible due to all the snow we're getting." My oldest sister replied, "No, I'm on my way to the cemetery to see if Mom's request about Douglas (our infant brother who had died at birth) can be fulfilled."

I then walked into the hospital and took Daniel to his occupational, physical, and speech therapy sessions (just as I used to do with his older brother Blake). Daniel's therapists all understood what I was going through because of my mom's condition, and they kindly suggested that I go up to the 9th floor to visit her while they consecutively administered Daniel's therapy sessions.

That morning, my mom's brother and his wife had also stopped by, and were in her hospital room until almost 11 a.m. I realized that I needed to leave to go get Daniel, who by then would be finished with his therapy sessions. I wanted to say a special private good-bye to Mom (which had—lately—become a daily ritual because I never knew if this "Good-bye" and "God Bless" might be the last) before I left. As soon as her brother and his wife stepped out of Mom's hospital room, I quickly slipped in to tell her that I needed to leave to go get Daniel on the hospital's 2nd floor. As she lay in a coma, Mom seemed to moan in reply.

Later that day, around 3 p.m., I received a call at home from my brother, who told me that I should come to the hospital right away since it seemed that "things had changed" regarding Mom's condition. As I drove to the hospital, sheets of heavy snow came down quickly. Even the main street that led to downtown (where the hospital was located) had two ruts in the snow; I'd managed to keep my vehicle's wheels in them, so that I wouldn't lose control. Traffic was slow, and while I was stopped at a red traffic signal, I looked up at the sky to watch the snow fall. It was at this moment that I felt an experience that I—to this day—can't totally describe. Something "strange" just came over me. The traffic light then turned green, and in the ruts of the snow—made by the other vehicles that drove ahead of me—I drove cautiously toward the hospital.

~ ~ ~ ~ ~ ~ ~ ~ ~ ~ ~

I parked my car, and then took the elevator—just as I had every day in recent weeks—to the hospital's 9th floor. But as I stepped off the elevator, I turned the corner and saw—halfway down the hallway—my brother and second-oldest sister embracing each other. I quickly took off my winter coat and practically ran down the hallway. As I approached my brother I asked him, "Is there still time?" And he—not sure of what I'd asked—nodded and said, "Yes. (He thought I'd said "Has she died?") I walked into the hospital room where I saw my two other sisters and my brother's girlfriend. Then my brother and my sister—whom I'd just met in the hospital hallway—came into the room, and joined us to gather around Mom's hospital bed.

When I realized that she had already died, I blurted—before I even knew what I'd said—"Mom, I'm just like you...I'm late!" She'd been known to be late so many times in her life—I even recalled that Mom had often said that she would probably be late for her own funeral! What's more, I'd remembered what Grandma had said to her daughter, Helen, during one of their last visits. While seated beside Mom's bed, Grandma had said that she now understood why Helen had been consistently late in life. It was because she'd had too much to do in the small amount of time she'd been given in life!!

I asked my siblings how long it had been since Mom had died, and was told that it had been about ten minutes before I'd arrived. I then realized that approximately ten minutes ago, I'd been at that snowy corner with the red light. She'd died while I'd waited for the traffic signal to change—and that indescribable feeling had come over me. My faith told me that it had been my mother's spirit passing over me in

113

farewell. In fact, my family explained to me that a few short moments before Mom died, she'd opened her eyes (which were quite yellow then due to the liver cancer), and looked at each person who stood in a circle around her bedside. She then closed her eyes—forever.

Perhaps she'd wanted one last look before she left this world?! On the other hand, maybe she could already see beyond…a few weeks earlier one of my sisters and I had stood at the foot of Mom's hospital bed and been advised by a priest (who'd come by to give her the Last Sacrament/Anointing of the Sick) that we shouldn't stand there. He said that the Angels appear at the foot of the bed when it comes time for the person to pass on (from this world). I guess we shall each come to know the truth of those "secrets" when our own time comes to pass.

I then realized that my step-father, John, was absent, and was told that just after Mom had died, he'd offered to go to her mother and gently break the sad news. The nurses told us that we could take as much time as was needed before we left the hospital room where Mom's body lay. By now, there was a blizzard outside, and sheets of white snow could be seen from the hospital room window. As I looked out the window—I thought how appropriate it was that her soul be lifted from where her body had rested under the warm white bed sheets to outside where white sheets of snow covered everything. In light of my faith, I felt it was a sign that Mom had been taken under the wings of the Angels from Heaven. Also notably, Mom died shortly after 3:30 p.m. during a two-day snowstorm—one of the top ten to ever hit Green Bay in history. What is more mysterious is that Mom had married John at 3:30 p.m., only three months earlier, when a different snowstorm had also hit our city!

I'd asked my oldest sister—whom I'd seen earlier that day in the hospital parking ramp as Daniel and I drove in for his therapy sessions—what she had learned when she'd gone to the cemetery regarding Mom's request. She told me that they'd said it could be done—and that our Dad was okay with this arrangement, too. I then learned that she'd shared this information with Mom about an hour before Mom died. When I heard this, it made me wonder if maybe this news was exactly what Mom had held out for! Perhaps she was finally able to let go once she

114

heard that her son, Douglas (who had died at birth), could be buried in the same plot. (They say that "the sense of hearing is the last to go.") Her casket would be placed next to his infant casket—just like a Mom!

It was around 7 p.m. when we left her hospital room for the final time. John and I had stayed behind, and we took one last look at her body as it lay there motionless, lifeless—it was so obvious that her spirit had definitely passed on. Exhausted from the past seven weeks (and aware that the next few days would be busy as Mom's funeral/Mass preparations became finalized), my siblings and I went to a local restaurant nearby for an adult bonding "time out." It was a place where we'd often enjoyed dinner with Mom through the years. It was difficult to process the idea that our Mom was really gone, but we were relieved that she no longer suffered in pain from the cancer. Still, there was also a deep feeling of grief as we longed for her continued physical presence in our lives.

~ ~ ~ ~ ~ ~ ~ ~ ~ ~ ~

NOTE: I'd often heard the song "One Sweet Day" on my car's radio in recent weeks when I'd driven to the hospital to visit Mom. Sung by Mariah Carey & Boyz II Men, it debuted—interestingly, nearly a year earlier to the date of her death—on March 16, 1996. The song was about the loss of a loved one, and the belief that eventually we can be together again in heaven one day. Because of my faith, it had special significance for me.

Three out of my four grandparents had lived well into their eighties and nineties, which included my maternal grandmother, who outlived my Mom. Consequently, I'd never really even thought about the possibility of losing Mom at her age—only 71!

CHAPTER TWENTY-ONE

MY MOM'S FATE AND FUNERAL

As fate would have it, Mom had died on Thursday, her funeral Mass was scheduled for the following Monday, and ironically (as well as unfortunately), this was Mom's mother's 96th birthday. Instead of celebrating her birthday, my grandmother now mourned the death of her beloved daughter, Helen, who—beyond just being her daughter—had truly been the physical caregiver among her children.

As the weekend progressed with funeral Mass preparations, I went over to Mom's house to help my sisters put together a collage of photos that depicted our mother's active, dynamic life; it would be on display at the funeral home. When I arrived at Mom's house, my oldest and youngest sisters, who both lived out of town, were in the back bedroom (my old room, which had become Mom's study after I'd grown up and married). They sorted out photos as I entered the room, and asked, "Where have you been?" I explained that I'd been delayed since I'd received calls from my neighbors and friends, who wanted to express their sympathy over Mom's death. I joined them to help sort out the photos of family memories we'd had of Mom.

I listened as they made remarks about our second-oldest sister. (She wasn't there with us because she was handling the music arrangements for Mom's funeral.) Negative comments were made about her ability to fulfill the funeral music job she'd been delegated. I'd heard negative comments (in previous weeks) made by my youngest sister to my second-oldest sister in the hallway outside of Mom's hospital room. Finally, I'd heard enough of such hurtful remarks—both in the nearby presence of our dying mom, and even now, while they prepared for her funeral.

A few months earlier (when I'd visited Mom at her cottage), she'd told me that my second-oldest sister and youngest sister—when they'd been there earlier that day—had had a sharp disagreement that really bothered her. Mom asked me if I was aware of some tension

116

between these two sisters, and I told her that I was. She then asked me if I would please do whatever I could to help them resolve their issues, and I promised Mom that I would.

So, I stood up for our second-oldest sister as I assured them that I was confident she would do whatever possible to handle the music for Mom's funeral. After all, she had music experience, and had often sung in the church choir for funerals. I asked them to give her a break…Mom had just died and we all needed to pull together, which was what she would want! Unfortunately, my two sisters did not respond positively to what I'd said. Nonetheless, we proceeded to sort the photos, and they made no more comments about our second-oldest sister. (I'd quickly learned that a parent's death could have a profound—even divisive—effect upon grown-up children to become critical of and/or judge one another.)

Late Sunday afternoon was the scheduled time for Mom's Wake Service at the funeral home. In the past, I'd been somewhat hesitant to walk into a room where the deceased was laid out—but today was different because I was somewhat anxious to see Mom. I was instantly relieved when I saw her in the dress that she'd worn when she married John—she looked like Mom again. There was no trace of the pain from cancer that we'd seen as Mom became frail, weak, and withdrawn. She had rarely—during the previous seven weeks until the time of her death—looked anything like her true self.

The Wake Service was attended by so many people that it made me realize how much of a positive impact Mom had had on those she'd known as a mother, daughter, sister, friend, teacher, etc., during her lifetime. I was touched to see most of my own local friends and neighbors show up—even my college friends, who'd travelled a long way to be there for me!

People were lined up to take their turn before Mom's casket, and right next to her casket stood Mom's beloved husband, John—just as he'd done often in recent weeks as she lay on a hospital gurney while she waited for chemo/radiation treatments. He'd lovingly cared for her until the very end, and only one week from her Wake Service, they would have celebrated their three-month wedding anniversary! Also, near

117

Mom's casket, her 96-year-old mother sat in a wheelchair, elegantly dressed, and also very stoic. Who would have thought that—at 96—her daughter would precede her in death?!?

I carried our 2 ½ year-old son, Daniel, in one arm, and held the hand of our 5 year-old son, Blake, as he stood on one side of me. Jay stood on the other side of Blake, and held his other hand as we walked up to the casket where Mom—their Gommy—lay. I then told the boys to say "Good-bye," and give Gommy their love for the last time that we would all see her. Before we walked away from the casket, the pictures that the boys had drawn for her (which had been on the wall in her hospital room) were tucked in the side of the casket. Mom had done this (with a note that she'd written for a deceased person who'd been close to her) before, and she had taught us all to do the same thing whenever a loved one died.

Mom had often mentioned that her father (to whom she was very close) had died unexpectedly when her two oldest children were five and two years old. (Coincidentally, the same ages of Blake and Daniel when their grandmother died.) She had also shared the story that my oldest sister, only two years old, had walked up and put a flower in her maternal grandfather's casket when he had died. (I find it interesting how adults can sometimes fear to attend a wake or a funeral more than a young child does. Could it be because the young child has recently arrived in the world from heaven, so death is not as fearsome? I would like to believe that this is the case.)

~ ~ ~ ~ ~ ~ ~ ~ ~ ~ ~

Visitation was scheduled for a period of time at the funeral home before we left for the church where the funeral Mass was to be held. Jay and I got into our car while my siblings and their children also got into their vehicles to line up for the funeral procession. In a motorcade behind the hearse, we drove by our childhood home, which was—as Mom had proudly said through the years—just "two doors" away from our catholic parish church. It made me think back to all the times when we'd walked to church with Mom. I realized that this would be the last time we would go anywhere physically with her in this lifetime and it almost felt surreal!

118

When the funeral procession motorcade arrived at the church, the funeral choir was to sing "What Are You Doing the Rest of Your Life?" before Mass. We all thought of it as "Mom and John's Song"—as it had been sung at their wedding. I later realized how the song's lyrics (written by Marilyn and Alan Bergman) were so fitting for them—even though their time together as husband and wife was, unfortunately, way too short-lived!

During her lifetime, Mom had often arrived late, and more than once she'd kiddingly said that she would probably be late for her own funeral! Ironically, that prediction came to be—we all arrived at the church late for her funeral. The church choir had already sung "Mom and John's Song," which had kept those seated in the church occupied until we arrived to begin the funeral procession.

Mom's casket proceeded down the main aisle of our family's parish church—accompanied by a select group of her closest friends on each side of her casket—just as she'd requested. Behind her casket, her children proceeded in chronological age. We, Mom's children, sat directly behind the first pew where her newlywed husband, John, was seated next to my grandmother, as were my uncle with his wife and my aunt with her second husband.

When the funeral Mass began, I looked around the church, which was packed with people who had somehow been touched by Mom during her lifetime—family, friends, neighbors, students, colleagues, etc. The priest who gave the eulogy was a friend of the family (he'd married Jay and me), and he spoke about Mom's life—more significantly, about her belief that "nothing was going to break her spirit!" No matter how difficult things in her life became. After Communion, a neighbor friend of the family sang the song Mom had told my second-oldest sister she wanted to be sung and dedicated to her own mother—if she should precede her own mom in death—which was "Wind Beneath My Wings" (written in 1982 by Jeff Silbar and Larry Henley). During her lifetime Mom had been an avid theatre/movie goer, and when she'd seen the movie *Beaches*, she said that the lyrics (recorded in 1988 by singer and actress Bette Midler for the original soundtrack to this film) summed up her feelings for—and relationship with—her mother.

119

As the funeral Mass came to its close, the group of Mom's closest friends once again gathered around her casket as they escorted it down the main aisle out of the church. Her family followed, and as I walked in that procession, I looked at people in the pews (which were filled to the back of the church) and felt so appreciative for what they'd meant to Mom—and what she had meant to them—during her lifetime. I was somewhat distracted by Jay's tears—I had tried to be strong for myself, but instead I found myself needing to be strong for him!?!

When we left the church, the procession of cars followed the hearse to the nearby Catholic cemetery where Mom would be buried in a plot next to her father, who had died 44 years earlier. After a short prayer service at the mausoleum, the family said our final farewell to her, and then we left her casket there so her burial arrangements could be completed.

It was Monday, and not many places were open to serve a funeral lunch. But since Mom's parents had been charter members of the Country Club for years, they made special arrangements to be open exclusively for Mom's funeral luncheon. The event was actually uplifting because the people who gathered there spoke about all the good times they'd shared with Mom during her lifetime. My brother and I, who were seated at the same table among funeral guests, commented that our mother (who had often mingled with the others at their tables) would now be able to be a part of *every* table's conversation. She'd always been very social, and had been able to contribute something enjoyable to any conversation. The words of Ralph Waldo Emerson—fittingly chosen for Mom's memorial prayer card—celebrated her life in loving memory: *"To laugh often and much; to win the respect of intelligent people and the affection of children; to earn the appreciation of honest critics and endure the betrayal of false friends; to appreciate beauty; to find the best in others; to leave the world a bit better whether by a healthy child, a garden patch, or a redeemed social condition; to know even one life has breathed easier because you have lived. This is to have succeeded."*

One of Mom's step-sisters mentioned to my second-oldest sister and me how we should continue to go to the theatre and see musicals (much as Mom had done with her children during her lifetime) because it would give us comfort after her death.

After the last of the luncheon guests had left the Country Club, I began to feel the full closure of Mom's death. I was exhausted from the seven preceding weeks—from her diagnosis, to her death, to all the days for funeral preparation and attendance—it had all finally caught up with me. The next morning I woke up to the finalization of my mom's death—the realization that I would never again be able to physically hug or see or talk to her *for the rest of my life*! I was 36 years old, had two small sons, and in recent weeks I'd been told that—due to the delayed development needs that our sons had displayed—our older son had "tendencies" of a mild autistic spectrum disorder. Plus—at that time— our younger son was questionable. On top of all this, it was becoming more difficult to deal with Jay and our strained marriage.

I kept it together as I reminded myself of the strength and stoicism my grandmother had managed to display. My stepfather, John, kept himself strong as he attended daily mass, and adopted the approach of—as he would say—"taking life one day at a time."

CHAPTER TWENTY-TWO

Tribute, Testament, and Testing vs. Treatment Results

Just weeks before Mom died, she'd called me to her bedside at home and told me that she wanted to donate a sum of money to the charity (which provided for the needs of children in the local area) where she and I had—for years—volunteered our time and service. The group's annual luncheon was scheduled for May, and she and I had planned to attend together to celebrate the completion of my five-year term. That was when I would officially—as she had years before—become an Associate. Unfortunately, she died in March—only two months before this occasion.

After Mom's death, I followed up on her request, and—since she'd made a monetary bequest—I was then asked to speak at the annual luncheon on her behalf. Initially, I'd felt reluctant to get up and speak, but with some encouragement from my friend, who was President of this women's service organization (plus my realization that Mom would want me to follow through), I decided to write the speech that I would deliver on her behalf.

On a Sunday afternoon, I sat down at our kitchen table, and began to write my speech. Mom had been a high school English teacher, and she spoke comfortably and taught from a podium daily in front of her students or in front of others whenever she gave a presentation. So in my thoughts I asked her, "What would you want me to say on your behalf, Mom? Please work through me as I write this speech." I then took my pen, a pad of paper, and began to write. I was surprised to find how easily the words came to me—in a way, I felt connected with Mom's spirit!

The event was held at the Country Club, and the last time I'd been there had been Mom's funeral luncheon, which had also been a celebration of her life. On this day, I was seated with her best friend and her sister as well as a few other women. When it came time for me to deliver my speech and make her donation, I was a bit nervous as I stepped up to the podium at the head table.

I placed my notes in front of me and began to speak. Every now and then I would look at the crowd of attendees—many of whom I recognized as either Mom's friends or "her" high school Junior English students—and I could feel how quiet the room was as the women listened to my every word. After I presented Mom's donation, I gathered my notes and began to walk back to my seat. Then my friend, who was President of this group and seated next to the podium, stood up and gave me a hug while the whole room of women stood up to give me a standing ovation. WOW! As I walked back to my seat, they continued to clap, and my Mom's best friend and sister said to me, "Your Mom is right here with you!" It gave me comfort—for all that Mom had done for me (including the time she'd babysat Blake and Daniel so I could accomplish my required "five years" of volunteer hours to benefit this charity)—that I could, in return, fulfill her one last request.

~~~~~~~~~~~~

During these difficult times—the loss of my Mom, as well as grief from the fact that both of our boys were developing atypically compared to their peers, and the gradual erosion of my closeness to Jay and his parents—I was fortunate to be able to rely on my supportive network of friends. One day my wonderful neighbor, whose daughters babysat for our boys, told me about a segment that she'd seen on a TV show (perhaps *20/20* or *60 Minutes*) that focused on "late-talking children"—particularly boys. She recommended that I pick up the book *Late-Talking Children* by Thomas Sowell—and I did.

His book truly gave me plenty to think about in light of the research studies and survey results that he referenced. The author was the father of a late-talking son, and his experiences led him to form a group of more than fifty sets of parents, all of whom had been anguished and frustrated as they struggled to cope with offspring who simply did not talk. He wrote: "Ideally, we would like an explanation not only concerning the central fact that our group of children talk late, but also concerning the associated phenomena—the overwhelmingly male group, the families with the analytical and musical talents…our children's brightness is concentrated in a particular slice of the intellectual spectrum, based on abilities known to be localized in the left half of the brain. The most unexpected—indeed startling—discovery from the survey of our group was that in 60% of these families the child had an engineer as a close relative…Our children seem more like engineers than like poets, more likely to master the computer than to master political intrigue…"

Obviously, as I read others' stories, I saw some similarities regarding our boys: "Luke understood what was said to him when it involved a concrete thing, but abstract concepts like 'waiting' did not seem to get through to him—or perhaps he just did not want to wait…not very patient when he has his mind set on something. He will often become frustrated and throw himself on the floor in frustration and resistance to us. All this is done without a word, except for crying and an occasional 'no'…has an excellent memory and does great with puzzles and objects that fit or stack together…loves animated videos or cartoons and will often act out the characters and do his best to sing along…is responsive to other children who want to play with him, but he likes playing by himself just as much, even when other children are around…"

This book provided consolation as well as hope when I read, "…perhaps what parents of late-talking children need to know above all is: You are not alone. Although late-talking in general has often been a sign of other serious and lasting problems, many parents of intelligent children who talk late have found light at the end of the tunnel— sometimes very bright light." Sally E. Shaywitz, M.D., Professor of Pediatrics, Yale University School of Medicine; Co-Director, Yale Center for the Study of Learning and Attention, wrote (about Thomas Sowell's book): "…*Late-Talking Children* gives parents the understanding, the confidence, and the fortitude to stand up and to fight for what is best for their child." As a "Battle-Maiden Mom," I felt empowered, and I was determined to learn how to navigate the systems (doctors, hospitals, insurance companies, schools, etc.) that would effectively serve both of our sons' best interests in light of their special needs.

During this same time period, we'd also received a report of our boys' lab results, which had been taken a few months earlier by the Biochemical Genetics Clinic. Blake's previous laboratory evaluation had (1) ruled out *fragile X syndrome*, (2) multiple metabolic tests performed were normal, and (3) unfortunately, they didn't have any other specific genetic or metabolic syndromes in mind that would explain Blake's problems. The consequent recommendations for Blake were: no further testing, and follow-up with a Pediatric Neurologist and Clinical Geneticist.

Similarly, Daniel's evaluation summarized that his metabolic testing to date had been very non-specific, and the studies didn't seem at all contributory to his problems; therefore (unfortunately), they didn't have any other specific genetic or metabolic diagnoses that would explain Daniel's problems. Recommendations for Daniel included: (1) no further testing at this time, (2) continue participation in the Birth-to-Three program, and (3) follow-up with Clinical Geneticist and Pediatric Neurologist as necessary.

A few days before Daniel's third birthday, the boys met with their Pediatric Neurologist, and we learned:

1) *The review of reports from occupational and speech therapists*

   clearly showed that many of the challenges that beset Blake in

   the past have slowly and steadily been overcome either because

   (a) intervention or

   (b) the natural history of his undiagnosed developmental disorder.

2) *He clearly had progressed "linguistically and in the sociocommuni-*

   cative domains" and was less challenged by sensory defensiveness.

3) *It was still important that his therapist recognize the continued need*

for him to receive remedial therapies.

4) *Unfortunately, a substrate, either anatomic, genetic, or biochemical couldn't be given for the developmental challenges faced by Blake, and perhaps more so, by Daniel.*

We were told that we'd been viewed as parents who weren't fully in agreement with many of the perspectives (neuropsychiatric) that were offered—we were quite understandably confused as well as concerned about the label of "mild autism." We'd discussed at great length: (1) the perspectives of many of the therapists and physicians involved, and (2) acknowledged that there was much confusion because of discrepant points of view. Consequently, it felt reasonable to say that the developmental diagnosis would be deferred at that time; however, "not being equivocal in stating that developmentally and historically" the Pediatric Neurologist concurred with (neuropsychiatric) opinion of an autistic spectrum disorder. We were told to focus upon the fact that "many children with mild autism had emerged beyond the challenges that permit this designation over time, and that it was a dynamic process influenced by many unknowns." A diagram was drawn for us that showed "the overlap symptomatology between Tourette's syndrome, autism, and ADHD in an attempt to demonstrate the psychological and biological influences of...sensory integration dysfunctions upon the behavior of children developmentally"—like Blake, and more so, Daniel.

In conclusion, we were told that further testing—such as an MRI or an EEG—wouldn't be productive at this time; instead, it was recommended that (over time) they maintain a level of therapeutic involvement.

We received these reports with mixed emotions—it was good to know that our boys didn't have Fragile X Syndrome and that metabolic testing brought normal results. But **the tiring "process of elimination" to determine what the boys don't have rather than decisively knowing what caused their developmental delays** in their speech, fine and gross motor skills, sensory defensiveness, etc., **still continued.** Our sons' pediatrician helped to soothe us by saying that although we didn't yet know the cause or condition concisely, the important factor was to deal with and/or treat the symptoms displayed. Fortunately, thanks to occupational, physical, and speech therapies, our sons were showing improvement.

~~ Early Intervention and Treatment Options ~~

EARLY INTERVENTION: Young children across the autism spectrum—including those labeled with autism, Asperger Syndrome, and other pervasive developmental disorders—receive an individualized approach that addresses their core deficits of ASD (i.e., academic difficulties, communication, sensory, social) and matches each family's preferences and needs. Critical features of appropriate early intervention services for young children with ASD include:

- **intensity** (Frequent opportunities to practice and be reinforced for engaging in adaptive skills—intervention should never be postponed. Focus is as important as time, which usually appears to be 20-40 hours per week.)

- **specialization** (Use of techniques that have been proven to be effective-based methodologies and therapists have experience with the unique disorder of ASD.)

- **individualization** (Focus on the individual child needs to be the basis of assessment, goal selection and treatment.)

- **family involvement** (Participation of family ensures generalization of skills learned, and also maximizes teaching time. Parents and caregivers need to feel empowered that they can make a positive difference in their child's life through their day-to-day interactions. These behavior strategies need to be user friendly and applicable to family life.)

- **natural environment** (While some skills may need to be taught in isolation, the sooner the child uses the ability in the natural environment, the sooner that child "owns" the skill.)

- **outcome-based focus** (Outcomes must be objectively measurable in order to ensure real growth. Data must indicate meaningful progress, and parents and caregivers need to see positive changes in the day-to-day life of their child for outcomes to be worthy of attention.)

In order for a young child with ASD to attain significant positive outcomes, there are several processing deficits that specifically relate to speech, language and communication, which must be the focus of early intervention. Concentrating on teaching a young child with ASD to process information efficiently must be differentiated from *skill acquisition*, which is teaching an isolated skill (such as body part identification or rote counting). Processing information involves multiple levels of brain function, including: attending to stimuli, acquiring new information, evaluating how the brain processes this information, and application of that information. *Significant processing deficits* in young children with ASD include *discrimination, imitation, social communication, symbolic/pretend play, and verbal speech.* Outcomes need to have significant impact on the life of the child and his or her family—the earlier the gaps in development are closed, the better the prognosis for the young child with ASD.

~ ~ ~ ~ ~ ~ ~ ~ ~ ~ ~ ~

The Birth-to-Three program is an example of **Early Intervention Services**. Once a child reaches the age of three, he or she can be enrolled in a local school-based Early Childhood Program. Often parents prefer to homeschool their young children with autism until it is felt that they are ready for a group setting. Another option is the Head Start program, a daycare program that is required to accept a certain number of children with disabilities (day care agencies in some communities will accept children with ASD). Some young children with ASD can benefit not only from individualized teaching, but also from settings in which caring and learning are fostered in a group.

SCHOOL AGE: All public schools must provide services for children with ASD from ages 3 through 21—they must evaluate the child for a suspected disability, develop an appropriate Individualized Educational Plan (IEP), and provide related services as needed. A child must have an educational evaluation in order to receive services in the public schools. Studies show that children with ASD respond well to highly-structured educational setting with appropriate support and accommodations tailored to individual needs. The educational program should build on the interests of the child, and use visuals to accompany instruction. When necessary, it should incorporate other services, such as speech or occupational therapy, to address motor skill development and sensory integration issues. A tailor-made, individualized IEP is critical for a child's success in school.

MOST COMMON TREATMENT OPTIONS

Educational - Includes Applied Behavioral Analysis (ABA), also known as Lovaas; Developmental, Individual-difference, Relationship-based (DIR), also known as Floor Time; Social Skills and Social Stories

Biomedical - Includes diets of Varying Types; Vitamin Therapies; Medication

Intensive Autism Services - Includes treatment provided by a team of individuals in the home, classroom, or community (may include ABA services)

Speech-Language Therapy - Includes Treatment for Auditory Processing Disorders; Oral Motor Treatment for Articulation

Communication - Includes Picture Exchange Communication System (PECS); American Sign Language (ASL); Visual Strategies; using pictures for communication; Facilitated Communication

Sensory Therapies - Includes Occupational; Sensory Integration; Auditory Integration Training; Developmental Optometry

OTHER RELATED APPROACHES: Complementary therapies that include music, art or animal therapies can help to increase communication skills, develop social interaction and provide a sense of accomplishment. Art therapy (which can provide a non-verbal, symbolic way for the child to express him or herself), and music therapy (which is good for speech development and language comprehension) are particularly useful in sensory integration, providing tactile, visual, and auditory stimulation. Animal therapy may include horseback riding, which therapeutically provides both physical and emotional benefits, and improves coordination and motor development, while creating a sense of well-being and increasing self-confidence. Unfortunately, little scientific research about these complementary approaches has been conducted to support these particular therapies.

CAUSES: There is no known single cause for autism spectrum disorder, but it is generally accepted that it is caused by abnormalities in brain structure and/or function. Brain scans show differences in the shape and structure of the brain in children with autism compared to those in neurotypical children. Researchers are investigating a number of theories, including the links among heredity, genetics and medical problems. In many families, there appears to be a pattern of autism or related disabilities, which further supports the theory that the disorder has a genetic base. While no one specific gene has been identified as causing autism, researchers are searching for irregular segments of genetic code that children with autism may have inherited. It also appears that some children are born with a susceptibility to autism, but researchers have not yet identified a single "trigger" that causes autism to develop. Other researchers are investigating environmental factors such as viral infections, metabolic imbalances, exposure to chemicals, and even gut bacteria issues.

(Source: http://www.autism-society.org)

Public Turn
of
The Tide

CHAPTER TWENTY-THREE

WAKE-UP CALL...TO ALL

One evening in mid-June, Jay and I were talking upstairs in our bedroom when he became upset and angrily shoved me to the floor. When I tried to get up, I realized that he'd pushed me so vehemently to the floor that my lower back was in real pain. I said, "I'm hurt...I am **really** hurt!" I realized that Jay was—obviously—out of control, and that (in light of Jay's angry outburst) I needed a third party to be present to prevent any further harm.

I tried to take a few steps and limped my way to the phone (which was on our bedroom's nightstand), but as I reached for the phone to call my sister who lived nearby, I felt Jay come behind me. He grabbed the phone out of my hand, and again shoved me—this time down onto the master bed. His anger had made him really strong, and as he held me down on our bed, all I could think of was to allow my body to go limp. My hope was that he would feel me surrender, and then let go of his hold on me. Instead, he just continued to hold me until I didn't know what else to do—so I said, "Fine, Jay, take me...then I'll be where my mother is now!"

He then shoved me—a third time—over on the bed while he said, "Go ahead..." I was in tears and stayed in a fetal position, while Jay then walked out of our master bedroom. I then slowly got up from the bed—and with my lower back in pain—I limped downstairs. I made it to the kitchen, and once more tried to call my sister for help, but as I did he showed up in the kitchen, and again grabbed the phone out of my hand. Naturally, I was terrified by Jay's behavior. Before I knew it, I was then backed up into the nearby family room, where he would not let me get past him. I even tried to crawl over our large, L-shaped sectional couch—despite my bruised, sore back—but I was barricaded in the family room with no way out!

Just then, Blake, who had been watching one of his favorite cartoons in the downstairs rec-room, came upstairs to the kitchen, and full of a six-year-old's curiosity, he asked what was going on. From the family room, Jay told him, "Nothing, Blake," while I pleaded with my son to call 9-1-1. Naturally, Blake looked confused. Distracted by Blake's unexpected presence, Jay tried to distract him, pretended that there wasn't any problem, and then took Blake back downstairs to play with him in the rec-room. When the two of them left, I was no longer "fenced in" the family room by Jay, so I tried to get back to the upstairs phone. My sister answered my call, and I urgently begged her, "Come over right away...no time to talk...come right now...Jay has hurt me!" Shortly after I'd hung up the phone, the doorbell rang.

As I painfully and slowly made my way back downstairs, I saw that Jay had already arrived at the front door. But when he opened the door, two police officers asked to come in. Jay said, "Everything's okay, Officers," but as the door opened wider, the officers saw me in pain and in tears. I said, "Officers, I think you'd better come in."

One of the policemen took Jay back to the family room for questioning, while the other talked with me in the front living room. I'd tried to sit down slowly in one of the wing-backed chairs, but the pain in my bruised tailbone—thanks to Jay—only allowed me to gently rest on the side of one of my hips. The uniformed officer noticed that I was in pain, and asked if I wanted any medical help. That would have been nice, but I was more concerned about the safety of my little boys, who were still in the house at this time. Daniel was already asleep in his crib upstairs in his bedroom, but I wasn't sure where Blake was in the house at the moment; so I asked the officer if he could please find my six-year-old to make sure that he was safe. Just then, the other policeman, who had questioned Jay, led him—in handcuffs—out of our house and into his patrol car.

The policemen told me that Jay had been arrested, and said they would come back later for a statement. By this time, my sister—who had seen Jay taken away in handcuffs and put in the police squad car—had shown up and asked what had happened. I told her as much as I knew at that time, and she asked me if Jay would get out on bail. Still stunned and overwhelmed by all that had taken place up to that moment (which I considered life-changing), I was hesitant to answer. My sister then told me that she would go ask our stepfather, John, to go with her to the jail.

Minutes after she left, the doorbell rang again. I slowly limped to the front door, and opened it to find one of my neighbors (also a good friend) standing there. She took one look at me, and asked, "Are you okay?!" Before I could reply, she offered to have her husband (who was an OB-GYN) come over to check out my pain.

The officer, who had arrested Jay, then returned to find out if I would give a statement. I asked him if I could first put Blake to bed. As I slowly followed my little boy upstairs to his bedroom, I tried to hide my pain from him. While I tucked Blake into his bed, he asked, "Mommy, why is the policeman here?"

I told him that the officer had some questions to ask, but he should try to go to sleep because it was late. I kissed Blake goodnight, and then checked in on Daniel—who was still asleep in his crib—before I slowly limped my way back downstairs to the kitchen where the policeman was waiting for my "statement."

Again, he asked me if I was ready. As I tried to gain control of myself (and my thoughts) in light of everything that had just happened to me, I asked him if the authorities had received a statement from Jay. The officer answered, "No, and it's your choice whether or not to give a statement." He then asked me if this was the first time that my husband had abused me. I told him, "No, this wasn't the first time—but it was one of the worst times that he hurt me physically." I recounted some of the other incidents of when I'd been physically abused by Jay, and wondered if perhaps this might finally be the wake-up call I needed.

The officer interrupted me and said, "Perhaps—after all, you know your husband. But I just have to say that the things I heard him say from the backseat of the police car were pretty disturbing!" Had Jay resisted his arrest? I later learned that he'd repeatedly demanded to know why he had been arrested. The officer explained that they would talk to him once they'd arrived at the police station. Then he heard Jay say, "Next time, I'll just say that she did it!" The policeman then explained that Jay wasn't to have any contact with me or the house, and if there

135

was any thought of having this order lifted, I would need to show up in court to make such a request. The police officer then left the house—and my marriage to Jay was essentially over.

~ ~ ~ ~ ~ ~ ~ ~ ~ ~ ~ ~

When I woke up the next morning, my memory—as well as my bruises—reminded me that what had happened the night before was neither a dream nor a nightmare. It had been real, and my life—and my sons'—would now take a treacherous turn. My sister called to tell me that Jay had been bailed out of jail, and he really wanted to see the boys—it was, after all, Father's Day.

Since Jay wasn't allowed to have any contact with the house or me, my sister offered to pick up the boys and bring them to a fast-food restaurant where Jay would be waiting. I got the boys ready to go and when my sister and my step-father arrived, they could see that I limped (thanks to the constant pain from the grapefruit-sized bruise on my tailbone). I thanked my sister for taking the boys to meet Jay, but I had mixed emotions. I wanted my sons to see their Dad on Father's Day, yet I realized that he was the same person who had been arrested for domestic violence/abuse toward me. Now he seemed like such a stranger to me—light years away from the loving husband I thought I'd married!

Since we'd had tickets to an event that we would no longer be able to attend (due to Jay's arrest), I called my oldest sister to offer them to her. But before I could get in a word, she started to scold me. I thought she would offer me her condolences and support—instead, I was blamed for Jay's arrest. She'd taken his side instead of mine—which really hurt especially since she hadn't even asked what had happened or taken the time to listen to my side of the story. I felt that I was being harshly judged when, in fact, I was the victim!

Within a week or so, I showed up in court with my stepfather at my side. The ban—which denied Jay contact with the house or me—was lifted at that time. I felt that *if* there were a chance for us as a couple, we needed (while still separated) to resume marriage counseling with our co-counselors. My level of trust in Jay, however, had nosedived. After every incident of physical abuse from Jay, he would try to apologize and promise me that it wouldn't happen again. But it always did—it was just a question of "when."

After he was bailed out of jail, Jay moved in with his parents and continued to live there during our separation. Following several weeks of co-counseling, I met with my counselor to discuss how the sessions had gone. She was straightforward, and told me that (a) she didn't think that Jay would change, and (b) I needed to decide whether to leave or stay with Jay. She also told me that for women in my situation more often than not, it was the wives who filed for divorce. They usually wanted to believe their marriages would work and that they would no longer be abused. But when the facts show them that things will not change, women accept the need to make a change and reluctantly file for divorce.

After more abusive incidents from Jay, I realized that our marriage had already come to an end. I could no longer trust his word (and when trust was gone, so was the marriage), so I distanced myself from him physically as well as sexually. I filed for divorce in late August 1997.

My mother's estate attorney recommended a female attorney I could use for my divorce. Meanwhile, Jay hired a well-known high-profile lawyer who would represent him in the upcoming divorce proceedings. This attorney was powerful and political in ways that were questionable and inappropriate, and his rumored "shady side" was revealed through the Family Court proceedings during our divorce, as well as afterwards.

I met with my attorney—a tall, slender woman with salt-and-pepper-colored hair that was cut short and close to her head. (She somewhat resembled—and therefore reminded me of—the "drill-sergeant" teacher I'd had in first grade.) Her office was located across the street from the courthouse in a building that—in past history—had housed the public library and the city's museum. For all the many times that my best friend and I had visited this building as young girls, it never occurred to me that later in life I would revisit this building for a different, heart-wrenching, life-changing purpose. Over the years, it had

137

been completely refurbished with various offices, including one for the attorney I would retain for my upcoming divorce proceedings.

When I met my attorney for the first time, she led me to what seemed to be a small boardroom where we sat down to discuss my petition to divorce Jay. My meetings with her began in late summer, and continued into the fall of 1997.

On Labor Day weekend of that year, my brother, three sisters, and I had heard the shocking and unfortunate news that Princess Diana had died in a car accident while we were gathered at Mom's house to sort through her belongings. She'd made it easy for us, and had previously written up a list of "which child should get what." We were somewhat surprised by this "advance planning" since her death had come so suddenly and unexpectedly. Perhaps because her own Mom was still alive and in her nineties, Mom had helped her with a similar list, and had been inspired to start one of her own. Mom's generous forethought was an unexpected blessing.

~ ~ ~ ~ ~ ~ ~ ~ ~ ~ ~ ~

NOTE: As a long-time Carly Simon fan, lyrics from her song "Like a River" describe a daughter's loss (fittingly for me) of her Mother.

CHAPTER TWENTY-FOUR

Months after Mom's Death—Dad Re-Enters My Life and Mom's Mom Dies at Ninety-Six

My siblings and I had grown more distant from our father in recent years due to a family intervention we'd had regarding our concern for him. He felt he didn't need the help, so it didn't turn out as successfully as we'd hoped. Consequently, each of his children was left to deal with "issues" with Dad as effectively as each of us felt we could at the time. Naturally, this resulted in strained relationships.

One afternoon in the fall of 1997, my father showed up (unexpectedly) at my house. I was in the garage when he got out of his car in my driveway, and as he approached me, the first thing he said was, "How are you doing, Dear?" I thought he was referring to my sorrow over Mom's recent and unexpected death, so with sadness I replied, "I'm doing…okay."

He then told me that he'd just come from Jay's parents' house, and they had asked him to come over to their house to discuss their kids' impending divorce. (Jay's parents were well aware of the strained relations between Dad and all of his children.) He agreed to meet them because he wanted to help in any way he could. My father told me that when he arrived, it was obvious that Jay's parents talked negatively about me—and only me—as well as my behavior. So Dad told Jay's parents, "I want to talk to Heidi…I'll get back to you." He then got into his car and drove straight to my house, where he now stood.

After I'd heard what Jay's parents had told him, I asked Dad to come in, sit down, and then I proceeded to tell him the truth about what had really happened. I let him know about the co-counseling, and the incidents of physical as well as emotional abuse by Jay that led up to his arrest. I explained that since then, we'd been separated and I had custody/placement of our sons. After my father heard all about what had truly happened, he said, "Given this information, Jay's parents don't deserve me bothering to get back to them…EVER!"

139

In spite of the earlier distance between us, I realized that he really did love me. Before Dad left, he said, "Heidi, I'm here for you and your boys. Now that I've learned about Jay's behavior, know that I support you in getting a divorce from him. I don't want him to ever hurt my daughter again." From that day forward, Dad had re-entered my life and stepped up to be present for me at each of the upcoming scheduled court dates for my divorce proceedings.

~ ~ ~ ~ ~ ~ ~ ~ ~ ~ ~

In early November, my 96 year-old maternal grandmother—who had enjoyed great health despite her limited eyesight due to macular degeneration—learned that her health was failing. Our family felt that since her daughter's (i.e., our Mom's) unexpected death from cancer in March of that year, our grandmother was simply dying of a broken heart.

I went to Grandma's house for what would become my last visit with her. For some years, she'd had a few women who worked in shifts, and cared for her in her own home. When I arrived that Saturday morning in early November, I saw Grandma lying in a hospital bed in her den. It now occupied the space where the couch had been for years. She seemed to have slipped into a coma, and was no longer able to communicate—I could hear her loud breaths, and since I'd been told that hearing is the last "sense" to go when a person dies—I told her what was in my heart.

"Grandma," I said, "You've always been a strong woman who endured life experiences—no matter how difficult or trying a situation would be like the loss of Grandpa, then the death of your second husband of over 25 years, and more recently the death of your daughter, Helen, just a few months ago. You always held your head high to convey your courage and integrity, which will always be remembered. Grandma, everyone admired your strength of character! Your daughter, Helen, (my mother) must have received this same character trait from you. Please, Grandma, continue to be with me in spirit—just as I believe my mother is—to keep me strong during this difficult time I've been faced with. Neither I nor my children can endure Jay's abusive behavior any longer. I've mustered up the strength to leave him and his abusive behavior for the boys' interests as well as my own!"

140

Tears rolled down my face as I looked at the physically weak but emotionally strong German woman with a caring, loving heart, who was—helplessly—dying a little bit with each beat of her weary heart. As other family members entered the den to see her, I said my last "Goodbye." It would be the last time I'd visited Grandma's house, which I'd known since childhood. Within hours, I received a call that let me know that Grandma had died, and funeral arrangements would be made.

~ ~ ~ ~ ~ ~ ~ ~ ~ ~ ~ ~

She was laid out in the same room at the funeral home where Mom had been only months earlier. I kept thinking of one of my visits to Grandma's house with my younger son Daniel, just weeks after Mom had died. I'd mentioned to Grandma that on our drive over to her house, we'd driven by the cemetery, which was on the way, and my little boy—then under three years old—would say "Gommy" (the name Mom had been given by her grandchildren). Grandma then asked, "You'll never forget your mother, will you?!" I was somewhat taken aback by this question, but I replied, "No way...how could we ever forget her?!"

As a girl, I'd grown up to admire and look to my mother's and my grandmother's guidance and wisdom. Through the years, I watched them manifest their strong faith, both during their lives, as well as when they faced death. Mom, much like her own mother, was faith-filled and showed compassion, which ultimately led them both to positively touch the lives of countless others during their lifetime. At the time of their deaths, each of these wonderful women displayed acceptance of God's will with grace and integrity. To this very day, my sons and I continue to miss both "Gommy" and Great-Grandma—their legacies live on!

Although Blake was six years old and Daniel was three years old during the year that both Mom and Grandma died, I'd continued to make sure that we not forget these two wonderful women who had graced our lives. Whether I was with the boys or alone, whenever I drove by the cemetery, I would take a moment to say a prayer or drive in and go to their gravesites (Mom's was next to her mother's—which was next to her father's).

One day, not long after Mom's death, I'd stopped and walked up to her grave—spring was in the air, temperatures weren't quite as cold, and since nobody was around, I spoke out loud to Mom as I stood before her grave. As I talked to her, I was distracted by a noise, which turned out to be what looked to me like a blackbird or crow up in a nearby tree. It continued to "caw" so much that I wanted to tell it to shut up. Just as I was about to do this, the thought of what Mom had told us before she died—"Don't feel that I've left you...look for me in small places"— came to mind, so I didn't "hush" the bird. I didn't really think that Mom was this blackbird or crow, but it did catch my attention and prompted me to think of her in spirit—which gave me a great deal of comfort. That type of thing happened a few other times...was it just a coincidence? I would like to think of it as more of a "God-incidence." I'd mentioned this to several of my family members, and some of them told me that over time they, too, had noticed the presence of a blackbird or crow in their "space" since Mom's death. In fact, one said that since Mom was such a "colorful" person in character as well as wardrobe, that a peacock—rather than a blackbird or crow—would be much more fitting!!

I later learned that crows are considered to be smart—and Mom was intelligent as well as practical, but never showy. (That was affirmed when one day—while I stood at Mom's grave—a cemetery groundskeeper commented that he'd seen Mom visit her father's grave through the years. She would often say a friendly "Hello" that brightened his day—Mom was always kind, sincere, and nonjudgmental.)

For what it's worth...I can add that after Grandma died, two blackbirds or crows would be sometimes present! Similarly, places have triggered a memory, and with the present-day technology of video cameras, memories made with our loved ones allow the departed to be remembered for how much love they had *within* themselves. They outwardly shared their affection and graced us with their love during their lifetime!

As the family members processed out of the Cathedral Church behind Grandma's casket, I noticed a group of women who had been Grandma's care providers in recent years, and even more in recent weeks as her health began to fail. As I passed them, I walked up to thank each woman for her care of Grandma, and for fulfilling her wish to be able to die at home. They responded graciously—and to my eyes, they all looked like gracious white-haired angels.

~ ~ ~ ~ ~ ~ ~ ~ ~ ~ ~ ~

NOTE: Although deaths, disabilities, and divorces can span across the length of a lifetime, I believe that my story is significantly different because **within a space of 42 weeks**, I'd suffered significant deaths and losses. These included not just that of Mom and Grandma's sudden deaths, but also my separation/divorce (due to an abusive husband), as well as the diagnosis that BOTH of our sons have an Autism Spectrum Disorder now. During that time, a deep, undeniable need to grieve and mourn came over me, and I felt that "the floor had come out from under me." Far too many times during those dark days I would ask myself, "How can I go on?"

"Courage isn't having the strength to go on—it is going on when you don't have strength." ~ Napoleon Bonaparte

CHAPTER TWENTY-FIVE

Divorce Depositions Disposed

There was simply no time to truly process the recent deaths since I had to keep up with our shattered little family's day-to-day activities. This included running the two boys to their Occupational and Speech Therapy sessions, driving Blake to kindergarten, and running to meet with my attorney to discuss divorce proceedings and issues. Our top concerns included placement and custody of the children, my physical abuse (which had resulted in my husband's arrest), and our grave concern—in light of his angry tantrums—about the boys being placed with their father. Since I was no longer available as a target for Jay to take his anger out on, he could (or would) transfer his fury onto the children.

When my female attorney said (regarding Jay's abuse), "There are women who have had it worse than you," I replied, "I'm sure there are, but that doesn't mean that what he did to me is acceptable!" From that moment forward, I began to have second thoughts about the wisdom of having her represent me in this divorce case.

By spring of 1998, depositions arrived for Jay and me to take at his attorney's office. In the presence of my attorney, Jay's attorney, and the Family Court-assigned Guardian ad Litem, I was the first to be deposed. His attorney asked me how often Jay had abused me.

I responded, "He beat me more than once...at least five instances." Then Jay's attorney proceeded to ask me about the first incident.

I replied, "There was an instance that took place in the counseling session with my first counselor, who was assigned by the Employee Assistance Program through Jay's employer. It was one of the last of ten sessions (a person is allowed that many before it is determined there's a need for ongoing counseling). As I recall, we were having a discussion with my counselor and the next thing I realized was that Jay slapped me across the face, which shocked me...and it shocked my counselor! The next thing I recalled was that my counselor said, 'Jay, you are going to have to leave the room!' Then she escorted him out of the room where we were having our counseling session with her. Within minutes, she returned to ask, 'Are you alright?!' I went on to say, 'I'm still in shock…I don't know!' She asked me if I felt okay/safe to go home with Jay. If I wasn't, she informed me that if Jay should ever hit/hurt me again, I needed to call 9-1-1 where the police would arrive and a record would be made."

I wanted to think that perhaps Jay was going through something upsetting—with his work, with his parents, etc.—because I couldn't figure out what had triggered him to slap me—especially in front of a counselor! Much like the stages of grief (first introduced by Elizabeth Kubler-Ross in her 1969 book, *On Death and Dying*), which I'd already experienced with Mom and Grandma's deaths—at first I felt shock and denial, and then I ultimately reached acceptance of the loss involved. Initially, I simply couldn't believe that my husband—whom I loved, and believed that he loved me—would hit or hurt me. With time, however, more instances followed, which made me realize that my marriage with Jay had morphed into a painful sham.

I added, "My counselor professionally recommended that Jay and I have ongoing counseling due to his behavior in my counseling session." As my deposition continued, Jay's attorney then asked me about the second instance where he had hurt me. I explained that we had been standing in the kitchen having a discussion that led to an argument, and he'd slapped me across the face so hard that my glasses fell off. When I knelt down to pick up my glasses, I saw that—due to his powerful slap—they were bent out of shape. Jay just walked out of the room with no further word about either his behavior or the incident. The next day, I just wore my contact lenses and went to the optometrist to have my glasses repaired.

My husband's attorney then proceeded to ask me about the third instance, which happened when Jay and I had a discussion regarding his parents. He became so upset that—as he stood in front of the kitchen microwave—he slammed the oak kitchen cupboard doors with such force that one actually fell off and dropped to the floor. I'd been seated at the kitchen table across the room, but seeing Jay's anger escalate as it had, I immediately got up and ran upstairs to our bedroom and locked the door. As I heard Jay run up the stairs to come after me, I could only go to the furthermost corner of the room. I'd hoped and prayed that he couldn't open the bedroom door, but the next thing I heard was him pounding on the master bedroom door. He kicked it so hard that his physical force broke down the locked six-panel oak door! When he realized what he'd done, the next thing I saw him do was to pull out the metal pegs in each of the door's hinges, and then he carried the door away!

I stood still in the corner of the bedroom to listen and wait—and finally I slowly made my way downstairs. As I walked into the kitchen, I saw Jay in the family room seated on the couch as he watched television. As for the six-panel oak door—I later found it propped up against a wall in the garage where he had placed it. (**NOTE**: The door stayed there until after our divorce, when Jay finally agreed to repair and reinstall it at his own expense. This was all done at the request of my Attorney, who—as I later learned—hadn't put that provision in the Findings in order to avoid embarrassing Jay. This door may have been "fixed and reinstalled," but—like victims of domestic violence/abuse—it still showed the scars, in spite of the glue used in an attempt attempt to make it look "fixed" and "okay.")

The fourth incident I spoke about during my deposition was when the police were anonymously called by a couple of our concerned neighbors (as I later learned from the officers), came to our house, and arrested Jay in mid-June of 1997. This was what prompted our separation. I was then asked about the fifth incident. I'd remembered a time from back when we were dating and explained, "We were at Jay's house when our discussion turned into an argument, so I got up from the couch to walk away, but Jay put his arm around me and squeezed me hard while he tried to move me around. I told him to stop it, which he did, and then he tried to hug me and said, 'I'm sorry...I didn't mean that.'" (This was the first incident, which by itself, gave me no indication of being a "red flag" about Jay's later behavior.)

It then became Jay's turn to be deposed. After he was duly sworn in, Jay was questioned about each of the five incidents that I'd previously described in my deposition. He admitted—in the presence of our attorneys (as well as our boys' attorney, the Guardian ad Litem)—that he recalled four out of the five incidents as I'd described them.

~~~~~~~~~~~~

Also, while I'd been previously deposed, Jay's lawyer—with reference to Jay's behavior toward our children—commented on the written recommendation by the Guardian ad Litem. It had revealed his belief that Jay had kicked one of our sons as he was saying his bedtime prayers, so the attorney asked me what happened.

I explained, "During this time of our separation leading up to the divorce, Jay was given the opportunity to come to the house to put the boys to bed on occasion—since he'd expressed that he 'always' put the boys to bed at night, and did not want to lose that time with them due to the separation/divorce." Then I went on to say that Jay and our son, Blake were in Blake's bedroom since it was bedtime. I noted that whenever Jay was over, I would either leave the house for a couple hours and return at the boys' bedtime when Jay was to leave OR I would excuse myself to do laundry—as I had done this time—in order to give them "bonding time." While I put away the clean laundry upstairs, I could hear Blake (then only six years old) crying and crying and crying. As I stood in our nearby bedroom, I wondered, *"What is going on in there?!?"* I stopped in my tracks as I realized that Jay was in there, and (since we were getting a divorce, and soon he would have to handle sticky situations with the boys on his own)—I didn't want interfere. But when I heard Blake getting more and more upset I became concerned, and took a pile of folded laundry in my arms that needed to be put away, and walked into Blake's bedroom. I tried to nonchalantly say, "Hey guys, what's going on in here?"

Blake said, "Mom, Dad kicked me!"

Before I could respond, Jay said, "I didn't kick him hard."

Blake said, "Yes, you did, Dad!" as he cried and rubbed his leg.

I then realized that I was in an awkward position between my son and husband, so I said to Blake, "Let me see, Honey."

Blake pulled up his pajama pant to show me. I rubbed his leg, and then I tried to soothe him while I tucked him into his bed. When Jay walked out of Blake's bedroom, I followed him, and asked him to step into the next bedroom. I then asked him to tell me what had just happened in Blake's bedroom.

Jay replied, "Well, he wouldn't say his prayers, so I kicked him!" He then turned, went down the stairs, and walked out the front door.

This reported information about Jay's abusive behavior toward me and our six year old Blake was now on file, as recorded by the deposition clerk. But none of this information (and its relevance to the custody/placement of Blake and Daniel) was ever presented to the Judge in the Family Court during our divorce proceedings.

The Guardian ad Litem's role—by definition—is to represent the best interests of the children (as determined by the GAL) through both the investigation and court process. Since the GAL investigates the facts that are relevant to the issues in a case—and then takes a position in court on the legal custody and placement of the children—our boys also met with their Pediatric Neurologist that spring. He suggested to our sons' attorney/GAL—that since their parents were in the process of a divorce—he be given the opportunity to revisit with them to familiarize himself with both their past and present status. In summary, we learned the following about our older son:

- *Blake was a seven-year-old child that he'd diagnosed in the*

  past as having an autistic spectrum disorder.

- *Blake was in the first grade, and benefitted from modeling*

  some of the positive behaviors of his peers. He has been

  doing well in many areas in school. It would be difficult

  to consider him to be at all autistic without the opportunity to know his past history and the way that his development unfolded.

- *Presently, he simply seems to be a slightly hyperactive child with auditory hypersensitivity, and one who has yet to master the pragmatics of language. He was still benefitting from occupational therapy and speech—since he speaks oddly and loudly, and does not have an inside voice, so to speak. He is still hypersensitive to things such as sounds and touch... rhythmically taps, and his mother wonders whether they should pursue drum lessons or percussion for him.*

Similarly, the Pediatric Neurologist was also contacted by the GAL, and before rendering an opinion, he had the opportunity to see how Daniel had developed and what progress, if any, had been made. The following was what we learned about our younger son:

- *Daniel, as a 3-1/2-year-old child, showed a variety of developmental challenges which included significant expressive and receptive language delay, atypical sensory thresholds, and apparent auditory processing as well as social delays, which have—in thePediatric Neurologist's opinion—permitted the designation of Daniel having an autistic spectrum disorder.*

- *Daniel continued to be challenged by linguistic limitations— much of his speech was echolalia, babble, and jargon.*

- He remained an easygoing child with a pleasant
temperament.

- With regard to sensory thresholds, he seemed to be a "hypo
responder" in that he has a very high threshold for pain,
seemed to be oblivious to situations that could harm him, and
was quite fearful.

- Daniel would initially gaze at people but then look aside
somewhat shy; but somewhat coyly seemed to play peek-a-
boo today. He evidenced emerging symbolic play...Daniel has
an autistic spectrum disorder.

The Pediatric Neurologist offered to visit with both of our sons
on an annual basis.

CHAPTER TWENTY-SIX

Fipst Days in Family Coupt

Ironically, as well as unfortunately, March 17th, which was the first anniversary of my Mom's funeral, was also the first day I was scheduled to appear in family court. I told my attorney about the date's significance, but didn't reschedule because my faith told me that Mom's spirit would be with me, as well as that of my Grandma (whose birthday was also March 17th)! As time drew nearer to this date of our first court appearance, however, my attorney told me that the court dates had been postponed until April.

Dad and my second-oldest sister, who both lived in town, said that they would be present for my future court dates. Since my brother lived in Texas and my youngest sister was in North Carolina, I understood they couldn't be in court. But when I'd called my oldest sister—who lived in a city that was just over a half hour away—to ask if she could be present, her husband interrupted our phone conversation to tell me, "She is not going to be there!" And then he hung up! After Jay's arrest and our separation, my oldest and youngest sisters had not supported me. Instead, they backed up Jay, which became evident as the court proceedings began. I felt betrayed and hurt by their decision to believe that Jay hadn't been physically as well as emotionally abusive to me—their own sister!

My attorney informed me that she would need to schedule an appointment for me with my sons' attorney. She instructed me to not speak about Jay—rather, about the boys, since he was their Guardian ad Litem. When I arrived at his office, he invited me in to take a seat, and then he sat down behind his large, imposing attorney's desk. He began his line of questioning, and when our conversation made reference to Jay, I recalled my attorney's advice. Since (as the boys' Guardian ad Litem) custody of the children—regarding where they would be physically placed after the divorce—was his concern, he asked me why

I'd requested (and why I felt that I should be granted) primary placement.

In my attempt to make an analogy, I answered, "My role in the boys' lives to date has been as their primary caretaker, the person who knows, understands, and tends to them (and their developmental needs) on a daily basis. I provide the consistency and constancy they need, and ultimately I manage them and their daily routine, which is far beyond what other 'typical' children of their age would need. While Jay—on the other hand—has managed a line of papermaking machinery on a daily basis as a mechanical engineer for his employer, and has done that since he was recruited out of college nearly 18 years ago. To take our sons out of primary placement with me would be similar to having someone else replace Jay at his job—someone else who would not have the experience or knowledge of this particular line of machinery and its idiosyncrasies. Jay gained his experience through the day-to-day maintenance of the equipment to position it to perform effectively and efficiently. Therefore, as with the line of machinery, so the boys' daily functioning, performance, and well-being would be significantly compromised. They need—beyond similar-aged children due to their special needs—consistency and constancy." The Guardian ad Litem seemingly missed—or perhaps just didn't want to acknowledge—the analogy I had tried to make and responded, "We're talking about children—not a line of machinery." Naturally, I felt frustrated and misunderstood.

The GAL was given lists—from both Jay and me—that detailed the time we'd each spent with our sons during the separation. I couldn't help but wonder why it is considered a "bonus" when the father spends time with his children whereas the mother's time is just expected or considered a "given."

When I met with my attorney to report how the interview with the Guardian ad Litem had gone, I expressed my frustration over the feeling that the GAL seemed biased toward Jay. I also told her that I'd followed her advice, but at a later date I found out that this "advice" had—in fact—worked against me, and (more upsetting) in Jay's favor. Evidently, the GAL had said, "If Heidi were concerned about Jay's abusive behavior that could affect the boys—should he get 50%

152

placement of the boys—why didn't she talk more about Jay?!" This comment from the GAL was another way in which I began to question my attorney's effectiveness.

~ ~ ~ ~ ~ ~ ~ ~ ~ ~ ~ ~

When the day came for our divorce case hearing before the Family Court Judge, I walked with my attorney to the County Courthouse, which was just across the street from her office. As we entered the assigned courtroom, Jay and his attorney were already seated at "their" table, so my attorney and I took our seats at the "other" one. I noticed something that seemed odd—Jay's parents were seated directly behind my attorney's table rather than behind his attorney's table. Typically, they were almost always seen beside their "boy," so why would they now choose to sit behind me?

My attorney assembled her legal paperwork on the table while I sat in silence and waited for the Judge to arrive in court, and for our case to get underway. My in-laws talked among themselves loudly enough so that I could hear Jay's mother's comment about me, "She should..." I just thought to myself how pitiful his parents were to be in such denial of their son's abusive behavior, and—instead—to blame others (like me) as a distraction from the truth, and a way to enable Jay. I then looked down at Mom's "Mother's ring," which I now wore, and made me think of her. Next, I looked up toward the ceiling of the courtroom with thoughts of how strongly I wished that Mom could be there physically. Given my faith, I thought, *Mom, I know that you are here with me in spirit,"* and that gave me a sense of comfort and strength during this difficult time.

Just then, I heard the Family Court Clerk announce that we were all to stand as the Judge entered the courtroom, and that's how the first day in Family Court began the process of the custody/placement determination of our sons Blake and Daniel. Each professional witness who was called forward to take the stand gave testimony, and they included the boys' medical specialists, pediatrician, teachers, therapists, etc.

Of the various witnesses called, one was a neighbor of ours who was a neonatologist at a local hospital. As this doctor testified, I could hear Jay's mom behind me say "Atta boy" as he'd stated that from his house/yard he could see Jay outside in our backyard with the boys "200 days a year!" The Judge challenged his answer, and then questioned the doctor's professional interface with our sons, who had significant special needs due to their diagnosis of developmental delays. The neonatologist admitted that he'd had none as a professional since his practice only treated babies from birth to age two, and our boys—now age 3 ½ and 6 ½—displayed developmental delays beyond the age of two.

It was a long day in court, and just before the Judge dismissed us all for the day, she remarked, "I want to see both attorneys in my chambers." I waited for my attorney to return from the Judge's chambers, but it was now late and I needed to get home to the boys and make dinner for them. I planned to follow up with my attorney the next morning. That evening, she called me to say that the Judge was upset— she asked me if I'd heard the Judge's voice from her chambers. I answered, "No, but because the meeting in the chambers had taken so long and it was late, I felt I needed to leave the courthouse and get home to the boys."

My attorney then told me that the Judge had stated that Jay's parents were barred from the courtroom for the rest of the divorce proceedings. Evidently, during one of the recesses that day, the Judge's clerk had brought to her attention what she'd seen as "improper behavior" on the part of Jay's parents in the courtroom. The Judge's reaction to this information was that she would be "on the lookout" as they resumed the rest of the first day's court proceedings. The Judge— beyond what her clerk had previously reported—did see their inappropriate behavior. So from then on, the two of them were refused admittance to the courtroom as the divorce proceedings continued.

~ ~ ~ ~ ~ ~ ~ ~ ~ ~ ~ ~

The next day, when my father, second-oldest sister, and I arrived at the courthouse together, we saw Jay's Mom and Dad seated in the vestibule area just outside of the courtroom. Thanks to the Judge's decision, for the rest of this court case, they were no longer allowed in the courtroom.

On the second day, more witnesses were called, and the proceedings included testimony from both Jay and me. When we broke for a brief recess requested by the Judge, one of my neighbors—a good friend who had been present in the courtroom—encouraged and supported me as we both approached my attorney. Together, we asked her when the information would be presented about Jay's arrest, and later, his abusive behavior toward Blake, who had been kicked and slapped across the face by him on separate occasions during our separation. It would be significant information since the Judge was due to decide on custody/placement of the boys. (Jay wanted 50/50 placement, and I longed to keep stability for the boys, and continue having primary custody. After all, I'd been their primary caretaker ever since they'd been diagnosed as "special needs" children. It was not that I'd wanted to keep the boys *from* their father—rather it was to keep them safe *from harm*—by their father.)

My attorney told us that information would not be presented. In shock and surprise, my friend and I asked in unison, "Why not?!?" She told us that that those issues were handled in "criminal" court, and this was "civil" court; and then she walked away. Stunned by her statement, my friend and I thought how inappropriate it was that this vital information would not be presented to the Family Court Judge. Blake and Daniel's best interests, safety, and well-being were at stake if they were placed with their father, who had already outwardly displayed his abusive behavior on more than one occasion!

I didn't know what to say or do at the time, and—unfortunately— this important "abuse issue" was not brought up again. In fact, when I'd met with my attorney, I'd been told, "When the Judge asks the question in court if this marriage is irreconcilable, you, Heidi, are to answer 'Yes'." It was some time later that I realized this was a clever way to not mention the domestic violence and abuse by Jay—it was enough for me to say that the marriage was irreconcilable. In a "no fault" divorce, which was allowable where Jay and I'd lived, the *reason* for the divorce didn't have to be stated. In hindsight, of course, this information could have been of great value regarding the consideration and decision of child custody.

155

Our case lasted before the Family Court Judge for 2 ½ days, and she then brought forth her ruling judgment regarding our divorce. She explained how she'd come to her decision regarding Custody and Physical Placement of our two sons in light of the various testimonies. Among other things she said was, "...I keep coming back to this—these children have done remarkably well during the pendency of this divorce. It's amazing how well they have done considering the trauma that they have experienced, considering their parents' separation, considering the death of a very close relative, and how that impacted on their mother. Blake is doing much better than anyone would have predicted had the parties stayed together..." Consequently, Custody and Physical Placement—as based on the Guardian ad Litem's proposed schedule—was decided and included the following:

"(1) **During the school year**, the respondent (father) shall have placement every other weekend, from Thursday at 3:30 p.m. until Monday morning. On those weekday mornings (every other Friday and Monday) that respondent has placement of the children, he shall drop off Blake at school and shall drop off Daniel at petitioner's (mother) residence. In addition, after his weekend he shall have Thursday evenings from 3:30 p.m. until 7:30 p.m. and Tuesdays before his weekend he shall have placement from 3:30 p.m. until 7:30 p.m. The petitioner shall have placement at all other times. In the event that Blake has speech therapy on either Tuesdays or Thursdays, the pick-up time shall be 4:30 p.m. (i.e. after the therapy).

(2) **During the summer months**, from the day after school

lets out until the Friday before school reconvenes, the petitioner shall have placement on every other weekend from Thursday at 3:30 p.m. until Monday morning. In addition, after her week-end she shall have Thursday evenings from at least 3:30 p.m. until 7:30 p.m. and the Tuesdays before her weekend she shall have 3:30 p.m. until 7:30 p.m. The respondent shall have placement at all other times. In the event that the petitioner has placement of the boys during the day because of respondent's work schedule, respondent shall pick up the boys from petitioner's residence on or before 4:30 p.m. on those days.

(3) Each party shall be allowed two (2) nonconsecutive full weeks of uninterrupted time per year with both boys upon sixty (60) day notice.

(4) The parties shall alternate the Christmas and Easter break from school, with the party scheduled to have that holiday be allowed the full week."

(The schedule for each of the holidays and the boys' birthdays rotated on an "odd" and "even" year basis.) My reaction was much like that of other adults who expressed the same sense of dismay over this schedule—it was quite complicated! The children had to move back and forth between their parents' houses on various days and times that weren't easy for adults to remember—much less children! What is more, could it truly accommodate and benefit children like ours with special needs? Witnesses for the boys had stated that they both had "a strong need for consistency and constancy of schedule, given their developmental delays and young ages." The Judge granted—as my attorney and I had requested—that the Guardian ad Litem revisit the boys in a year and "review the situation" as to how this custody/placement schedule worked for them. Especially since both boys were both "special needs" children.

~ ~ ~ ~ ~ ~ ~ ~ ~ ~ ~ ~

NOTE: Our divorce became finalized eleven years, one month, and one day after our wedding day. I thought it was ironic that these are all a series of the number one, but also significant with regard to our marriage because the two of us had never been able to become one together. The Biblical reading Genesis 2:24—often included at weddings—states, "For this reason a man shall leave his father and mother, and be joined to his wife; and they shall become one flesh." At our wedding rehearsal, it had been read mistakenly with the words mixed up. Perhaps the "mixed up" version was a foreshadowing—something that wasn't necessarily foreseeable at the time, but unfortunately it may have sealed the fate for our marriage.

CHAPTER TWENTY-SEVEN

WHO CAN I TURN TO?

Since I'd received primary physical placement of our sons, Blake and Daniel, I felt that perhaps the boys and I could finally begin to move forward with our lives. But, unfortunately, Jay continually hurt me whenever it was time for him to pick up the boys at my house.

For instance, there had been a couple of already-packed boxes of his personal things that I'd put in the garage for Jay to take. One time when he'd come to pick up the boys, he became upset as he talked to me, and then he lifted up one of the boxes and raised it to throw at me. Fortunately, I stood in the doorway and my reflexes were quick enough for me to shut the door.

Another time, Jay had come into my kitchen, and started to argue with me. As his hand grabbed at my face, I tried to defend myself and pushed Jay away. He then said to Blake (who was nearby), "Come on, we're leaving!" As he walked out the door that led to the garage, I realized that my lip was cut and bleeding due to the way he'd grabbed my face. I quickly ran out the door to the garage, and out on the driveway where Jay and the boys had gotten into his car. I went up to the driver's window and quietly said, "Look, look what you've done!" as I pointed to my bloodied lip. But Jay just looked the other way, and backed his car out of the driveway with the boys in the backseat.

As I walked back to the garage, I realized that due to my sense of urgency to catch up with Jay, the door to the house had closed on me, and I was locked out! I could hear the dog bark inside the house through the screen door off the kitchen to the backyard deck. This meant that the door to get back into the house was unlocked, but, unfortunately—the backyard fence gate was locked. I thought about climbing over the fence, but it was a seven-foot white picket privacy fence, so I decided to instead try to pry open the gate's hardware lock/handle. Since I couldn't find any tools in the garage, I looked across the street and noticed that a neighbor's garage door was open, so I went over to ask if I could borrow something to help me pry the gate open.

When one of the neighbor's daughters answered the door, I covered my bloody lip with my hand so not to upset the little girl, and then asked her if her mom would come to the door. When my neighbor approached, she saw my bloodied lip and offered to lend me some tools. She also suggested that her husband—who was expected home shortly—come over to help me get back inside my house.

As I tried to remove the gate's hardware with the neighbor's tools, my lip continued to bleed. Shortly afterwards, I saw her husband arrive and drive into their garage, but he didn't come over to help me. This wasn't really a surprise since he'd testified for Jay when he took the stand during our divorce court proceedings. I was finally able to remove the gate's hardware, open the gate to enter the backyard, and get back in the house. And as soon as I was inside, I managed to stop the bleeding from the cut—thanks to Jay—on my lip.

I called my attorney's office to tell her about what had happened during the times when Jay arrived at my house to pick up the boys. But her secretary simply told me that the attorney's recommendation was for me to take the boys and their belongings (like Blake's backpack and Daniel's diaper bag) out to Jay's car whenever he arrived for the boys. That way, (1) he would be less likely to enter my house and hurt me any further, plus (2) he would be kept in the "public eye" where he wouldn't be as likely to hurt me. From then on, each time that Jay picked up our sons, I carried their belongings outside and led them both by the hand to his car. I'd been told to work *around* Jay's abusive behavior—wasn't that enabling by avoidance? On the other hand, if this was the only way to be safe *from* his abusiveness towards me, I would do it.

One time—after I'd brought the boys and their belongings out to Jay's car (which was parked on the driveway)—I'd only turned to walk back into the garage when I heard Jay say something. I stopped to look back, and not sure what he'd said—I thought perhaps the boys had forgotten something in the house—I asked, "What is it?" Before I could finish my sentence, Jay stuck his head out of his car's rolled-down window and said, "Look in the mirror!" Puzzled by his remark, I

160

replied, "What? Look in the mirror??" He then yelled, "Yeah, pretty ugly…aren't you?!" and then he drove his car—with the boys in the backseat—out of the driveway.

We still had our family dog, Bailey, and our Marital Settlement Agreement had stated, "The parties' dog will go back and forth between the households depending on which party has placement." But Jay had other ideas. Blake wanted Bailey to go along with him and Daniel whenever their father picked them up. So after I brought Daniel to Jay's car, I would get Bailey's food and crate ready and take them outside, while Blake brought Bailey on her leash outside to the car. I stepped back in the house and shortly afterwards, Jay was at the front door waiting to hand over Bailey—on her leash—back to me. He said, "I'm not taking the dog," and then brought Bailey's belongings to me. Understandably, Blake was in tears, but his father just ordered him to get in the car with his younger brother. How sad—as a boy, Jay had grown up having a dog, and yet he was refusing Blake (and Daniel) to have that same opportunity.

Within the next couple of weeks, I was able to connect with my attorney and told her how Jay had not followed our stated court orders—which also included his mandatory meetings with his counselor for anger management. Her only response was, "Heidi, I'm no longer your attorney." I was shocked by this and asked, "Why?" Then, without further explanation, she hung up the phone on me.

I was beside myself—to say the least! She had been my attorney for the entire year regarding both the divorce and custody issues, and legal fees had amounted to nearly $30,000. My attorney had now "left the scene" just when I most needed the court orders to be enforced with Jay and his attorney. I was despondent because she not only walked away from my case, but she'd walked out on me!

~ ~ ~ ~ ~ ~ ~ ~ ~ ~ ~ ~

When I shared this devastating and disappointing news with my Dad, he suggested that we meet with his attorney. When we did so, Dad's lawyer asked about my case in order to be brought up to date, and

161

then he said, "What a complicated mess!" He reassured us that he would look into it and get back to my Dad in a few days.

Dad had used this attorney for his divorce from Mom thirteen years earlier, and the lawyer had commented on "how similar" I was to my mother. I realized that this statement was made sarcastically, and I remembered that Mom had told us (after she and Dad had gone through their divorce), that she neither liked his attorney nor the way their divorce had been handled. Dad's attorney also told us that Jay's lawyer had once worked at his law firm. Soon Dad told me that his attorney would not take my case, and I could read between the lines.

In my local newspaper, I'd read that "Former spouses ignore court orders because they wish to perpetuate conflicts, and quickly learn that if they do not comply with court orders, chances are that they can get away with it (this behavior) without much fear of reprisal from the courts." The article excerpted from "Flying Solo" (which provided information for people whose lives had been changed by divorce or separation…of a spouse) suggested that I take my ex back to court one more time and hire a "no-nonsense, experienced lawyer."

So my search began to find that type of attorney. But—inevitably—when they asked which lawyers and guardian ad litem had been involved in the case, they would excuse themselves and not take my case. I even met with a prominent woman attorney, who was considered by some to be the "female version" of Jay's attorney. She skimmed over the information I'd provided, and I soon realized that she hurriedly created excuses to *not* take my case. So that neither of us wasted each other's time, I began to gather my paperwork and said, "I can see that you're not willing to take my case. Thank you for your time." I then added, "It makes me wonder how attorneys like Jay's can sleep at night, especially when his sons are similar in age to ours." She looked surprised that I'd stood up—literally as well as figuratively—and then I stepped out of her office. I felt that I'd figured out her priorities, and decided to walk out on her—before she (as the attorney she was supposedly known to be) would get the chance to refuse taking my case.

By this point, I wasn't quite sure to where or whom I could turn next—I no longer had access to legal representation in order to make Jay

162

follow the court orders. And then I read a helpful article—in our local newspaper—in Ann Landers' column:

"**Dear Ann:** I am a Domestic Violence Outreach specialist/advocate and I assist victims of domestic violence...Too often the question asked is, "Why does she stay?" instead of "Why does he batter?" Victims of domestic violence are like puppets on a string, and invariably the abuser sadistically toys with his victim. I refer to domestic violence as "the death of the soul." The physical abuse is bad, but in time, the bruises go away and the bones heal. The emotional abuse is something that does NOT go away. I am a survivor of domestic violence. I am glad I can say these words...YOU MUST GET HELP. Outside intervention is your key to freedom. It could save your life. – A.P., Leesville, La.

Dear Leesville: Thanks for encouraging all victims of domestic violence to seek help immediately. Shelters...are listed in the telephone book, or you can call the Domestic Violence Hotline...for a referral."

Then on August 18, 1999, I read an article in our local newspaper titled "New Domestic-Violence Law Pushed." Proposed by our state's Attorney General, it stated "A person who commits domestic violence in front of a child could face felony charges and as many as two years in prison...We know a child who witnesses his mother being beaten is likely to be 1,000 times more violent...We need to break that cycle...hopes the bill will become law by Jan. 1, 2000...the goal is not unrealistic...statistics showed that children are present during 75 percent of domestic incidents...executive director of the Family Violence Center in Green Bay, thinks the legislation is necessary to reduce domestic violence...When a young person sees real violence carried out on their mother, that violence has an immediate effect on them...what they are seeing is real. It has an enormous, long-term, lifelong effect on the children that observed it."

When I read that advice column and the domestic-violence law articles, it was as if the authors knew exactly what I had lived through. So I felt compelled to contact my local Family Violence Center, and report my concern about my sons' safety in light of their father's abusive behavior. When I arrived for my scheduled appointment, everything

163

seemed somewhat surreal—up to this time I'd come to know the Family Violence Center (where my Mom had donated clothes) as one of the children's charities that she and I had served through our volunteer hours as members of the women's service organization. Now my children and I had become beneficiaries—I'd honestly never thought that we would be in such a position!

~ ~ ~ ~ ~ ~ ~ ~ ~ ~ ~

On our boys' follow-up appointment with their Pediatric Neurologist on June 2, 1999, we learned that Blake:

1)   *evidenced atypical and uneven development with a pattern of strength and weaknesses and sensory intolerances, which have permitted the diagnosis of an autism spectrum disorder.*

2)   *over time his strengths have emerged, and so dominated his development that it has become increasingly more difficult to place him anywhere along the autism spectrum disorder; yet his somewhat restricted range of interests, perseverativeness, social and physical maladroitness, and other issues do distinguish him from most children his age in the eyes of developmental specialists and those with an understanding of the subtleties of autism.*

3)   *is doing wonderfully from an academic standpoint of view in his parochial school, but it is felt by some of his interventionists that he might fare better and make more social gains in a different environment, especially if given the opportunity to have more intensive speech therapy.*

We'd appreciated the time the Pediatric Neurologist had spent with us regarding our concerns as Blake's parents, but we'd been told that without collateral, educational, and remedial data available to him, many of the very important questions we asked could not be answered.

Similarly, the Pediatric Neurologist (who had last evaluated him in February of 1998) reassessed our younger son and told us that Daniel—as a five year old with "autistic spectrum disorder"—was noticed (in the 16 month interval) to have gained much, but there remained concerns about him. This is what we learned about Daniel:

1) *While in many ways his development resembled his older sibling's, his linguistic abilities seemed to be relatively deficient, and he was a bit more impulsive as well as aggressive, and seemed to respond less well than his sibling to gentle reprimand as well as the establishment and setting of limits.*

2) *With regard to his educational prognosis and prognosis for overcoming the challenges of autism, his somewhat superficial and preliminary impression—based upon conversation with us parents, observations of Daniel, and knowledge of his past development—would be that the obstacles might be more high for Daniel than they had been for Blake, but yet not insurmountable.*

3) *Daniel may be a candidate for one of the intensive behavior modification programs offered through the state—a program such as this might foster more socially-appropriate behaviors, and allow for a strategy to develop, establish, and maintain limits on some socially-unacceptable behaviors.*

4) *With regard to general neurologic status, Daniel had regressed somewhat with regard to toilet-training. He had not regressed visually, auditorially, motorically, or in terms of coordination,* (although he was noticed to have the tendency of walking on his tip-toes whenever he wasn't wearing shoes), *and had made some progress linguistically and socially.*

Subsequently, the experts felt that Daniel—at this point—would not require repeats of any of the studies done or any new testing.

CHAPTER TWENTY-EIGHT

Déjà-vu All Over Again, So Soon

"The measure of life, after all, is not its duration, but its donation"

~ *Corrie ten Boom*

In the first month of the new millennial year, I'd received the news that my stepfather, John, (who had moved back to Florida within a year of Mom's death) had been diagnosed with cancer. It was a strain of the disease that was somewhat similar to Mom's, and he only had weeks to live. Since it was the same month during which Mom had been diagnosed three years earlier, I had a strange sense of gloomy *déjà-vu*. In his phone call to me from Florida, he sadly told me that he had chosen to not take treatments (as he'd seen how that route had made Mom so much weaker during her own cancer fight). Instead, he planned to spend the time that remained for him with his daughter, who lived in California. John died the following month, and his funeral took place back in his hometown in Indiana.

My second-oldest sister and I (with Blake) flew from Green Bay, and we met our other siblings (as well as John's daughter and son) to attend his wake at the funeral home. He was laid out in a dark suit (probably the one he'd worn when he'd married Mom), and his daughter pointed out that his tie was the one he'd received from me not even two months earlier as a Christmas gift. At the head of John's casket stood the framed wedding picture of John and Mom—they looked so happy together! The only comfort we could take away with faith from John's funeral was that he and Mom were reunited once again—this time in heaven. They had courted each other for three fun-loving years before their marriage—which had sadly (due to Mom's death from cancer) lasted less than three months. No matter how short-lived their married life had been, their connection lives on eternally in the song—from Mom and John's era—"(Our) Love Is Here To Stay" (written by George Gershwin, lyrics by Ira Gershwin).

After John's funeral service, we numbly flew back home. Within a relatively short period of time, I'd lost three of the most loving, positive people in my life—Mom, Grandma, and now, John. What is more, I was also feeling battered by my sons' losses due to their autism diagnoses, as well as by the ugly disintegration of my marriage.

As I tucked Blake into bed that first night back home, he had questions about John's funeral, which seemed to bring back what memory he had with Gommy before she'd died. Blake then told me that he felt that ever since Gommy had died, things for us hadn't been the same—they'd become much worse. I told Blake that one of the last things I remembered Gommy telling me was how much she would miss rocking him and Daniel in her arms. She'd so enjoyed that during their first years of life.

~~~~~~~~~~~~

NOTE: In light of our faith that Gommy was still with us in spirit, "our song" for Blake and me had become "You Are Not Alone" (an "R&B ballad about love and isolation" written by Robert Kelly "after the loss of close people in his life" and produced by both Kelly and Michael Jackson. It had been released in August 1995—less than two years before Mom's death).

167

CHAPTER TWENTY-NINE

What I Feared, Happened

Jay continued—in a variety of ways—to hurt me after our divorce. Here are a few instances: (1) Just as one of Blake's soccer games ended, Jay threw one of our son's bottles at me, (2) when he picked up the boys at my house after work—he put the car in reverse, so that the car door slammed into me as I buckled the seatbelt for our younger son in the backseat of Jay's car, (3) because normal communication truly was impossible, it was recommended that we use a notebook to write any information or instructions regarding the boys, and then transfer it whenever the boys were scheduled to be picked up. I once tried (unsuccessfully) to point out a couple of important items in the notebook while we stood on the driveway and the boys were in Jay's car. But when he refused to look at the pages, I walked back in my garage to go in the house.

To my surprise, he followed me into the garage, so I backed up and said "Get out of here"—two times—and then turned to walk back in the house. Jay then grabbed me from behind by my right arm, and pulled me toward him. As he grabbed at the notebook in my left hand, he scratched me on my right forearm, swiped the area by my right eye, and his watch left indentation marks as he gripped my left wrist. To free myself from his hold—he'd had my back against the front of his body, which limited my ability to get away from him—my only option was to squeeze him in his groin area. That unexpected defensive move worked like a charm and he then released me, and I immediately ran out of the garage. Jay ran after me out onto the driveway, and grabbed me again. On the other side of his car, Blake—who was then eight years old—had climbed out of Jay's car, and ran up to his Dad to try to stop him. As Jay looked down at our son, it was as if he suddenly "came to," and realized his own abusive behavior. Jay then got into his car, acted as if nothing had happened, and drove away with the boys. I slowly walked back into my house, fell to my knees on the kitchen floor, and sobbed—for me as well as for my boys—over the fact that our lives had come to this.

For relief (and with assistance of the Family Violence Center), I petitioned for a restraining order. The court took my side, but I almost couldn't believe it when they also granted Jay's request for a restraining order. My Family Violence Center Advocate told me to not take it personally, since she had seen this happen before—it was considered a way to "diffuse" the situation. It was the only way to be safe from Jay's abusive behavior.

Not long afterwards, Blake told me about other incidents when he had been hit and/or hurt by his Dad. Once, while he did his homework at Jay's kitchen table, he asked if he could take a break, and when Jay shouted, "No!" Blake began to cry. Jay then loudly told him, "Snap out of it, Blake!" which only made him cry more. Then Jay hit Blake's arm. When he got home, Blake made a fist, pointed to his upper arm, and asked me, "Why does Dad hit me?"

A few weeks later, Blake told me that his Dad had hit him again after his birthday party—he and his younger brother had been arguing about the yo-yo that Blake had received as a birthday gift. They were in the kitchen while Jay was cooking—and with a fist—he hit Blake on his arm. Blake also told me that after each of these incidents his Dad would say, "Oh, Blake, I didn't mean it." But with the honesty of an eight-year-old, Blake explained to me, "Dad shouldn't hurt me—I'm his son."

Due to Blake's conversation with his school's counselor/psychologist about he'd been hit by his Dad a few times, the Principal informed me that a call had been made to Child Protective Services. Blake was assigned to a psychologist at Family Services, and I was told that an attorney's subpoena would bring the school's logbook forward for review.

One night, as I put Daniel to bed, he told me that he only used the potty at Mom's house—not at Dad's. This explained why Daniel had become "impacted," and needed to see his pediatrician for relief. The following week, at Blake's annual check-up, the pediatrician asked how placement was going with the boys. As I tried to explain the placement schedule, he—like other professionals—expressed concern. When he asked how Daniel was doing—Blake interrupted the doctor and said,

169

"Grandma says if Daniel poops in his pants, then he's a bad boy." (Daniel had earlier told me the same thing.)

More recently, Daniel had been receiving in-home autism therapy. A bruise in the hip area of his upper thigh (coupled with his behavior) concerned both his in-home therapist and me. It was Friday afternoon of Jay's weekend, and Daniel's therapist said that if she were me, she wouldn't let Daniel go to his father's house for his weekend of placement. With the assistance of my Advocate from the Family Violence Center, she and I met with my future second attorney—a referral from the boys' Guardian ad Litem—to discuss our concerns regarding Blake and Daniel's safety when in their father's care.

We discussed the option of getting a restraining order in place to protect the boys from their father, but my Advocate explained that this wasn't a recommended strategy. Why? Because her professional experience revealed that in court, the mother is then more likely to be "put in a bad light," i.e., viewed as being vindictive toward the ex-husband. My new Attorney then explained about—and gave me a copy of—WI Statute 948.31 (4), which outlined legal basis to withhold the boys from placement with their father: "It is an affirmative defense to prosecution for violation of this section if the action: 1. Is taken by a parent...to protect his or her child in a situation in which the parent...reasonably believes that there is a threat of physical harm...to the child;"

My Attorney also explained that it was now May 2000, and May 26th would bring the two-year time period, after which I could return to Family Court with our concerns. He told us that he would put together the needed Motion so we could proceed to Family Court right after May 26, 2000.

Much to our surprise, Jay's Attorney drafted up a motion to the Family Court for Order to Show Cause for Revision of Judgment, and it was filed on June 1, 2000. My Attorney, my Family Violence Center Advocate, and I attended the scheduled hearing on June 13, 2000, before the Family Court Commissioner. Jay's Attorney—on behalf of his client—proceeded with documentation, etc., to show cause for revision of Judgment. He went as far as to request that an Injunction be placed on

170

me for withholding—when it had been Jay's time of placement—the boys for two weekends to date. My Attorney then spoke on my behalf as his client—but he neither had the documentation to forward to the Family Court Commissioner (regarding WI Statute 948.31 (4) as the basis for any "withholding" as argued), nor had he yet written/filed the Notice of Motion and Motion for Revision of Judgment on my behalf (which he, my Family Violence Center Advocate, and I had agreed upon in previous weeks at his office)!

The Family Court Commissioner stated that she would grant the Motion made by Jay's Attorney for the Revision of Judgment on his client's behalf, AND the Injunction on me. She said this was because my Attorney didn't have any documentation before her!?! (My Attorney didn't get around to filing a Motion on my behalf to the Family Court until August 7, 2000—almost three months later after we had discussed and decided back in mid-May—before the two-year waiting period expired!!)

We were initially scheduled to appear in court on August 21st, but due to the psychological evaluations of the boys and of the parties—it was postponed until October 3, 2000. Supposedly, the "findings" were not yet processed or completed, and a rush decision for this case was not warranted!

~ ~ ~ ~ ~ ~ ~ ~ ~ ~ ~

On September 22nd, I was informed by my Attorney's office that the following Wednesday, September 27th, and Thursday, September 28th, Jay's Attorney had subpoenaed (1) the noted Psychologist regarding Autism, who had evaluated our younger son relative to his diagnosed condition, and (2) the Family Services Psychologist, who had been assigned to counsel/treat our older son relative to the recommendation made by Child Protective Services.

Mid-afternoon of September 27th, I received a call from my Attorney's office to inform me that the subpoenaed deposition scheduled for that evening had been cancelled since two of the three attorneys couldn't make it. This deposition would have been for the Psychologist—assigned back in May1999—who'd evaluated Daniel for

171

further refinement of the diagnosis of Autistic Disorder (as well as other concerns included in the type of visitation and placement needed by Daniel). I was told that this Psychologist had been contacted regarding the cancellation due to Attorney circumstances, and that he'd been asked if he would be deposed the following evening after the Family Services Psychologist's scheduled deposition.

The next evening—it was after hours at Jay's Attorney's office—the Family Services Psychologist arrived to take her deposition among the Court Reporter, Jay and his Attorney, the GAL, my Attorney, and me. (I was later informed that Jay's Attorney was the Family Services Psychologist's personal attorney as well—perhaps that's why her responses seemed vague?? Perhaps a conflict of interests??) My Attorney told me—on the side—that he felt what was important was that she'd said that she believed Blake, who "was steadfast that Dad did hurt/punch him twice." She also said, "I don't think he was coached." (I recalled that when I'd first explained to her all that had been going on—regarding Jay's abusive behavior towards me and then to Blake—she'd responded with real fear and concern for our safety.)

When the Family Services Psychologist had finished her deposition, Jay's Attorney told her that he would walk her out of the office building. While the rest of us waited to see if the Psychologist—who'd evaluated Daniel—would arrive in the next twenty minutes or so, I approached the GAL and asked if/or when he would be meeting with our boys as their Attorney. (He hadn't yet met with the boys. The Motion had been made back on June 13th when he was reassigned as their GAL, and this evening was Thursday, Sept. 28th. Plus our case was scheduled before the Family Court Commissioner on the following Tuesday, October 3rd at 9 a.m.!!) His response was vague, and he didn't really give me an answer.

By that time, Jay's Attorney had returned to the conference room where we had waited (1) while he'd escorted the Family Services Psychologist out of his office building and (2) for the arrival of Daniel's Psychologist's for his rescheduled deposition. It was then decided that we all should pack up and leave—since it seemed that the Psychologist wasn't going to show up. As my Attorney and I walked out of the office building onto the parking lot, we could hear someone's voice say, "Excuse me...Excuse me...I've been locked out and have been out here waiting..." It was the Psychologist who evaluated Daniel!! My Attorney asked him if he would still have his deposition taken that evening, since the other two Attorneys were still in Jay's Attorney's office building. He replied, "Sure" since that had been the whole purpose for him to have arrived as he had.

The Psychologist, the Court Reporter, my Attorney, and I then went back into the office building. Just as we came off the elevator, we met the GAL, who had been waiting for the down elevator. My Attorney explained to the GAL how the Psychologist had been locked out of the office building, and then asked the GAL if his deposition could be taken since we all were still there. The GAL responded by shaking his head back and forth "No," and then stepped into the elevator. My Attorney asked if he and Jay's Attorney could take the deposition. The GAL shrugged his shoulders, and then the elevator doors closed.

My Attorney went behind an office door to update Jay's Attorney about how the Psychologist had been found locked outside, but was willing to take his deposition since he was there. We could hear the conversation between the two Attorneys—Jay's Attorney said, "No!" and my attorney responded, "Then YOU come out and tell the gentleman that!" Out came the two Attorneys to where the rest of us had stood, and Jay's Attorney said to the Psychologist, "Hey...sorry about your being locked out...it's a new office building...Hey can I buy you lunch?!" We all were given no option but to leave.

When we'd gone outside in the parking lot, I asked my Attorney, "Now what do we do?" (The Psychologist who'd evaluated Daniel had stated in his evaluation/report that he was in favor of our legal position regarding custody/placement in this case.) My Attorney then asked him if he would be willing to come to court on Tuesday morning to testify, and he agreed.

The next morning was Friday—the GAL had not yet met with our boys and our case was scheduled before the Family Court Commissioner on Tuesday morning—so I contacted the GAL's office. I was told by his receptionist that I could bring the boys after school that day to meet with him. He spent some time with Blake and less time with Daniel. After we left the appointment, Blake told me that he'd said what was in his heart, that he didn't want to be hit or hurt by his father again, and really wanted to primarily stay with his Mom.

~~ Notable "Breakthroughs" from Recent Studies and Helpful Hints ~~

Findings of a new study—released in January of 2014—by Vanderbilt University researchers in the *Journal of Neuroscience* unveiled clues as to why autistic children have communication problems and trouble bonding with people. It's because speech is out of sync for many children with autism. The autistic children have trouble identifying instantaneous sound and visual stimuli—they do not instantaneously connect noises with sources or relate the words they hear with the speakers. "It's like they are watching a foreign film that was badly dubbed—the auditory and visual signals do not match in their brains," said Stephen Camarata, professor of hearing and speech sciences at Vanderbilt. "One of the classic pictures of children with autism is they have their hands over their ears," said Mark Wallace, a neurobiologist who is director of the Vanderbilt Brain Institute. "We believe that one reason for this may be that they are trying to compensate for their changes in sensory function by simply looking at one sense at a time. This may be a strategy to minimize the confusion between the senses."

Additionally, one of the researchers said that sound processing is delayed in autism—so the children see the picture about half a second before they hear the sound. Part of the therapy is to try to speed up auditory processing, to get sight and sound to match better. The research suggests that computer games to enhance sensory perception should be a primary focus in early intervention therapy. Researchers at Vanderbilt are also investigating how autistic children perceive touch. "A lot of what we are working on in the lab is what we call the tactile, the touch domain, to see if these same kind of things happen with sight and hearing also extend into the realm of touch," Wallace said.

On May 15, 2014, an article posted online by Mike Nace at BioNews Texas stated that a researcher at the University of Texas Health Science Center at Houston (UTHealth) discovered that certain professions may be linked to a higher rate of children placed on the autism spectrum. The new data and conclusions...reveal that fathers with technical professions are in fact more likely to have children who present autism spectrum disorder...the data bore out a noticeable trend that jobs deemed as technical among fathers correlated with a higher instance of ASD diagnoses in their children. According to a recent UTHealth news release, the children of fathers who work as engineers were two times more likely to have been diagnosed with ASD, while children of fathers working in the financial sector presented with ASD four times the norm. And those fathers, who worked in healthcare, were six time more likely to have a child with autism. Dr. Aisha S. Dickerson, a researcher at UTHealth's Center for Clinical and Transitional Sciences who served as first author of this study reported that results suggest yet one more clue for determining what in fact causes autism. "Parental occupation could be indicative of autistic-like behaviors and preference, and serve as another factor in a clinician's diagnosis of a child with suspected autism."

~ ~ ~ ~ ~ ~ ~ ~ ~ ~ ~ ~

HELPFUL HINTS FOR INTERACTIONS
WITH INDIVIDUALS WITH AUTISM
~ For more information, call 800-3AUTISM (Autism Society) ~
- ~ Use simple language; speak slowly and clearly.
- ~ Use concrete terms and ideas.
- ~ Repeat simple questions, and allow time (10-15 seconds) for a response.
- ~ Proceed slowly, and give praise and encouragement.
- ~ Do not attempt to physically stop self-stimulating behavior.
- ~ REMEMBER: Each individual with autism is unique and may act or react differently.
- ~ PLEASE contact a responsible person who is familiar with the individual.

AUTISM
COMMUNICATION: *May* be non-verbal or have very limited verbal abilities ~ *May* appear deaf; may not respond to verbal cues ~ *May*

repeat words or phrases in place of normal communications ~ *May* have difficulties expressing needs; uses gestures or points.

BEHAVIOR: *May* have tantrums—display extreme distress for no apparent reason ~ *May* exhibit inappropriate laughing or giggling ~ *May* show no real fear of dangers ~ *May* have little or no eye contact ~ *May* appear insensitive to pain ~ *May* be sensitive to touch, sound, or bright lights ~ *May* exhibit self-stimulating behaviors, i.e., hand flapping.

IN CRIMINAL JUSTICE SITUATIONS: *May* not understand rights ~ *May* have difficulty remembering facts or details of offenses ~ *May* become anxious in new situations ~ *May* not understand consequences of their actions.

Learning to Fight
to the Finish

CHAPTER THIRTY

Second Time Around—In Family Court

My Attorney kindly requested that the Guardian ad Litem (on September 28th) provide a preliminary recommendation based on the findings from the Court-ordered Psychologist. But the GAL's Preliminary Recommendation was given to us parents *within only minutes before* we were seen by the Family Court Commissioner—a lower level than Family Court Judge—on the morning of Tuesday, October 3, 2000. (The GAL had met with our boys only once—on September 29th—between the dates of June 13th through October 3rd of that year.) From the time he met with our boys until that day's court appearance meant that *only one business day* of time was used to evaluate our boys' feedback for his Preliminary Recommendation! I couldn't help but wonder why the GAL had not (to date) visited our boys at either my home or Jay's house—others who'd been divorced had questioned me about this as well, since the GAL had visited their children at both parents' homes.)

The Psychologist, who had evaluated Daniel, appeared in court that day to testify—only to be personally attacked by Jay's Attorney as well as by the Guardian ad Litem. They tried to discredit him by asking, "You know there's a *court-ordered psychologist* who's to make the determination to the Court." The Psychologist replied, "Yes, I'm aware of that." He continued to explain that in light of Autism—especially with regard to Daniel, who was younger—he was trying (with his professional expertise in Autism) to convey to the Family Court that he had an understanding of the concerns/issues that Daniel faced. His goal was for a placement decision that would better accommodate what would best serve the interests of a child like Daniel...and Blake. This was, of course, why this case was in Court.

After the hearing, I followed up with the Psychologist later that day. But before I could even finish my sentence, he interrupted me to ask, "Who were those attorneys in court today?" He continued to say that he'd been in court many times before to testify, but he had never been publicly demeaned the way he'd been in court that day! He also added that after he'd walked out of the courthouse, he had to sit quietly in his car for quite some time to decompress before he could go on with his day. He even (essentially) told me that attorneys like that should be reported to the Bar!

Another healthcare/medical provider, i.e., our sons' Pediatrician—who referred each of our boys to other specialists as needed due to their developmental delays, needs for speech/occupational therapy, etc.—was scheduled as one of the witnesses to testify that day. When it came time for his telephone testimonial, my Attorney asked me, "Should we still call on him?" I was somewhat dumbfounded by his question and said, "Well, you're my Attorney...what do you think?" Ultimately, the Pediatrician was NOT asked to testify—WHY?!? He, like the Psychologist, was a strong advocate for the boys to remain in my primary care—among others who'd testified.

Jay's Attorney had only one witness testify on his behalf—a neighbor whose children had played with our boys. However, she and Jay had rarely interfaced directly (she hadn't really spent enough time inside his house or with him) to justify testifying about how well he parented our boys. How could her testimony and Jay's sway the Court to decide on 50/50 placement (six months on/off with each parent)? Especially when given what the Psychologist had conveyed to the Court in his testimony about the developmental delays/challenges our boys had despite his being attacked?

It was also unsettling that the Pediatrician hadn't been called upon to testify—when, in fact, he'd scheduled himself as a witness with the Court. (At a later office visit for the boys, he expressed how "put out" he felt after scheduling his day around his telephone testimony. He never got a call to provide testimony to the Court, which had been initiated and requested by the Court and the Attorneys!)

The Family Services Psychologist's transcript from her deposition was submitted to the court on stipulation. What is more, the psychological evaluation prepared by the *Court-ordered Psychologist* had been submitted *in lieu of testimony from her*. Why hadn't she been "grilled" on the stand by the Attorneys as the Psychologist had?!?

On November 17ᵗʰ, I testified with the presence of my Family Violence Advocates in the courtroom (one of whom had recently become the Executive Director of the Family Violence Center). My direct examination as a witness lasted nearly two hours. When it came to my cross-examination, both the opposing counsel (Jay's Attorney, whom I was later informed served on the Board of Directors for the Family Violence Center, yet consented to represent as his client, my ex-husband—in spite of his criminal complaint, arrest, and divorce brought before the County Circuit Family Court!!) and the GAL stated that they had no questions. I was the final witness, and Court was adjourned after the Family Court Commissioner announced when her decision would become available. Jay's Attorney then suggested that the Closing Arguments *be written to and not stated before* the Court Commissioner. Surprisingly, she agreed.

After we were all dismissed, both of my Family Violence Center Advocates came up to me and expressed how well I'd done. They said I'd testified straightforwardly, factually, and to the point regarding the circumstances/situations that affected the placement of our sons. One of my witnesses also informed me that while I wasn't present in the courthouse lobby waiting area earlier that day, Jay's Attorney had approached the two Family Violence Center Advocates (who were there on my behalf), and had said to them, "…you're getting close to the edge…you'd better watch it!!"

What is more, what Jay's Attorney had said to the Family Violence Center Advocates seemed an outwardly, direct, unethical way to intimidate others. He'd used/misused his political position on the Family Violence Board (for his/his client's own personal gains). Plus, in retrospect, it certainly seemed to be a conflict of interests that went "against the grain" of what the Family Violence Center and its employees as well as its Board of Directors stand for and uphold professionally!

~ ~ ~ ~ ~ ~ ~ ~ ~ ~ ~ ~

As we waited for the Family Court Commissioner's decision regarding placement, another incident occurred. After school one day, Blake had told both me and his brother's in-home therapist that he had been hit again by his father. This time, it was a slap across the face for not turning off the play station game before he'd left for school. I'd put in a call to the GAL's office to inform him of what had occurred, but when I'd called, I was informed by his secretary that he couldn't take my call. I explained about the urgency of the circumstances, but was told was that the GAL would call me back—yet he never did!

The in-home therapist—who said that she'd had previous work experience at a domestic violence shelter—encouraged me to call the police. So I did, and shortly afterward, a Sheriff's Department Officer (who had arrived once before regarding an incident with Daniel and his father) and his Sergeant showed up at my home. The Officer spoke to Blake while the Sergeant spoke to me in another room. Upon the Sergeant's request, I explained what I'd been told by Blake about what had happened, but he said that being hit across the face was not abuse. As he walked out of the room, he told me that the boys' father and I needed to get on the same wavelength regarding discipline. WOW!? (I thought to myself about the "line"—when bad parenting crossed over to harm!) He then talked to the Officer, and they both agreed that the boys should stay with me for the weekend—despite it being Jay's placement. Blake then told them about a function that was scheduled for the next day that his Dad was to bring him to—and the Officer told him that it wouldn't be safe to go with his father. The Officers then told us that they were going to Jay's house to inform him of their decision regarding visitation.

When they arrived at Jay's, he showed them the injunction that his Attorney had sought from the Court Commissioner. Within a half-hour of them leaving my house, the Officers returned, and told us that the boys were to now go to their father's house for the weekend. Less than an hour earlier, these same officers had told the boys that they weren't to go to their father's house because they wouldn't be safe with him! How conflicted and confusing was this message?! In this case, the very lesson that children and others are taught through the D.A.R.E. school programs (regarding domestic violence), were neither applied nor enforced by the Sheriff's Department Officers.

The GAL also "brushed off" this incident. At the suggestion of my Advocate at the Family Violence Center, I forwarded the cassette tape—as she'd instructed and recommended—with a note to the boys' GAL. This cassette recorded the reality of six separate incidents that had happened during the summer months (when Jay usually had the boys most of the time and overnights from June 28 through August 8, 2000). That's when Daniel verbalized his reluctance to go to his Dad's house. Due to the injunction that Jay's Attorney had filed against me (to force the boys go to their Dad's house against their will), my last resort was to take both boys out on my front porch, give them my Good-bye hugs and kisses, and then step back inside my house, and shut/lock the front door. (I'd had to reassure Blake that he would be safe—even though I definitely wasn't reassured!). Under this revised arrangement, Jay would then get out of his car, come up to the front porch, literally pick Daniel up and carry him to his car—despite Daniel's physical and verbal resistance. In the last instance on the cassette tape, Daniel can be heard pounding on my front door!! This particular way of "picking up" the boys—particularly Daniel—had been seen by my neighbors, who later expressed their concern and sadness for my boys when they testified in court. Again, no further follow-up was taken by the GAL—and we were left to wait for the Commissioner's placement decision.

On December 18, 2000, we received the Family Court Commissioner's Decision and Order Amending Judgment, which said "the Court can only modify the current custody and placement Orders upon a finding that a *substantial* change in circumstances has occurred since the entry of the current order, and that *any modification is in the best interests of the minor children*. The substantial change in circumstances burden is met. The progress that both children have attained since the Divorce Judgment was entered is sufficient upon which to modify the current Order...Although the progress continues, the transitions under the current Order continue to cause stress for the children...I've reviewed in detail all information submitted by each of these parties, in addition to the testimony presented by each of the parties and their witnesses. In particular, I have carefully reviewed (the Court-ordered Psychologist's) exhaustive psychological evaluation completed in this matter...(the Court-ordered Psychologist) had access to (Daniel's Psychologist's) psychological evaluation and considered it and incorporated it in reaching her own opinions and recommendations. Despite the special needs of the children, I am satisfied that a shared placement schedule is in the best interests of the minor children...My decision is based on the assumption that in-home therapy for Daniel will continue in each of the parties' homes...both parents must acknowledge the importance of this treatment for Daniel. Furthermore, both parties must continue to coordinate and follow through on any therapy recommended for Blake."

With all this said, the Family Court Commissioner ordered shared physical placement of the minor children on a yearly basis. Joint placement would mean **alternate primary physical placement** on a <u>**six-month basis**</u>! The exchange time was to occur at the semester break from school (January of each year) and the same date in the following July of each year. Commencing with the semester break in January 2001, I was awarded primary physical placement—which would allow for continuation of ongoing therapy services that were already provided and in place in my home. Subsequently, Jay would have primary physical placement of the boys, which would start six months later. (As much as their father testified to the court about his desire to have the boys half of the time in order to spend time with them, etc., Jay had been offered the first six-month period of placement—but he was not interested!)

Each of us would have alternating weekends of placement during our respective non-primary placement, which would start on Fridays after school until Monday morning—when the boys would be returned to school. The non-primary placement parent would also have one weeknight as agreed (Wednesday by default) from after school until 7:30 PM. Holiday schedule remained the same as set forth in the original Divorce Judgment.

My Attorney informed me that—due to the on-going concerns regarding the boys' safety and well-being during placement with their father—we could appeal the decision. He further told me (as he had in his letter dated October 9, 2000) that "any decision can be reviewed *'de novo'* upon proper application within ten (10) days", but I was later told that this wasn't true.

184

The Family Court Commissioner allowed time for our attorneys to gather and provide financial information from us. Often, during the Christmas holidays—and even into the New Year—I placed call after call to my Attorney's office with no response! Soon it was mid-January, yet my Attorney had still not scheduled me to get our financial information to the Court Commissioner, who had requested (by letter) "to do so within 7 days of the date of this letter" (dated January 16, 2001). Since my lawyer had not done so in a timely manner, my Financial Disclosure wasn't even presented to be considered by the Court Commissioner. The child support amount was greatly skewed in favor of Jay, and I wasn't given a chance to oppose Jay's (and his Attorney's) financial proposal. I'd received a major double-dose of let-down! Both of these decisions (child custody/placement as well as financial support) seemed to only benefit Jay—but what about the best interests and well-being of the boys? I had (as did several others) grave concern that Blake and Daniel—who as "special needs" children with an Autistic Spectrum Disorder—were now at even more risk!

CHAPTER THIRTY-ONE

The Search Goes On...

In so many ways, my second lawyer (also) failed to work on my behalf, or represent me the way an attorney should. Thanks to his inattention, there were way too many missed opportunities, ignored deadlines, legal miscues, etc. Consequently, vital facts regarding my case were obstructed or overlooked and, ultimately, the Family Court's decision was affected. And this meant that the outcome continued to put our sons at physical and emotional risk during their time with their father.

Finally, Blake's Counselor/Psychologist with Family Services directly expressed her concern regarding this 50/50, 6-month on/off placement decision for both Blake and Daniel. She addressed the Family Court Commissioner in February 2001 to voice her concerns about the potentially dangerous situation that Blake and Daniel faced. Concerns included:

1) The court had not grasped the significance of what it meant to meet the needs of a special needs child, and that she was not a proponent of the alternating 6 months with each parent rotation...

2) Concern remained for Blake, who'd been consistent in his description of events, had not wavered from his recitation, and had confronted his father...about the hitting incidents. Sadly, no accommodations appear to protect Blake's rights and safety.

3) This issue is weighing sufficiently heavy on Blake—calling 9-1-1 has been discussed; he fears he would not be able to do this at his father's house; exiting the house has also been discussed, again he feels that is not possible.

4) Essentially, Blake is anxious about the placement plan, confused, angry and fearful of his father's behavior toward

him, and there appears to be no remedy. Her opinion was that Blake is distressed to the point that at times he is experiencing emotional abuse from his father....

5) This case has been deeply troubling—to other professionals as well who have been involved in it...The real question is—how to minimize the potential and real damage sustained by Blake and Daniel...

My negligent second Attorney then referred me (i.e., passed me off) to another lawyer—to pursue the appeal/trial *de novo*—but my calls were never returned. I continued to approach/meet/seek help from at least ten other attorneys regarding our case inside—and even outside—the county. But with each visit, it became apparent that for an attorney to take this case back to court would mean more than the issue of our boys' placement. Doing so might place particular attorneys in a negative light with the Court—due to their earlier misconduct. The new appeal might highlight unethical ways that they'd handled themselves/their clients/witnesses. Questions could be raised concerning how they'd conducted themselves "behind the scenes"—personally as well as professionally. If they'd made political and monetary gains—at the expense of our two boys receiving a just placement decision from the Family Court that would truly serve the boys' utmost best interests, rather than those of their parents, or attorneys—it would be shameful. Our sons had been left behind—not only initially (due to their parents' divorce), but more significantly by a "legal system" that had put everyone else's interests above the boys' best interests. Sadly, in this custody situation, politics and power seemed more important than serving justice!

~~~~~~~~~~~~~

Blake was in fifth grade when he and his classmates were introduced to the D.A.R.E. program. On the night of the students' graduation from this program, the Officer told those in attendance—which included parents, relatives, and others—that D.A.R.E. had a valuable objective. It had opened the door for children to start the awareness/education of domestic violence, drugs, etc., but it was up to the parents to continue to keep this message with their children. I thought

187

that this seemed like a mixed message for our family situation due to the domestic abuse that Jay had inflicted. Blake later told me that he'd asked the Officer—during one of D.A.R.E.'s earlier classes—about parents who hit and/or abused their children. He was told that the parent would probably be arrested. (This sent a mixed message to Blake since incidents reported about and by Blake regarding his father's abuse toward him and his younger brother had still not received attention.) Blake then asked me, "Why do people not believe me or you, Mom, about what Dad has done to hurt us?"

All I could do was tell him that I wished I knew why. The next day I contacted this D.A.R.E Officer, who (fortunately) took the time to listen to concerns about the boys' experience with abuse by Jay. In response, he offered to make himself personally available to Blake—he asked Blake to call him so they could perhaps spend some time together. He discouraged the idea of Blake asking for a "Big Brother" (from the eponymous program) because Jay might resent it, which could work against Blake.

In the months that followed, Blake kept up with dance lessons that he'd started taking from a local dance centre. The spring recital was to include a performance by the students with their fathers. In our "parent notebook"—used as our means of communication as parents— Jay stated that "Blake can join me (Jay)" for dance practices before the recital, which also included two special practices and a dress rehearsal. Jay then laid out "his" plans regarding when he would pick up Blake over the days scheduled for the recital performances, which would take place over the Memorial Day weekend.

When Blake had been dropped off to my house after one of the recitals, he told me that his Dad told him he wouldn't be at the next recital performance. How could Jay say that when he'd been through all dance practices with Blake? How could he decide to bow out at the last moment?! I tried to reassure a very disappointed Blake, and calmly suggested that if his Dad hadn't arrived to the theatre before their father/son dance number, to just inform his dance instructor so she could handle the situation. After all, the show must go on!

As my sister and I sat in the audience, I told her about Blake's potential predicament, and we both hoped that Blake's Dad would not let him down. When the father/son dance number began, I held my breath and watched the fathers come onstage, only to see that Blake was left without his Dad to join him! Fortunately, one of the other fathers stepped up (and stepped in) to dance with Blake as well as with his own child. It was a kind attempt to improvise due to Jay's absence. Blake looked confused and tried to go on but as soon as the dance was done, Blake—understandably—ran off the stage in tears. It was the last dance number before the intermission, so I told my sister that I needed to go backstage, find Blake and console him. When I found Blake, he cried through his tears, "Dad didn't show up to dance with me!" He was so upset that he just wanted to go home. I found his dance instructor—who understood Blake's situation—and she told us it was okay for him not to stay for the second half of the recital program.

~ ~ ~ ~ ~ ~ ~ ~ ~ ~ ~

One of Jay's "parental notebook" entries commented on how he was not going to split the cost for our sons' clothes that were "worn at my house." The boys had told me that once they arrived at their Dad's house, they were told to change out of the clothes they'd worn "from Mom's house," and told to put on clothes "from Dad's house!" Jay added that he would, however, split the cost for things that went between houses; therefore, he would pay for half of their shoe costs!

What became more troubling for Blake and Daniel was that any gift they received from Jay for their birthdays, Christmas, etc., would have to remain at "Dad's house" and couldn't be taken to "Mom's house." I'd overheard Blake tell one of his friends about this, and how much it bothered him. His friend agreed, and didn't understand why this rule had been made. Blake had even tried to sneak a new toy he'd received from his Dad into his backpack to take it out of Dad's house, but was caught and punished. Later, Jay refused to let Blake use a cell phone, and would take it away from him as well—he could only call by their Dad's landline phone. Jay even reprimanded me to not send that cellphone with Blake to his house again.

189

Blake became emotionally abused through Jay's controlling and manipulative behavior which frightened and intimidated him. Blake continued to be physically abused by his Dad—beyond "just" being hit and/or slapped across the face. Once, when Blake was so tired that he flopped on his bed at Jay's house, he heard an ominous "cracking sound." Blake became so scared that he quickly got off the bed and down onto the floor. Jay had heard the noise, came into Blake's bedroom to yell "Get up! Get up!" at him, and he stomped on Blake's feet as he was screaming.

~~~~~~~~~~~~

My sons and I had found comfort as we received counseling services at the Family Violence Center, and we soon learned about another type of "shelter." Our family dog Bailey had been "put down" due to old age, and both boys were at the perfect age to again have a dog to run and play with in the backyard. So we considered getting another Sheltie to join our family. We found out that the Rescue Shelter group would walk in our city's Christmas parade, and this gave us a chance to meet Holly—a one-year-old tri-colored sheltie. We were told that she had been recently brought to the Rescue Shelter because her owner (who already owned a sheltie) wanted a second one. But when they adopted Holly, the two shelties "fed off" each other's barking, and the owner chose to only keep one dog. Since Holly was the newer one in their household, they decided to give her to the Rescue Shelter. As soon as we met her, Holly took to the boys just as they had to her—she instantly became a treasured part of our family.

The boys wanted to take Holly with them whenever it was time to go to Dad's house. But as before—despite court orders—their father wanted no part of taking the dog with the boys. We'd been in occasional contact with the Rescue Shelter, and during one of our conversations I'd mentioned how the boys longed to have Holly go with them to their father's house—but he wasn't interested. When the rescue lady learned that my sons' father (since the time of our separation and divorce) had been physically abusive—especially to our older son—she told me that they would have to come and pick up Holly. She needed to be taken from us, and returned to the shelter. I was shocked by her remark, and questioned why that would have to happen. She responded that should Holly be in harm's way, the Rescue Shelter would then have to take her back—after all, their purpose was to protect the shelties.

Needless to say, the boys and I were sobbing when she showed up at our front door to take our beloved pet away from us. As much as the Rescue Shelter's purpose made sense objectively, it brought to light how a dog would be "sheltered" and protected from potential harm, but our Family Court System failed to do the same for Blake and Daniel. Rather than *protect* our sons from being placed with their abusive father, the Family Court had instead recently *increased* their placement time with him by up to 50%! To this day, the boys and I still miss Holly—we will never forget her—and we continue to try and forgive their father for causing her removal.

Our local District Attorney recommended that I file a grievance with the Supreme Court of Wisconsin's Office of Lawyer Regulation. Actually, two separate submittals were filed—one on June 6, 2003 and the other on July 7, 2003—in which I described in detail and provided as many as 38 supporting documents to substantiate widespread grave concerns about attorney conduct and behavior in our court case. Just four days later—on July 11, 2003—I received correspondence that said the matter was closed. It seemed to me that the attorneys had "cozy relationships" and considered themselves the "gatekeepers" of what information was (and what was not) introduced to the Family Court Judge and/or Commissioner. And that then became the basis for them to ultimately decide custody/placement of the children. What doesn't get introduced in Family Court can't be considered by the Judge and/or Court Commissioner. When withheld, those findings could be crucial to the custody/placement decision for the children's best interests and well-being. *Never, never be afraid to do what's right,*

> *especially if the well-being of a person or animal is at stake.*
>
> *Society's punishments are small compared to the wounds*
>
> *we inflict on our soul when we look the other way.*

~ *Martin Luther King, Jr.*

191

CHAPTER THIRTY-TWO

Meeting with a Medium Provides Meaning

At this point in my life I couldn't help but feel that practically everything and everyone I'd ever loved had been taken away from me. More and more, I came to realize that one thing I needed in order to survive was my faith in God. The other thing was the support I received from my network of true friends who showed up to be there for me (as well as for my sons). One of my friends even offered me a referral to a local well-respected Christian clairvoyant who might help me access my own Inner Guidance, and heal through connection with my Angels and Spirit Guides.

When I met the medium, she invited me into her home and had me lie down on a massage table; she then started to ask questions. I decided to keep many of my issues to myself so I could better evaluate what she knew about me due to her "special sense" that most of us don't have. She asked me if I was a teacher and I replied, "No—but my Mom was. My professional background is in Business." She then asked me if I was divorced—I wasn't wearing a wedding ring, which could have also meant that I was single—and I answered, "Yes." I was then asked how many children I had, so I told her "Two." She said, "Your oldest is a girl." I replied, "No, I have two sons." She then asked, "You don't have a daughter who's around thirteen years old?" I said, "No." But I then realized that our first child had been a miscarriage—and would have been thirteen at that time. And although the gender had not been identified, I'd always felt that it had been a girl. I then started to really pay attention to this woman—because how else would she have known that? So I told her that I had miscarried during my first pregnancy, and then I'd had two sons.

She went on to say that she didn't see me in denial, but rather as a "counselor" or "healer." The "One Supreme Being" that had power over me for good—she counseled—"is the Holy Spirit." Essentially, I needed to do some self-healing, and not allow others to transfer their self-inadequacies to me, i.e., not let anyone walk over me ever again and never blame myself for what had happened.

This session provided me with some comfort—as well as surprises—since I'd only just met this woman. As much as I thought she would talk about our Blake and his relationship with his abusive dad, her focus was—instead—on our younger son. She told me that he was the son that "the Guides" wanted to talk about, "He's much like you," she said. "He came into this life to be himself." It's the same learning lesson she told me that I have, which is "I don't want to be like that." She explained, "Sometimes when we come into a family, children can pick and choose the qualities of each parent that they want." She felt that our younger son has a more karmatic path with his father—he does not have to do what his Dad does. The younger son was supposed to be a free spirit—i.e., be his own person—and he was coming into himself just at that time. In her words, "He's too compassionate and trusting so he has to learn to trust in himself and feel strong. Perhaps taking martial arts would teach him how to protect himself—and swimming, which is soothing, might be like an umbilical state that offers a sense of safety. He needs to know that he's safe here, and you can help to tell him that in many ways." I added that neither boy felt safe with his father.

She responded, "In the next three or four years their father will have to face up to his own responsibility for his own life. I see him as he 'slips under the door on a skateboard' as if he's on a 'free ride.' But he's going to get hit hard if he doesn't face responsibility for his own life—he could have a health problem or something…Trust me." I remembered that almost everything had been "taken care of" for him in life—especially by his parents. And whatever he hadn't wanted to do, I was forced to do—and then he would blame me or criticize my efforts.

~ ~ ~ ~ ~ ~ ~ ~ ~ ~ ~

She continued, "You are the protector of the children. Anything that he's not doing (decreed by the judge's orders) you can bring him into a court of law and have it reversed. Your sons' father is in a 'destiny year'—he has to face the Judge, just as he needs to face his responsibilities. He's not going to be a parent. The *only* way he can have power over you is with *money*. And it may not be through you that he learns his lesson. You need to look for—and find—a Judge who will listen to your children," she said.

I told her that a new Guardian ad Litem would be assigned soon. (The last Guardian ad Litem hadn't done much of anything when Blake told him how he'd been hurt by his Dad.) The police had been called regarding concerns of the boys' being hurt by their father, but for whatever reason, they refused to pay attention to what was really happening.

I also explained how I'd been advised to get a restraining order because my ex-husband had continued to hurt me—emotionally and physically—after our divorce. Meanwhile, Jay had come up with some bogus photo (which had obviously been taken at his parents' house). In it, he showed a sad face while pointing to a (barely visible) scratch on his arm that he claimed I caused. It was a creative but incriminating set-up by my ex and his parents. The Court—not wanting to deal with such petty behavior—gave each of us a restraining order so they could move on to the next case.

"Treat him as if he doesn't exist—you don't need him—not even monetarily. Relieve yourself of any control that he has over you," the medium told me. Her recommendation was that I talk to my new attorney, and ask what could be done. I needed to be monetarily independent from my ex-husband, and regain primary custody because the boys simply did not want to live with their Dad. It was important that they get the opportunity to talk directly to the Judge.

She was concerned about our younger son, and told me to get him into reality, since his father neglects him and allows him to sit in front of the computer all the time. I told her how sad I was that both boys had not only lost their parents to divorce, but they'd also lost their primary caretaker, who—as special needs children—they depended on. And that person was me. My sense has been that the Court's twist was to say that their mom was standing in the way of their Dad being able to bond with his children. But in reality, it was the other way around.

I brought up the instance that had happened after Blake's band concert—it had been their time with their dad. I'd attended with my father—who told me that he felt that Jay's parents and his girlfriend were keeping Daniel away from me. When the band concert had ended, my Dad and I walked out of the grade school's gym with the crowd. When we stepped into the lobby, Daniel could be seen standing between two soda machines with Jay's parents—almost as if they stood guard over Daniel. As we walked by, Daniel saw me, and I reached in between Jay's parents to say "Hello" to and touch my younger son. But at that moment, I felt someone from behind physically grab me by my arm and shove me aside. At first, I thought it was just the regular push of the crowd toward the lobby, but when I looked back, it was Jay's girlfriend who tried to stop me from greeting my own child. I was shocked by her hostile behavior—especially in a public place. In the confusion, Daniel ran to me, and I brought him over to where my Dad was standing in the lobby. Blake then came up to me—obviously, neither boy wanted to leave with his Dad. But because of the injunction, there was nothing I could do except to escort them out to Jay's car.

I then walked over to the driver's side of the car, and quietly told Jay to tell his girlfriend to keep her hands off of me as well as our children. He just smirked, and then drove away—with the boys. My Dad and I were beside ourselves after that public display of physically aggressive behavior in front of our boys by Jay, his girlfriend, and his parents. What concerned us even more was the way in which the boys would be treated after they arrived at their dad's house following this evening of sad, emotionally-fraught events. I added that my counselor had told me that Jay was passive-aggressive (i.e., he stirs things up to then just walk away, and "acts like it never happened"), which was similar to what our older son has noticed. Blake's comment had been, "Dad says he doesn't remember."

The medium suggested that I keep a record of events that took place with the children as they related to their father because there would be a "pattern." She told me that she felt that I could make it on my own without Jay—who wanted a string attached in order to keep control. She also said that next year—especially during the summer, i.e., July—Jay would be forced to take responsibility for himself. She said, "You need to stand up and say, 'This man has no power over me' and get it out of your system—which will empower you and make you more productive."

195

~~~~~~~~~~~~

Additionally, I was told that there was simply nothing more I could do to protect my sons. It was time "to not get into my head so much," because I needed to learn my lesson in life. She said, "As you learn to turn it over to God TOTALLY with every layer of yourself— mind, body, and spirit—things will then start to move in your favor. Visualize what you want to happen in that courtroom for the highest good of your boys. These children weren't just accidentally born to this man who is trying to control them—this play has already been written for a higher purpose for all of you. It doesn't mean that it's wonderful, but it does give everyone an opportunity to grow and learn. If your ex-husband can't go to his heart and not have control, then he's going to replay the same scene again that he's played in other experiences with his soul. The boys are learning, and will grow to be stronger—given what they've learned in order to deal with their father. It's not about tough love, but rather it's about understanding that the higher power (God) and the great spirit (Holy Spirit) are around that child—there are no accidents. No mother wants her children to be abused or mistreated. I commend you on all the things that you've done or have gone through— it's very difficult to stand up to society. But you can free yourself of emotion, and find peace within your heart. There are people around you who will help you with this very strongly."

I told her that a number of individuals had come up to me and encouraged me to let somebody—like the media—know what has truly been going on regarding my sons and me. While others had discouraged me, and said that—instead—it could backfire, and really screw things up.

She responded, "I think you're an advocate—bring it to the higher good—because there is a purpose for this. Faith does not come easy for any of us—have faith in the higher power (God) that it will be turned to good. You have to attack each thought as a fear—look at it as 'What's the worst thing that could possibly happen?' You have to look at the positives that are around you. Thoughts and beliefs create our reality. If you believe you're powerful, and you believe that God is powerful, then no ex-husband (or anyone else) can attack you—because you will have come through alright. Stay in the moment and stop returning to the past—this is the NOW—so that the right outcome can come about.

We all have lessons—the difficult part is to realize what those are, and then tackle them. When you think that maybe you should be in charge of something, and have done what you could—remember, that's the time to surrender to a higher spiritual base (God) rather than to the others, i.e., attorneys, etc. Accept and understand that you can't do any more. And if you can't do anything, then it means that it's not up to you to do it. You have control in your life *as long as you work with God because you've surrendered.* We may not understand why this is happening, but we do believe that God will turn it to good. God is good—and if you're on the highest path of spirituality—everyone is protected in difficult situations. Empowerment (i.e., power used rightly) comes directly from God—not from the way that others use it."

She continued, "I believe that you're here not just for yourself and your children, but for other women. This is your way of doing it—has it been fun? A good trip? No, but when you look back at all of this you'll say 'Aah, this has been one of my life's main purposes because it's bringing the truth out.' What do you want to tell the world about this? What do you want to do to make a difference for other people? Many times that's what happens with people who go through their own and/or their children's pain in life. They then step out beyond their own life and start something big—like John Walsh, whose son was kidnapped and killed, and then he created a TV show as an advocate for other missing children. He has done wonderful work on behalf of others through the years, and I feel that you're going to step out and help others, too. Natural steps for a humanitarian are (1) help the family, (2) then go out and help strangers (because that's the natural step for all God's children), and (3) overcome really being hurt in order to see that there's a need. You qualify under all these prerequisites to step out and help some other little child as well as your sons. It becomes very personal and internal for those who have gone through hellacious times, but when it can be turned to good for others, you have more than completed your mission in this lifetime. You are more powerful than the men in your life because they are not using their heart—wisely.

197

Power comes through the heart and intent. You will help other women become self-empowered, too. Most advocates have been hurt in their lifetime—connect yourself with women like you, and do something about the issue—there's power in numbers. I see you working with some seminars or books to help bring about self-empowerment. You are definitely going to be a catalyst for other women—but it's not time yet. Strengthen yourself spiritually, and then you'll clearly see when to take action and when to let things rest. Feeling that you're to move forward in a powerful way is not seeking revenge. Ask God 'What am I doing here?' and you will see signs if you are supposed to take some action. Nothing is complete until we leave this earth—when we get everything done down here (fulfill our purpose), then we can leave. You're not ready to do that yet—we want you to raise those boys—so you want to stay around here since things are not yet in perfect order. Continue to raise your children well—it's your gift as their mother."

~ ~ ~ ~ ~ ~ ~ ~ ~ ~ ~ ~

As we wrapped up our session, she suggested that I should go to my Church, and surrender to God's will for my sons. I was told to light a candle, then kneel, and turn over all my maternal concerns—regarding my sons' safety and well-being when with their father—to Blessed Mother Mary. She instructed me to honor Her, pray, and say, "I don't know what to do anymore. I've done everything I could possibly do for my sons' best interests, but it's not enough. Therefore, as their mother, I ask for Your help, trust in You, and turn over to You, Blessed Mother Mary, my two sons." I was told to say each of my son's full name as I visualized placing my boys' hands into Hers—into Her care as our Heavenly Mother for the highest good—and see them happy with Her. (I later did just as she had instructed—many times—and found myself in tears. But I also felt great comfort.)

We talked about my Mom before I left my session, and she said, "The main thing to know is that her love is around you. This was a lady who loved her children...she really loved people—and think about her that way. Ask yourself, 'What would Mom tell me to do?' She was a good person. I sense her as an instructor of some kind mentoring others now."

198

~~~~~~~~~~~~

NOTE: The song "Mother, I Miss You" (lyrics by John Tesh, Edith Dalia Reid, Leroy Nelson Reid) expresses my wish that time together with my mother would have been much longer—especially since she was suddenly gone long before her time. There has been so much that I (and my sons as they've grown up) would have liked to show and share with her. How deeply I miss her—not being able to laugh and talk again as we had—but in light of my faith, I hold onto the belief that I will see her again (when it is my time to join her and other loved ones who have passed on).

CHAPTER THIRTY-THREE

FALLOUT FOLLOWING FIFTY/FIFTY CUSTODY OF CHILDREN

After our divorce in 1998, a new law emerged that promoted "father's rights." It seemed to aid Family Court's tendency towards 50/50 shared custody where the children of divorced parents would spend half of the time with each parent. It was somewhat new. The aftermath of the Family Court Commissioner's decision in favor of this type of placement ultimately showed that its consideration of the father's rights didn't benefit the children's rights—especially children with special needs, like Blake and Daniel.

Jay was a professional engineer who worked full-time as a Manager for one of the local papermaking companies. Although his boss had testified in Family Court that Jay's hours were flexible for family needs, that didn't prove to be the case. His work schedule—frequently—included evenings and out-of-town trips. He came to rely on either the help of his girlfriend (who later became his third wife, and had two sons older than ours; these boys also "cared for" our sons at times), or more often, his parents. None of these caregivers had (or were interested in having) an understanding of our sons' Asperger Syndrome. (I'd been told that they were often yelled at while in the care of Jay's "helpers"). And when he did go out with the boys, his parents often came along to assist him with taking care of our boys.

As I look back, when I married Jay it was as if I'd joined his family, and his parents wanted to parent us—my husband didn't become a grown-up father/parent, but rather his parents continued to parent him as well as his sons. Also, over time Jay showed that he would listen to and side with his mother over me, his wife, and allow her to come between us. One of my friends had commented about this behavior and asked me if I'd ever watched the TV show *Everybody Loves Raymond.* I told her that I hadn't because I didn't get the chance to view television since much of my time was spent either caring for my two "special needs" sons or keeping up with household matters, etc. She told me that my situation sounded a lot like this TV show—the storyline and characters very much "mirrored" my family life with Jay, his brother, and his parents. At her suggestion, I tuned into this sitcom and learned that it truly did seem to resemble my situation—it was as if the show's creators had known the inter-relationships among Jay, his family and me!

Jay went as far as to have Daniel's in-home therapists not only pick up Daniel from school—but also Blake—and then bring them both back to his house for Daniel's in-home occupational and speech therapies. I was informed by my counselor that, legally, the therapists should not be driving and taking care of Blake because he was not their assigned patient/client. Sadly, Jay's increased reliance on the in-home therapists (since he wasn't available due to his work schedule) proved to be more for his convenience than for our boys' best interests. This was ironic because initially, Jay had not allowed any in-home therapy for Daniel in his house. Essentially, Jay provided minimal care for the boys and had them passed around between numerous caregivers, which adversely affected the boys' high need for routine. So much for the "one-on-one" time Jay had insisted on when he'd requested 50% custody. In reality, Jay was hardly available to our boys during his time of placement. Additionally, he'd shown failure to follow the "right of first refusal" clause, which stipulated that I would have the children on weekdays whenever he was working or otherwise unable to take care of them. This had been part of our Divorce Judgment. Instead, Jay would often have his parents babysit Blake and Daniel while he was at work during the week without my knowledge, which meant there was no way for me to invoke my "right of first refusal."

After the decision had been made by the Family Court Commissioner to grant Jay an increase to 50% shared placement of our sons, my Family Violence Advocate evidently followed up personally with the Guardian ad Litem. He was asked to listen to cassette tapes that contained disturbing expressions made by our younger son at times when he had to go to his dad's house for placement. In pursuing this action, my Family Violence Advocate hoped that there might be some reconsideration of (a) the 50/50 shared placement (which had become the new court order) and/or (b) the GAL's decision to step down from this case. Dismayed, my Advocate told me that the GAL refused both.

My Family Violence Advocate later contacted me to say that she was going to attend a conference in Madison—our state's capitol—where a particular aspect of Family Court Legislation was up for consideration. She asked me to write up my account of the abuse my children and I had experienced from Jay since our separation/divorce. It would be relative to the "Legislation for consideration of domestic violence/abuse issues when making placement decisions that should be made *in the best interests of the children*." I took my hand-written document to the Family Violence Center in September 2001, and she took excerpts from my documented account to this conference.

~ ~ ~ ~ ~ ~ ~ ~ ~ ~ ~

At the recommendations of others, I continued the search for a new lawyer in a county outside of ours, and eventually retained my third Attorney to bring our case back to Family Court. I had met with him late in the fall of 2002, when I'd brought him up to date with the 50/50 placement that was failing our sons. Initially, my third Attorney was hesitant to file a motion at that time because he felt that timing was an important issue. He explained that if our filed motion came before the Court during my six months of placement, our addressed concerns with the current custody Order might appear somewhat moot. He also said, "...the burden is now on you to change the current placement...Back in the year 2000, the burden was on the father to change placement, and he did so." My new Attorney suggested that he review my file again sometime in the spring of 2003. This was easy for him to say, but it meant more months of waiting while Blake and Daniel continued to be—and feel—unsafe when with their abusive father.

As I'd been instructed by the Christian clairvoyant, I decided to turn over my children to our Heavenly Mother in prayer—as a way to let go of my maternal worries. There were times when—after Blake and Daniel had left my house with their father (as court-ordered, but against their will)—I would close the door and cry so hard that I could hear myself gasp for breath. During those episodes I felt utterly helpless as a mother who could not protect my own young children.

I'd seen some of my friends in tears when their child left home to attend college—which I could understand. But I also realized that it was

202

their children's next longed-for chapter in life. As parents, the adults had done their job of childrearing, and as a young 18-year-old adult, college would provide their grown child positive, productive (and pleasurable) years. In contrast, my two sons—at the young ages of eight and eleven—begged me not to make them go. But due to Family Court Orders they were forced against their will to stay at a place (their father's house) that been proven to be unsafe for them. Those forced visits definitely did not benefit either of our boys' best interests or their well-being. In my nightly prayers, faith told me to trust that my sons were in the hands of God, who would protect them from the pain in the world— even from their own father. Still, unfortunately, there were way too many times when I cried myself to sleep. One night before falling asleep, I listened to Delilah who played the song "If I Could"—sung by artist Regina Belle—which really resonated with me.

I'd even come to terms with—as I'd shared with my Counselor— the fact that (as much as I would dread it), if a police officer arrived at my door to tell me that something terrible had happened to one or both of my boys, i.e., if Jay went so far as to commit murder—I would learn to accept it because I could then know that my son (or sons) would be at peace. My son would then be free from any further harm imposed on him by his father, and he would be in a safe place with his Heavenly Father—rather than with his own father here on earth, who had angrily abused him. I told my Counselor that I knew it sounded like a terrible thing for a mother to say, but I'd hoped she understood in light of my position of helplessness. She told me that she totally did.

Since the Family Violence Center and I had both expressed continued concern for the boys' safety and well-being, a much-needed "referral" was finally received. The boys were assigned to a well-regarded local Clinical Psychologist who had experience with, training for, and understanding about children with Asperger Syndrome. I met with her and explained what had happened to date regarding the placement of our sons ever since the separation/divorce. I especially related the concerns about the recent change to 50/50 custody as well their father's passive-aggressive, abusive behavior toward the children. This autism expert would (hopefully) become a catalyst for the judge to understand the real truth about my boys' precarious situation, and I hoped that (as their Clinical Psychologist) she would stand up for their best interests. Her report, which would be submitted to the Court-Ordered Psychologist, would be pivotal.

As previously suggested, I contacted my third attorney in spring of 2003, to meet and update him about the legal developments since we'd met in fall 2002. After reviewing my file, he agreed to become my third Attorney and take our case back to Family Court. When I asked him what had ultimately made him decide to take my case, which had only become more complicated with time, he responded, "Because I can see how passionate you are as a mother for your children." I told him that I took his response as a compliment, and he replied, "I meant it to be." Then I said, "It's interesting that you compliment me regarding my passion for my children, when my ex-husband and his attorney have twisted that same quality to portray me negatively to the Family Court. They claim I'm too overprotective regarding my children."

~ ~ ~ ~ ~ ~ ~ ~ ~ ~ ~ ~

My third Attorney filed the "Notice of Motion and Motion to Amend Judgment of Divorce" and its supporting "Affidavit" with the Family Court in July 2003. As Petitioner, my Affidavit—of nearly 24 statements—regarding substantial change of circumstances and modification needed to serve the best interests of the children included:

- *At the time of the last hearing, (Father) argued that since he*

    lived near my home, he should be awarded 50/50 placement—

    but since that time he has built a home that is a 40 minute

    drive from my home as well as a 35-40 minute drive from

    Daniel's current school. My home, on the other hand, is

    only two blocks from Daniel's school.

- *Both boys, who have a form of autism, continue to have anxiety*

    with the new living conditions when placed with their father.

204

- *The boys now have different school schedules—if the current 50/50 placement scheduled continued—while placed with their father, it would mean that the children would have to awaken much earlier than in the past to be driven from their father's house to school on time, and perhaps even need day care or babysitters. WHEREAS if they were placed with me during the school year, the boys' routine would not be interrupted— they would continue to attend school as they always had in the past.*

- *On a number of occasions the boys had expressed that their desire is to live with me—which also offers them access to their friends, (who are located in my neighborhood) as well as their school. As their mother, I have always been (and continue to be) available, to schedule and transport the children to their medical appointments and extra-curricular activities.*

- *The father's work schedule (including evenings and out of town trips) has not allowed him to be equally involved with the children. I have had placement of the boys during the father's placement time on almost a daily basis from after school until he gets home from work.*

- *Even though the current Judgment indicates such, the father had not allowed the children to initiate telephone contact from*

his house to my house when the children have requested.

- Currently, the father does not allow the boys' toys or clothing

to be transported between the homes—he indicates that what

is at his house stays. Additionally, the father will not allow

their pet dog to travel with them to his residence—despite the

current order—which has greatly upset the boys.

Although we were scheduled to appear before the Family Court Commissioner—the same one we'd had before—on August 25, 2003, it was postponed to a later date due to the appointment of a new Guardian ad Litem, and discussions regarding consideration for *new* psychological evaluations from the parties for the Court-Ordered Psychologist. So, it wasn't until January 21, 2004 that we finally appeared before the Family Court Commissioner once again, and received an Order Amending Judgment, which included the following:

- Both parties are directed to comply with the Court's original

Judgment of Divorce as relates to a right of first refusal with

regards to daycare—each party shall have the right of first

refusal with regard to daycare…(mother) shall have

placement of children on weekdays when (father) is working

or otherwise unable to take care of the children.

*- Petitioner's (mother's) motions **denied** regarding: 1) father's*

counseling, 2) telephone contact by the minor children,

3) parties' dog to be transferred between households.

- Petitioner's (mother's) Counsel shall contact Court-Ordered Psychologist's office for a status of evaluations. All attorneys shall schedule a scheduling conference with the Commissioner's Office after parties and Guardian ad Litem have interviewed with the Counselor (Clinical Psychologist) who has appropriate skill in Autism and has been treating the boys.

Three months later we received additional court orders from the Family Court Commissioner that included our final hearing dates in June 2004 (which would be scheduled before her) and the following:

- The Petitioner's (mother's) Motion requesting that the children be evaluated by a doctor who specializes in autism is denied. (NOTE: I'd been told that the Court-Ordered Psychologist did not necessarily have expertise or specialize in autism.)

*- The Petitioner's (mother's) Motion to dismiss without prejudice the Petitioner to refile in order for the March 13, 2004 law regarding domestic abuse (specifically, new law – Act 130 {Wis. Stats. 767.24}) to be in effect for the purposes of this hearing, is **denied**.*

- As it pertains to the final hearing, the court will not base its

decision using the new law regarding domestic violence

(specifically new law Act 130) because this matter was filed

prior to the March 13, 2004 effective date of the new law.

How frustrating it was to hear that the *very law* (which my Family Violence Advocate, who had presented excerpts from *my* written account that had *supposedly helped* to get this legislation *passed* by our state's Senate as 2003 Assembly Bill 279) that *should have helped us*, could **not be used**! This law "related to creating a rebuttable presumption against awarding a parent joint or sole legal custody if the court finds that the parent has engaged in a pattern or serious incident of abuse, requiring a guardian ad litem and a mediator to have training related to domestic violence, requiring a guardian ad litem to investigate whether a party in an action affecting the family engaged in domestic violence, and requiring screening for domestic abuse at the initial mediation session." What was also of significance for me—regarding this law—was March13, 2004; exactly seven years from the date when my Mom had passed away!

CHAPTER THIRTY-FOUR

CUSTODY CASE BROUGHT TO BETTER TERMS FOR THE BOYS?

On January 21, 2004, the Family Court Commissioner had ordered that Blake, Daniel, Jay, and I each be scheduled for a meeting with the Court-Ordered Psychologist—who could also choose to evaluate Jay's third wife (whom he'd married in July 2003). It was also ordered that the Guardian ad Litem be the *only* person to provide the Court-Ordered Psychologist with additional and supplemental information. Only the court, the attorneys, and the parties named would have access to the Court-Ordered Psychologist's report, which was for the purpose of evaluating "custody and placement of the minor children" and would "be admitted into evidence without further foundation."

With these stipulated guidelines, my third Attorney informed Jay's Attorney that he intended to (1) depose the Court-Ordered Psychologist, (2) depose his client, (3) discuss the parameters of discovery, and (4) schedule a status conference, should it be deemed necessary.

Jay's Attorney responded to say that Jay was willing to discuss a modification of the *6 months on/6 months off shared placement*, which had been recommended earlier by the Court-Ordered Psychologist, and incorporated into the Family Court Commissioner's most recent decision relative to placement. Jay was most interested in a week-to-week alternation *or* a split-week alternation. At that point in time, he was *not* interested in exploring a shared placement scenario where the children would be primarily physically placed for the school year (with me) versus the summer months (with Jay). My proposal offered overall consistency and constancy (since primarily placed with me), which the boys needed because it served *their* best interests/well-being (as proven in the past).

Meanwhile, we were informed by the GAL that both the boys' Clinical Psychologist and she agreed that it was best that neither of the Attorneys request copies of her records. Their thinking was that the child might feel less free to open up to her if he believed that the parent would have direct access to the records. My Attorney agreed with the GAL's statement that the boys might feel less free to open up to their Clinical Psychologist if they believed that the parent would have direct access to her records. However, he was concerned that in order to assist these children in the long run, it may be necessary for the attorneys and/or the parties to at least be aware of what type of treatment was ongoing with the Clinical Psychologist. She not only saw these children one or two times for the purposes of an evaluation but she was also their treating physician. Based upon this fact, my Attorney expressed (as a parent himself) that he would want to know (a) what type of treatment his child was receiving, and (b) how he could assist his child in any problems they were experiencing.

In a letter to the new GAL, Jay's Attorney stated that he could not assure either her or my Attorney that he would withhold secured records relative to our case from his client. His position was that the best course of conduct in this case was to agree with her original suggestion that nobody sees the children's Clinical Psychologist records other than the Court-Ordered Psychologist. While our Attorneys continued to send correspondence back and forth, the new GAL had both of us parents agree (while we were in a meeting with our children's Clinical Psychologist) that we would not request written documents from the doctor, who believed that this was very important.

My Attorney then requested that the GAL verify with the Court-Ordered Psychologist—since neither of our attorneys could speak to her—that she would include the children's Clinical Psychologist's findings with her own, and her "game plan" on how she anticipated conducting the court-ordered psychological evaluations. The protocol of her "game plan" was described—in part—as (1) she would certainly be interested in viewing the children's Clinical Psychologist's records, and (2) she might speak with her as well. She supposedly appreciated the Clinical Psychologist's concern about allowing the children's records (in this case) to be viewed by parents since she also expressed in agreement that it could have an inhibitive effect upon the boys' therapy.

~ ~ ~ ~ ~ ~ ~ ~ ~ ~ ~

In late February 2004, my Attorney included a letter to Jay's that stated it had been brought to his attention that Daniel was currently scheduled for both an EKG and an EEG at the hospital due to a referral from the child's pediatrician. Daniel had been experiencing chest pains on an ongoing basis. My Attorney understood (from me) that I had contacted Jay so that we both—as parents—were aware of these procedures for Daniel. In early March 2004, my attorney and I—as well as the GAL—were informed by Jay's Attorney that Jay was *quite surprised,* and reported that Daniel had *never* experienced chest pains during his placement at Jay's residence. (Note: Remember the lesson taught that when the word "never" is used—BEWARE—because it's probably an untruth.) Was this Jay's denial or was it parental ignorance?

The psychological evaluations took place, and a disturbing situation arose. My Attorney addressed the GAL to inform her that Daniel reported that his father continued to tell him that the (Court-Ordered Psychologist) had been informing his father (Jay) of what Daniel had told his Clinical Psychologist. The child was having a lot of anxiety over the fact his father continued to instruct him about what to say at the counseling sessions with either the Court-Ordered Psychologist or the boys' Clinical Psychologist. Daniel felt uncomfortable with the idea that either doctor might share the issues that he brought to the table with his father.

Secondly, Daniel had also reported that his father continued to get upset (including yelling) when assisting the child with his toileting. All of us were aware that Daniel had ongoing self-care issues—he'd reported that his father yelled at him while he'd helped Daniel cleanse himself. Although these might be mere allegations, my Attorney asked the GAL to follow up with these concerns. It was also understood that the GAL might not have met with the children in quite some time. (Like the previous GAL, no visits had been made to either of the parents' homes.) A number of months had passed since the last meeting with the GAL, so my Attorney asked Jay's Attorney to discuss his client's conduct as well as instruct his client to cease and desist these types of actions immediately. He restated what we had all previously agreed to-- **that it would be appropriate for neither (Court-Ordered Psychologist) nor (the children's Clinical Psychologist) to provide**

211

specific information to the assessment early on, in order to prevent the parents from using this information with the children. Since this obviously had become a concern for both my Attorney and me, we asked that Jay's attorney kindly discuss this matter with his client, and then confirm with my Attorney's office that these very important issues had been addressed.

Less than a month later, my Attorney followed up with Jay and his Attorney to tell them that a message had been received from a very concerned mother (me) in this matter. He reminded them: (1) the parties continued to communicate through a notebook, and (2) the youngest child had been currently instructed by (his Pediatrician) to take Miralax on a regular basis in order to address some health concerns. My Attorney pointed out that (1) in the past week Jay had indicated in the notebook that the boys' mother (me) should stop sending the Miralax to his house, and (2) Jay had also recently indicated in the notebook that he would not administer this medication to the child just for the sake of doing so.

Furthermore, my Attorney informed them (on my behalf) that I did not wish to give this child any type of medication that was not needed or instructed by a physician. However, based upon the child's medical condition, the pediatrician had indicated that this medication was not only appropriate, but **necessary**. The fact that Jay *chose not* to follow through with administering this medication to our younger son was obviously of great concern. My Attorney asked Jay's Attorney to discuss this matter with his client, and also said that the GAL would, as well, be informed regarding this unhealthy situation. He added that he would ask the GAL to set up a time to meet with the boys, and give (both attorneys) some preliminary thoughts on this matter well before the hearing, and if possible, before the depositions scheduled—which was for early June 2004.

Depositions of both parents as well as the Court-Ordered Psychologist took place at Jay's Attorney's office. Instead of going through with the hearing dates scheduled later that month, we spent time with our attorneys, who wrote up a draft of our desires (i.e., what we would agree to change regarding the current custody and placement from the 6-months on/off between parents current schedule—on that, we could both agree!) The attorneys also felt that it put us in a better light before the Family Court Commissioner, who executed the new Stipulation and Order on June 21, 2004, which can be found in Appendix B.

The good news was that the placement was no longer six months on/off which had definitely not served the boys' well-being. Additionally, this new custody arrangement put a "safety net" in place whereby the boys' Clinical Psychologist could address concerns (things that the boys expressed regarding a parent in a counseling session) directly with the parent and the boy(s). This would insure that the parent be held accountable for actions that didn't serve the boys' best interests. The new arrangement could, however, pose more of a challenge since it now became one week on/off. Would the boys adjust to a more rigorous routine as they moved between each of their parents' homes on a weekly basis—especially with their condition of ASD (in which routine is much needed)?? As before—only time would tell if these new terms of custody would address the boys' best interests and improve their well-being.

CHAPTER THIRTY-FIVE

SON SEEKS SAFETY—BECOMES SUICIDAL

After the recently updated court Order, Jay's Attorney informed the Guardian ad Litem that Jay had secured a counselor to address issues relative to placement of our minor children with him. Jay returned to the Counselor that he'd used when we had been in co-counseling at the time of our separation, and the GAL opined that Jay's Counselor was "extremely appropriate to provide the needed therapy."

In February 2005 (on Blake's 14th birthday), my Attorney requested that the boys' GAL contact his office to briefly discuss concerns that pertained to counseling. He wanted to discuss her thoughts regarding a particular paragraph of the current Order, which indicated that she was to meet with the counselors and verify that the appropriate counseling was being followed through by all parties, as well as by the children. My Attorney informed the GAL that it has been brought to his attention that the boys' Clinical Psychologist had been in the process of trying to contact the GAL to discuss the ongoing counseling she had been having with the boys. It was understood that Jay might not be following through with the court-ordered counseling as it pertained to the boys. He added that he didn't have any knowledge as to whether or not Jay had continued with—or completed—any type of counseling with his own counselor as stated in another paragraph of the Court Order.

He also informed the GAL that there had been at least one—if not more—incidences of some type of inappropriate behavior on the behalf of the father towards the oldest son, Blake, where he'd hit the child in the diaphragm, which had caused the child to fall to the ground. (Blake had later told me that this incident happened in front of his grandparents and stepbrothers when he tried to "stand his ground" because he didn't want his hair cut by his stepmother. Blake added that his father told him—in front of all of them—to get up and stop faking.) This incident was brought to the Clinical Psychologist's attention, and a report was made to Social Services. Also, there were believed to be some ongoing issues regarding Daniel's medications and/or other health issues that his parents have had difficulty agreeing on to handle.

On March 11, 2005, the boys' Guardian ad Litem was reappointed by the Family Court Commissioner in our case, and stated the GAL was directed to "Submit to the Family Court Commissioner— and to the parties—a preliminary recommendation within 90 days of the appointment effective date unless extended by the Court." After she had been reappointed, the GAL was scheduled to meet with our boys *in the presence* of their Clinical Psychologist, who had the professional expertise and knowledge of Autism Spectrum Disorders. I waited in the lobby of the Clinical Psychologist's office until the boys finished this appointment.

As we drove home in the car, Blake spoke up to say that he'd told the GAL that he wanted to live with me most of the time, since he didn't feel safe with either his Dad or his Dad's new wife. He then went on to say that when he'd told the GAL this, she told him that he—as well as his mom—would be arrested. He said that he then told her that he would run away from his Dad's house. Blake added she told him that he wouldn't he be able to decide where he wants to live until the age of eighteen. He said that he was also told by the GAL that he wouldn't be allowed (as a fourteen year old) to talk directly to the Family Court Judge/Commissioner regarding his placement request. Blake was visibly upset after speaking to the GAL. It was discouraging—even questionable—that the GAL wouldn't grant Blake his request to talk to the Family Court Judge/Commissioner one-on-one, when others had suggested this recourse to him—and the fact that he wanted to so strongly.

When I shared this information with my Family Violence Advocate, she told me that she was truly shocked. She was—to say the least—upset that a GAL would say those things and speak that way to Blake.

The following Friday, I received a call from a counselor at Blake's middle school, who expressed concern that he seemed suicidal, and suggested that I should come immediately and pick him up. I told her that I would be right over, hung up the phone, but I could hardly

215

register the impact of this life-changing call. How could things be so bad that my older son would want to take his own life? As I drove across town to his school, I was flooded with a wide array of emotions and thoughts—as any mother would be. I prayed to Blessed Mother Mary for her intercessory help, which I knew I would need. When I arrived, I was directed to the school counselor's office where I found Blake, immediately hugged him, and—not knowing what else to do—asked her for guidance regarding what could be done for Blake in light of his present state of mind. She instructed me—as Blake's mom—to take him to our area's juvenile psychiatric center.

While Blake was being admitted, he said that he was afraid that his Dad would come and take him away. That weekend was Jay's custody time, but Blake told the admitting nurse that he would rather stay at the juvenile psychiatric center than be with his father. She told him that—since he was only fourteen—he could not be forced to leave because he'd been admitted voluntarily. (How interesting it was to learn that at age fourteen an individual can request and receive psychiatric treatment yet—disturbingly enough—cannot request or control where he or she would feel safely placed in a custody case!) The admitting nurse assured Blake that if his father showed up there, necessary arrangements would be made for them to meet in the lobby area—a place where his Dad could be watched and ushered out, if necessary.

Blake was then asked to surrender any items he had beyond the clothes that he was wearing—he even had to remove the shoelaces from his tennis shoes. We were told that this was customary upon intake because patients were not allowed access to anything that could be used to commit suicide. Blake and I were then shown a room where all the walls were padded—for safety (we were told). It was reserved for patients who became behaviorally "out of control," and needed to be put in such a room to avoid harming themselves. As Blake and I were led down the hall to what would become "his room," I felt that what was happening to us had suddenly become surreal. Had Blake felt there was no other way out? Had what the GAL told him the previous week pushed him to the limit, and caused him to feel so desperate?

When we arrived at the assigned room, he was introduced to his roommate who looked a bit older than Blake. I was told that I would be allowed one hour of visitation each day during Blake's stay—he was scheduled to initially be there for five days. That would include the weekend, Monday and Tuesday, at which time he would be able to meet with his assigned doctor/psychologist, who would then make a determination as to whether or not Blake would stay on or be discharged. Once he was settled in his assigned room, I was then told it was time for me to leave. I tried to assure my son—and reassure myself—that everything would be okay. I gave him a big goodbye hug, and told him that I would see him the next day—for my one hour of allowed visitation.

~ ~ ~ ~ ~ ~ ~ ~ ~ ~ ~ ~

As I slowly walked out to my car, I felt the need to believe that what had happened in the past few hours of that horrific Friday afternoon had not really occurred. My mind was reeling with questions (as well as concerns) about my older son and his well-being. The isolated feeling of being alone—for Blake as well as for me—was the worst thing! And now Daniel would also be alone at his Dad's for the weekend, since it was his time of placement.

This particular weekend also included my godson's wedding, and some of my siblings were in town that evening. We'd already made plans for all of us to go out to dinner with my Dad. At first, I didn't feel like going, due to what my day had been like. Finally, however, I decided to join them—after all, I couldn't be with either of my sons due to circumstances beyond my control, but I could at least catch up with my Dad and siblings. I told myself that the dinner would be a distraction from feeling alone, helpless, and nearly hopeless!

When I arrived for dinner, we had the largest round table in the middle of the tiny but quaint restaurant. When everyone asked where my boys were, I was hesitant to tell them—at first—but then I felt the need to share what had happened that day for Blake. As I explained the situation, I could sense varied reactions from my family members—some just continued eating, others looked concerned but were not sure what to say, and they asked if I planned to be at the next day's wedding. As much as I looked forward—and wanted—to attend my godson's wedding, I honestly didn't feel that I could attend, since my own son Blake needed me now more than ever. Even though I could get only *one hour* of visitation each day with my son over the next few days, I felt the need to stand by—even if it could only be in spirit.

I would have never imagined myself or my older son being in such a horrible position! I spent each day of that weekend's allowable one-hour daily visitation with my fourteen-year-old son, but seeing him on Sunday evening was particularly difficult—even heart-wrenching. I'd said my good-bye and hugged Blake—he was built like a football line-backer, and since he was now taller than I was, I had to reach up to him as he bent down toward me. I realized that he was crying—uncontrollably—on my shoulder. When I asked him to tell me what was wrong, Blake replied that he was really concerned about and scared for his younger brother, Daniel. He explained that he knew Daniel wasn't safe—while at the juvenile psychiatric center, he'd realized that Daniel was all alone with Jay and his new wife. Blake continued to tell me that ever since he'd been admitted to the center, he could not protect his younger brother! As much as I'd been concerned about this as well, I tried to comfort and stay strong for Blake.

A nurse, who stood behind the desk in the lobby of this section of the facility, spoke up to say, "I'm sorry, since visitation time is over it is time for you to leave." I felt that visiting hours limited me from being with my son (whom I loved and who needed me most right now), but I quietly answered, "I understand." Blake and I then stood back from each other's embrace as we both tried to wipe away our tears. I went up to the nurse behind the desk to ask if I could call back in an hour to be sure that he was okay, and had been able to settle in for the night after his teary breakdown. She told me that she felt bad for Blake—and for me—and that it would be okay for me to call. She also gave us both a bit of encouragement by suggesting that the next day (Monday) I should contact Blake's case manager, and ask that we both meet with her. Since he had been admitted on Friday afternoon (and after the weekend, the regular staff would be in the office), it might benefit him. After all, she had seen the depth of concern he'd expressed that evening, so I shared her encouraging suggestion with Blake as we hugged each other and said our goodbyes. As I left, I told him that I would call the desk in an hour to see how he was doing. I tried my best to reassure him—and myself—that (somehow) everything would be okay.

An hour later, when I made that call from home, the nurse told me that Blake had settled in for the night and seemed to be alright. I thanked her profusely for granting my phone call request, and she again expressed her concern for Blake and for me. She also said that she was deeply troubled to see what an unfortunate position we were in, and reminded me to contact Blake's assigned case manager the next morning. As I hung up the phone, I inwardly acknowledged that I was relieved to learn that Blake had been able to settle in for the night. But I still—understandably—had a hard time falling asleep that night because I felt so helpless and hindered as a Mom. Thoughts were reeling in my mind out of concern for my fourteen year-old son, who was trying to be strong and stand up for himself. Blake had willingly admitted himself to a juvenile psychiatric center—a place where he was forced to be alone, and could not protect his younger brother while Daniel was staying at their Dad's house. I, too, wondered how Daniel was managing without the emotional support of his big brother, Blake, whom he looked to (and up to) in a daily way.

~ ~ ~ ~ ~ ~ ~ ~ ~ ~ ~

It was such a low and lonely moment for me—as well as my sons—and I felt the need to ask God "Why have you forsaken me...and my boys?" I then thought about the movie *The Passion of the Christ*, which I'd watched only weeks earlier during Easter. The scenes of Mary—as she bravely stated that she "needed to see her Son," and then watched in a daze as she followed the crowd who jeered at Jesus as he carried the heavy wooden cross—really touched me. Mary heard and saw her Son's suffering when He fell, and ran to Him to say "I'm here" just as she'd done when Jesus had fallen as a boy—she'd known for years that this situation would be in store for Him. At the site of the crucifixion, she saw her Son bullied by the guards, and nailed to the cross. She then walked toward Jesus, kissed his feet, and said, "Flesh of my flesh, heart of my heart, my Son let me die with You." Mary experienced overwhelming grief when she witnessed the crucifixion and death of her divine Son. With compassionate eyes and aware of the sorrow she felt, she simply said, "My Son." And Jesus replied, "Don't be afraid."

As a mother, like Mary, I couldn't help but be concerned about (and in pain for) my discouraged, suffering child. And now—separated from Daniel—he felt both alone and lost in a disturbing situation simply because he didn't feel safe when with his Dad. How noble of Blake—at only fourteen years old—to show such great bravery and stand up for himself. In my eyes, he was a true hero! The lyrics from the song "Hero"—written by and produced by singer/songwriter Mariah Carey and Walter Afanasieff—seem fitting.

As Mary asked Jesus (in the movie *The Passion of the Christ*), "My Son, where, when, how will You be delivered from this?," I, too, had thoughts like that as I prayed for the God-given saving answer for my son's grave situation. Her motherly love for Jesus was so great—yet she'd realized she would give it over to His Heavenly Father, who was great enough to handle any burden. I learned from Mary's example that I needed to—as before—give Blake over to Him as well.

Just as Blake had displayed courage, so I hoped to find mine as I faced this horrendous situation. My faith told me that Jesus was walking at our sides—He was no stranger to suffering and adversity—which meant everything! With courage, hope, faith, we would venture forth tomorrow and respond to this latest dilemma—these crises—that we faced. That's when we would meet with Blake's assigned case manager.

"Worry does not empty tomorrow of its sorrow. It empties today of its strength."

~ *Corrie ten Boom*

CHAPTER THIRTY-SIX

ENOUGH IS ENOUGH

When I arrived to see Blake the next morning, the two of us then asked to meet with his assigned case manager. She brought us into her office, and told us—in a very matter of fact manner—that Blake was doing well enough to be discharged as soon as that day. This totally took us both by surprise. I asked, "How can that be? When Blake was admitted on Friday, we were told that he would be here at least through Tuesday. What could have changed so drastically from Friday afternoon until now—Monday morning—to reach that conclusion?"

She didn't answer my questions, but merely repeated that Blake would be discharged to go home with his Dad. Blake's face showed fear, and I was astonished to hear what she'd just said. I then asked, "Why would he be discharged to his father when, in fact, upon his admittance here Blake expressed that he didn't feel safe—and was even suicidal—when placed with his Dad? Blake sought safety here to be protected from his father, and you're willing to let him go directly back to what sent him here in the first place?! There MUST be something you can do!" She seemingly "wiped her hands of the situation"—a parallel to Pontius Pilate in *The Passion of the Christ*—and gave me the referral to another community agency to see if Blake could be given an extension to stay until the next day (as had been originally stated). As for her and her staff, they planned to discharge him as she'd told us earlier.

Blake was in tears, and I was in disbelief. I tried to comfort my son—I told him that I would contact the other agency as well as his Clinical Psychologist. The boys' Clinical Psychologist (as well as their Dad's Counselor) had offices that were adjacent to this juvenile psychiatric center. When I finally got through to Blake's Clinical Psychologist, she listened as I updated her with all that had happened since Friday, and then told me she would look into the situation.

I also drove to the agency that was located downtown, and met with a woman who took the time to listen attentively as I explained

Blake's situation to her. Her response was one of genuine concern for him—and for me as his distraught mother. I was told that a call would be made to allow Blake to stay one more night where he was—as originally stated in the original plan—and that she would have someone from their agency meet with him personally at the center the next morning to see what could be done. I sincerely thanked her for that much needed understanding and concern, and then I went to tell Blake about everything that she'd said. He seemed somewhat relieved (and hopeful) when he heard this news.

The next morning (Tuesday), I received a call from the new agency, and was told that they would NOT be seeing Blake after all. I asked them why, and how had that been determined since yesterday afternoon—when I'd been told otherwise. Without any straight answers to my questions, they said that Blake would be discharged—into his father's care—that day! I couldn't believe what I'd just been told—our son had been suicidal due to (a) his fear of being hurt by his father, and (b) the feeling that there was no way out!

Blake's time there was over the weekend (i.e., with a "skeleton" staff), yet he was told that he was okay to be discharged immediately after the weekend? I'd met with the referral agency, which was compassionate for Blake's cause and concern, but somehow the appointment they'd scheduled with him for the next day—as well as the call made to the psychiatric center to grant Blake an extra-night stay—had now been replaced by a ruling that the meeting would not take place afterall?!

None of this made sense—but what was, however, pretty clear to me was that someone or something had stepped in to change everything to Blake's disadvantage, and (conversely) to his Dad's favor. Once the weekend had passed and offices were opened, it would make sense that Jay had put in a call to his Attorney and/or Counselor whose office was located adjacent to this psychiatric center. Together, they would have the "clout" to dissuade the staff from treating Blake because it would show—which I'd found out years earlier when he'd abused me—that Jay had abused his son.

Unfortunately, there was nothing I could do. And it would be pointless for me to try and convince Blake that he would be okay when, in fact, nothing could be assured. I was present at the signing of his discharge, and immediately afterwards I called the Clinical Psychologist to ask her what could be done for Blake. The "silver lining" I received—and clung to—was that she told me she totally understood. She promised to invite Jay into Blake's counseling sessions with her to address Blake's concerns, fears, etc. She would make Jay see that he was accountable for his abusive actions toward Blake. She added that—unfortunately—this could take time, which I felt could potentially put both Blake's safety and well-being at risk!

Being utterly helpless—unable to protect my own son from his father—and dependent on others, just didn't feel natural. Even at the animal level, a mother instinctively protects her young. And my basic instincts as a Mom regarding the safety and well-being of my sons were the same! I began to question "Why am I here? What difference do I make? What is my life's purpose?" I was caught in the midst of twists and turns of unexpected turbulence in an intimidating situation, but then I remembered in Psalm 144 that God is "my rock,…my fortress, my stronghold, my deliverer, my shield in whom I take refuge…" I was inspired to put on my "full armor" and look to the Holy Spirit (my true Compass and Guide) through my own worries and troubles as well as through the pain that my son faced. My faith also told me to look to and call upon the Angels, whose task was to safeguard us in our battles. Sometimes at the darkest hour, the light will come forth. I had to rely on and trust in this "leap of faith" because I had no other choice at this time. Everything about our future was up to look to the professionals—particularly my sons' Clinical Psychologist. All I could do was hold them to accountability, which was easier said than done when it involved my children's safety and well-being.

Patience and prayer—things that others couldn't prevent me from doing paved the way, in time, for the truth. As much as Blake and I had truthfully told people about Jay's abuse toward us, others neither wanted to hear nor believe what we had to say. However, eventually, the facts could no longer be dismissed.

~ ~ ~ ~ ~ ~ ~ ~ ~ ~ ~

On August 31, 2005, the boys' Clinical Psychologist informed their reappointed GAL that she—on behalf of her patient Blake—had concerns about his relationship with his father.   Another incident in which Jay was physical with Blake had occurred. Even though—during their therapy sessions—it had been made very clear that physical force or discipline was *not* an option. This had been established for the safety of the children, as well as for Jay's benefit. This latest incident was the second violation of that established rule. She added that she had met with Jay individually after the first incident and reinforced the expectations.

Additionally, Blake had been assigned to write a paper for his summer school health class, and the topic was events that had had an impact on him.   Here is a paragraph from Blake's original draft:

"Also at this time, my parents are going through a divorce. I

remember, very clearly of this day. I was downstairs, in the

basement, watching one of my favorite TV shows, when I

heard some racket going on upstairs. I went upstairs and I

saw Dad beating the crap out of my mom. My Mom is yelling,

"Call 9-1-1! Call 9-1-1!" But I did not know what that meant.

Then later, I saw my Dad being taken away by the police, and I

saw Mom coming down with bruises and I had no idea what

happened. She just told me to go upstairs and sleep and so I

did. A few days later, I found out that my Mom and Dad were

separated and getting a divorce. I was five years old when

this happened."

At some point, Jay asked to read the paper and Blake agreed. Blake remembered hearing his father yelling that night. It was probably around

10:30 p.m., and Blake was already in bed. Early the next morning (while Blake was still asleep), Jay burst into his room, yelled at him to get up, and Jay stripped the blankets on Blake's bed. Jay insisted that Blake rewrite the paper before he went to summer school. According to Blake, while seated at the computer, Jay grabbed his jaw and pushed Blake's head until it was bent backwards against the chair. Jay held Blake's head there while continuing to yell at him, and accused Blake of writing lies. Jay proceeded to shame Blake by saying, "Grandma and Grandpa would cry if they saw this." Apparently, Jay also told Blake that the truth was what Jay said it was. Daniel validated the incident since he'd been awakened by the yelling. Blake told his father "This is the truth, I saw it, I remember." But Jay insisted that his essay was a lie, and never happened. Even Blake's stepmother became involved and told him that he was not supposed to lie. So Blake apologized to his father because he felt he was the cause of his father's anger, and in order to keep the peace.

Another incidence was that over the same weekend, there had been a few arguments between Blake and his stepmother. The frustration kept building, but instead of working to de-escalate the situation, it appeared to be fueled. At one point, she told Blake to get off the phone, which he did. She then asked him if he was calling a girlfriend, and he said, "No." She continued to ask if it was a girlfriend, and he again said, "No." She told him it sounded like a girl, but Blake explained that it was his friend (who was a male). She kept taunting him until he said "Screw you." When she then grounded him to his room for one hour, Blake angrily retorted, "Why don't you just keep me in my room all day?" Jay came in, told him he was grounded, and asked for the case of X-box games. Blake then threw them at his father, but they went over the stairs. When Jay insisted, Blake angrily retrieved them, and then he was ordered to apologize to his stepmother. This really threw Blake "over the edge" figuratively as well as literally—he threw his leg over the stair railing as if he were going to jump. Jay told him to go ahead and do it. (Blake later told me that at that moment he realized what he was about to do—which caught him just in time from jumping over the upstairs railing.)

Jay then followed Blake into his bedroom, taunted him to go ahead and hit him (Jay). His stepmother came in and told Blake that he was to stay in his room. She came in later (after Blake had calmed down) and asked if he wanted to talk now. She stated that his father was going through a lot of stress, which Blake interpreted as the excuse/reason for Jay's behavior.

The next day, there was another incident—regarding Daniel—in which Blake felt that he needed to intervene. Apparently, Daniel was supposed to get dressed, but stayed at the computer too long. He managed to get dressed in the timeframe given, but did not eat breakfast. Daniel was hungry, so both his stepbrother and Blake told him to go and get a cereal bar. But when Daniel asked his stepmother, she said, "No"— he couldn't have anything because it had been his decision to not eat. Jay also told Daniel "No." Blake realized that Daniel had not understood the timeline and decided to get Daniel something to eat. But his stepmother again said "No"—it had been Daniel's choice. Blake spoke to his father, explained the situation to him, and then Jay told Blake that it would be okay for Daniel to have a cereal bar. Later, when they were in the car, their father and stepmom began to argue in front of both boys about Daniel having nothing to eat and that whether it had been "his choice." Blake felt obligated to jump in and take the blame.

After that weekend, Daniel said that he did not want to go to his father's house—he'd overheard Blake say that he was going to kill himself, as well as Jay telling Blake to hit him. Daniel was worried about his father getting mad, yelling, and about what would happen.

Jay had *not* continued with his Counselor's anger management sessions. Anyone can manage his anger when things go smoothly and others comply with what is requested. The true indication of the ability to effectively handle anger is when emotions escalate and there is disagreement. Clearly, Jay did not appear to have that particular skill. The immature taunting of his son to hit him or to go ahead and jump was—at minimal—poor parenting. And this behavior had been of grave concern in light of (a) the tension about homework during the school year, (b) Blake's level of ability to tolerate frustration, and (c) the ongoing question of Jay's anger and alleged abuse.

The Clinical Psychologist also expressed concern about the message to Blake—i.e., that what Blake said that he remembered was "a lie" but what his father said was "the truth." There were many healthy ways to discuss disagreements about what had happened in the past. But Jay's reaction only served to reinforce for Blake—and possibly Daniel—that their father's anger might escalate out of control and he could become physical. Blake had begun to feel responsible to act as an advocate for his brother, and he should not have to take on this role.

Jay was asked to come in and discuss her concerns—without the boys. Blake was worried that he would have to go with his father that evening for his weeklong placement, and that Jay would become angry and out of control. (This had been a precedent in the past—she reminded the GAL about the time when the Court-Ordered Psychologist had shared with the boys' father some of their concerns about visiting him. Jay turned around and reprimanded the boys about what they had said when they'd met with the Court-Ordered Psychologist.)

The Clinical Psychologist concluded and suggested that Jay allow Blake—and possibly Daniel—to begin their visitation on Monday rather than Friday to give their father time to cool off.

CHAPTER THIRTY-SEVEN

OUTREACH TO OTHERS

"A woman's strength isn't just

about how much she can handle

before she breaks.

It's also about how much she must handle after she's broken."

Author ~ J. S. Scott

I'd become increasingly concerned about my sons' safety and well-being since the new placement schedule began in July 2004. Based on what the boys had told me—as well as written communication I'd had with Jay—I admitted to my Counselor that I felt helpless. My sons were obviously at risk whenever they were placed with their father and, consequently, I genuinely questioned Jay's ability to provide a physically and emotionally safe environment for Blake and Daniel. She informed the GAL that my goal since our divorce was for the boys to have a healthy relationship with their father and successfully transition between our homes.

Why not FIRST enforce Jay to attend anger management sessions, and THEN let him have placement of our sons? That would be a motivating factor for him to get the help he needed, which would mean less damage to our sons. Mistakenly and unfortunately, my passion and concern for my children's well-being had been twisted by my ex-husband and his Attorney as "an inability to manage anger." I saw this as a cruel attempt to distract from Jay's deep-seated anger management issues. He'd been a hurtful husband, and then became a "bullying" father due to both his damaging denial and unrealistic expectations regarding our special needs sons. Jay couldn't handle them wisely. Instead, he ruined his chances for a solid father-and-sons relationship as they became his outlet (aside from me) for his disappointment. As it presently stood, our boys continued to be at obvious risk from their father's abusive behavior.

Others had expressed their concern to the GAL, including the Family Violence Center Advocate who had been attending our court hearings with me. She admitted that she was not an expert in autism, but she said that through her work as a Social Worker, she had witnessed the negative impact on (any) children who had been placed with parents on *alternating* weeks. She also believed that "The literature would also indicate for this to be especially true when there has been a history of violence in the home." She added, *"Considering children with special needs are more likely to need a more structured and consistent living environment, the alternating of weeks cannot possibly be in their best interest. I was shocked at the last Guardian ad Litem's recommendations and the court's decision regarding the placement of these children (six months on/off with each parent). The abusive behavior of their father toward not only their mother, but towards his children, particularly Blake was—in my opinion—not taken seriously when the court made its ruling. Abusiveness is incompatible with truly positive parenting, as the literature will corroborate (i.e., Lundy Bancroft, The Batterer as a Parent)…These children need a positive voice to help protect them. I urge you to listen to these boys, ask them direct questions, and believe in what they tell you."* (**Note**: This letter was sent to the GAL a couple weeks *before* the GAL met with our sons in the presence of their Clinical Psychologist—*afterwards* Blake showed suicidal tendencies, and was admitted to the juvenile psychiatric center.)

~ ~ ~ ~ ~ ~ ~ ~ ~ ~ ~

Rather than follow the "beaten path" (which led to being abused or bullied), I chose to "beat it"—with reference to Robert Frost's poem *The Road Not Taken*—and try a (different) "path less traveled" with the hope that it would make "all the difference." Essentially, I dared because I cared. And I was persistent in pursuing the court system until both of my boys received the safety and peace they needed to grow up functionally—in spite of their parents' dysfunctional divorce. With passion for my sons (as well as for justice) and encouragement from others, I reached out to notable others who might lend their voice to my cause, as well. On August 8, 2005, I sent an email to Oprah titled *Cry for Help*: *"HELP!!...was what I heard you, Oprah, say in your message to the viewing audience by looking straight into the camera nearly every time you went to a commercial break during the first segment (woman confronting her father/brother with the abuse she suffered by them) of your show 'Family Secrets' on Tuesday, September 30, 2003...I was present in your audience."* (as were three of my friends whom I'd invited when I won four tickets at our parish school's annual auction—they and I were hopeful that this particular show would be Oprah's "Favorite Things"—unfortunately, it wasn't. But fortunately, for me, it provided a direct message relative to my family situation). *"You made such an impression on me by stressing that anyone who is watching this show—whether adult OR child—who is suffering from any kind of abuse, to keep going, and going, and going, etc...until someone hears your cry for help, will listen to you, and help!*

I have to wonder if this was truly God answering my prayers and providing me with a purpose to be personally in your audience that day to hear this message from you, Oprah! I believe your purpose is "Communicator of Causes" as THE VOICE to create the awareness needed to make a positive difference. Especially in the lives of those suffering from abuse (you've said as you did when you were younger). So I come to you and ask you to please listen to my—but more, my sons'—cry for help!!" (I continued to explain my situation and that of my sons).

Others suggested that I also contact my government officials. In my letter to our state's Lt. Governor, I began, *"I come to you as...1) a state citizen, 2) a woman to woman, 3) a mother to mother...with a cry for HELP! I sincerely ask that you PLEASE listen to my, but more, my sons' cry for HELP!!"* I continued to make the points as I had in my email to Oprah—but I also included the following information: *"Aware of your recent appearance in town, I applaud you as a woman and a leader at the state level for your efforts to empower women at the local level. Your efforts 'to support and expand opportunities for all women and girls to help them be healthy, safe from violence, to learn, to achieve, to compete, to realize their dreams...' is very admirable and very much appreciated. I have been encouraged by others locally to* come to you to make you aware of my experience living in our local community as a wife who has been battered/domestically abused by my husband, and the repercussions I, as well as my sons, have had to go through given the behavior of our county's 'legal system' in this family court case."

In closing, I also repeated what was stated on her website about her: "...has some old-fashioned beliefs about government. She believes those things that must be done as a community should drive government's agenda, that we work to support the commonwealth. She asks for your observations, insights, suggestions to make government work better where you live."

Almost a year after I'd written to Oprah and our Lt. Governor, I learned that she had been invited back to our city as an Honorary Chair for the second annual networking luncheon, and this time I sent a letter to request a possible ten-minute meeting after this event. I emailed: "In reviewing your website as our state's Lieutenant Governor, I find that you mention that from your mother, Helen, you 'learned a great deal...She comes from a different era and may have had a different style, but she always found a way to continue to advance the level in which she used her natural gifts.' If I may make a comparison, I too somewhat underestimated my mother's power...and her name was Helen as well. As an English teacher, my mother not only taught English/Grammar for over 18 years at a local all-girl high school, but (even more) wanted to impress upon her students that, as females, they have value. She wanted them to hold and understand their value in their personal/professional, societal/community lives! I learned my mother's value when many of her students and friends (to this day) recount how, even after her unexpected death to cancer almost ten years ago, she positively "touched' their lives. Why I bring this up to your attention is that as much as she was a teacher, she was my mother from whom I learned the life lesson to stand up for one's self and for what is right—no matter how difficult it may be. Perhaps you recall who I am from the letter I sent to your attention within the last year...It was the life lessons that I learned from my mother to **not give up**, but rather **stand up for what is right**. And what could be more right but my sons' entitlement to be safe...even when it's

231

from their own father—who emotionally and physically abuses his own boys!"

I added that since I'd sent my previous letter to her, I had also approached our Congressman, who had then brought the issue to the attention of the Family Court Judge, who had initially resided over our case nearly ten years before. I also shared with her that ever since the legal system/GAL had walked away without finishing court orders of the GAL last year at this time, my sons' Clinical Psychologist continued to see/treat my sons due to her continued concern for the boys' ongoing 50/50 placement with their abusive father. Ultimately, as of May 1, 2006, the boys' Clinical Psychologist had presented their father with an agreement, and he'd signed off his placement. Now he sees the boys every other weekend from 10 a.m. Saturday until 6:30 p.m. Sunday (for a total of four days per month). Since the new placement is proving to serve the boys' best interests, I'd recently filed—with the assistance of my Advocate from the Family Violence Center—a motion with the Court Commissioner's office whereby we will appear in court next month for revision of the Judgment, so that the child support fits the current placement (which is no longer 50/50). If the Commissioner does not hear/denies, I will then appeal/de novo the decision (as is my understanding within 30 days), to appear before our initial Family Court Judge for her decision.

~ ~ ~ ~ ~ ~ ~ ~ ~ ~ ~

As the boys' Mom, I now had to represent myself in court since I could no longer afford attorney fees. I'd already spent over $85,000.00 to date—money that I'd inherited from my Mom and Grandma—a gift that was much-needed for what better use than to provide safety for my sons? My third—and last—Attorney informed me (as the WI Statutes state) that I, as a party in this case, had the right to ask for a "status conference hearing" by going to the Family Court Commissioner's office to make the request. The response I received was signed by the Court Commissioner (who presided over this case each time it came before the Family Court Commissioner to date), yet ruled the status conference would be heard before yet *another* Family Court Commissioner— someone totally new without any knowledge of the history of our case!

The Guardian ad Litem did NOT present her preliminary post-investigation recommendation (as the court had ordered her) before—OR at—our status conference hearing. The GAL only mentioned that the boys and the parties were continuing counseling. Nothing was mentioned about how our older son had been admitted in May 2005 to the juvenile psychiatric center as an inpatient with suicidal tendencies. All of which was due to his experience of physical/psychological/verbal abuse by his father! When I brought the Clinical Psychologist's report—which explicitly stated incidents where the boys were abused by their father—the *new* Commissioner told me that I needed to file *another* Motion. And then she said that if I didn't know how to file a motion myself, I should seek another attorney.

I explained to her that I could no longer afford an attorney. She made a flippant remark to me with reference to what the GAL had told her about me. It didn't seem appropriate for a professional to say that, and made me feel very intimidated by her. The *new* Commissioner then stated that the GAL could be dismissed (without being enforced to follow out court orders stated of her), and to settle up her bill regarding her costs in this case! She then left the courtroom with the GAL, who quickly exited the courtroom behind her.

CHAPTER THIRTY-EIGHT

CHAMPION FOR THE CAUSE

The lyrics from the song "Not While I'm Around"—written by Stephen Sondheim and sung by Barbra Streisand—became my "battle cry." There was a little voice inside that told me I had untapped abilities, as well as the greatest motivation in the world—my boundless love for my sons Blake and Daniel. With the assistance of my Advocate from the Family Violence Center, I filed a Motion before the Family Court Commissioner's office. I'd received a Notice of Hearing (signed by our original Court Commissioner), which also stated the case would be held before her.

What I'd learned from my experience in Family Court was that it was hard enough to have to gain the courage to step out of an abusive relationship, but dealing with court professionals who treated you in an intimidating manner—so that the truth would be withheld—was the biggest challenge of all. In fact, it was quite similar to the powerless feeling of being controlled, intimidated, and manipulated when in an abusive situation. The abuser—undeservedly—gets what he wants, and the aftermath (for the victim) can be worse than the actual act of abuse—you're the one blamed and who gets judged. I felt that my sons and I had really been betrayed by the (court) system.

But despite efforts to shut me up and/or shut me down (whether by my abusive ex-husband or from a court/legal professional), I stood up for what was right—to serve the best interests and well-being of my boys. After all, they (just like everyone else) have rights to be protected from physical/psychological/verbal abuse.

~ ~ ~ ~ ~ ~ ~ ~ ~ ~ ~

This is what I wanted to say to my boys...Blake and Daniel, I will fight for you—what other choice do I have? You're my sons, and when you're suffering so am I—my heart is *always* with you. I will do whatever it takes—seek out the answers, research, and connect (as I had with your doctors regarding your ASD), so that you no longer suffer in silence because I have a passion for you, as well as for justice. Conversely—and unfortunately—my sons' court-appointed GAL (as well as the Family Court Commissioner) would not. Instead, they ignored us and walked away—without any accountability or responsibility—as quickly as possible. This left victims—like the three of us—voiceless despite attempts to stand up for their rights against abuse/violence. Below, I've excerpted this fitting "Anonymous" stanza that follows:

COURAGE

Courage is the strength to stand up

When it's easier to fall down and lose hold.

It's the conviction to explore new horizons

When it's easier to believe what we've been told.

Courage is the desire to maintain our integrity

When it's easier to look the other way.

~ ~ ~ ~ ~ ~ ~ ~ ~ ~ ~

Slowly and hesitantly, but with growing courage and determination (just as I'd relentlessly questioned medical experts in the past), I'd begun to research the state statutes in preparation for legally representing myself–with my Family Violence Advocate present— before the Family Court Commissioner. My Dad—who had followed and been present for our case for almost ten years—had occasionally mentioned that he thought I "should have been a lawyer." (I'd graduated from Marquette University with a Business—not a Law—degree; but college had taught me how to stand tall, and face life's challenges with determination and promise.) Rather than be silenced, I chose to walk into the courtroom on November 27, 2006, and take my seat beside my Advocate, while Jay and his Attorney took theirs at the other end of the table.

When the Family Court Commissioner stepped into the courtroom and took her seat, she asked me to present my case. Jay's Attorney had scheduled this hearing, which it allowed no *more than a half hour of time* to present my case, since 12 noon was the start of the lunch hour for courthouse personnel. Therefore, I realized I needed to state my case succinctly.

With my notes before me, I said, *"This motion is brought forward to serve the needs and best interests of our sons, Blake and Daniel. It regards the <u>child support</u> that they deserve and is <u>not about maintenance</u>. There has been a 'substantial change in circumstances' regarding placement and consequently, there's a need for the child support to be adjusted so that it fits the placement schedule. Our two sons—with their clinical psychologist—have requested, and their father has agreed and voluntarily signed off on an Agreement drafted by the sons' clinical psychologist.* (I provided a copy to the Court Commissioner). *Since that date of May 1, 2006, our sons spend two overnights per month, which is less time spent with their father than the primary physical placement as originally ordered by the Judge.*

Since it's no longer 50/50 placement, the child support should no longer be based on 50/50, but rather a percentage—as was originally court ordered by the Judge at the time of the divorce when I, their mother, was given primary physical placement. (I then provided a copy of the original court orders and placement schedule for the Court Commissioner's review.) I proceeded to explain my earning power: *"Before I met Jay, I'd lived in the Fox River Valley and had sales territory in Chicago, Madison, and Milwaukee in light of my degree earned at Marquette University. When we became engaged to be married, we decided—as a couple—that I would give up my career, move to Green Bay (where he had been employed as an engineer). We then decided—again as a couple—that since our two children had 'special needs,' I would become an 'at-home' mom, which I have been for nearly 15 years. The boys continue to be considered 'special needs' due to their current IEP (Individualized Educational Plan) and need for Speech/Language therapists—our younger son had been diagnosed with autism before the divorce.*

236

The previous Court Orders were 'financially based on Jay's income and made an assumption of my making $30,000' annually—in real terms 1) I have had my resume in circulation via the internet, replied to newspaper ads, and used employment agencies, 2) I had a temporary part-time marketing position with a local construction company, 3) but reality has shown that the Green Bay community is an industrialized area that has not offered me the opportunity to make the court-assumed annual income of $30,000." (Financial Disclosure Statements were provided to the Court Commissioner for her review.)

I looked at the clock to make sure that I'd concluded the presentation of my case within just a few minutes before 12 Noon. After the Court Commissioner adjourned the hearing and got up to leave the courtroom, Jay and his attorney then left as well. As I gathered my paperwork, I looked over at my Advocate beside me. I wasn't sure about the look on her face, so I then asked her, "How did I do?" She and I were the only people left in the courtroom—she sat back in her chair and asked me if I'd seen the looks on my ex-husband's and his Attorney's faces. I told her that I hadn't because (a) I knew this hearing had limited time constraints, so (b) I'd focused on my notes as well as trying to look the Court Commissioner "in the eye" when I addressed her.

My Advocate then told me that she wished I'd been able to see the looks on their faces because they had been "totally blown away" by my presentation. I was in disbelief, but she continued to reinforce that I could not have done better. I'd like to think that perhaps my courtroom strength reflected Exodus 14:13 *"Fear not! Stand your ground, and you will see the victory the Lord will win for you today."* as well as Rick Warren's words: *"When you have been refined by trials, people can see Jesus' reflection in you."* As much as I'd felt alone when I walked into the courtroom that day—through my faith—I received the strength and inspiration needed to act upon God's purpose for me. In my pain, I'd discovered encouragement to persevere in faith from Hebrews 11:1 *"Now Faith is the substance of things hoped for, the evidence of things not seen."* It is "more than meets the eye"—or in other words from Martin Luther King, Jr.: *"Faith is taking the first step even when you don't see the whole staircase."* With reference to John 14:16 *"And I will give you another advocate to help you and be with you..."*—the Holy

Spirit—a paraclete (someone who helps in the legal context) was with and within me in order to have the needed strength to make my case convincingly to the Court (Commissioner).

In January 2007, I received the Family Court Commissioner's written decision, which ruled that I would be granted child support payments that were more in line with the primary placement I'd had of Blake and Daniel. I was hopeful that after nearly ten years (until our divorce I'd been married over eleven) of battling with the court system—and my ex-husband—to receive the placement deserved by our "special needs" children, I could now (finally) EXHALE!!

~~ Asperger Syndrome ~~

(Source:
http://www.medicinenet.com/script/main/art.asp?articlekey=104252)

Asperger Syndrome is named for Dr. Hans Asperger, an Austrian pediatrician, who first described the condition in 1944. Dr. Asperger described four boys who showed a "lack of empathy, little ability to form friendships, one-sided conversation, intense absorption in a special interest, and clumsy movements." Because of their obsessive interests in and knowledge of particular subjects, he termed the boys "little professors."...Today, many experts in the field stress the particular gifts and positive aspects of Asperger Syndrome and consider it to represent a different, but not necessarily defective, way of thinking. Positive characteristics...described as beneficial in many professions include:
- increased ability to focus on details
- capacity to persevere in specific interests without being swayed by others' opinions
- ability to work independently
- the recognition of patterns that may be missed by others
- intensity
- an original way of thinking

PROGNOSIS for ASPERGER SYNDROME:
An estimation...is difficult, if not impossible, since affected individuals have variable degrees of impairment, and the provision of treatment can dramatically improve the long-term outlook for people with Asperger Syndrome.

INTERVENTIONS that have shown to be of benefit include:
- efforts to reduce overstimulation or overload of sensory input
- supporting executive function skills by provision of an environment that is predictable, structured, and organized
- organization skills training
- speech/language therapy that addresses the ambiguous use of language and the use of language in social settings

- social skills training programs, including training in the awareness of social cognition, use of gestures and facial expressions, and conversational language
- adaptive skills or life-skills training
- educational supports such as assistance with organization, note-taking, allowing oral rather than written testing, use of scripts, and assistance with reading comprehension and subtlety of language
- self-advocacy training

~ ~ ~ ~ ~ ~ ~ ~ ~ ~ ~ ~

Autism Spectrum Disorder and Media Exposure

- *Parenthood*—a television series—premiered on NBC in March 2010 with a storyline that focused heavily on a family's journey to accept and help their son who was diagnosed with Asperger Syndrome. The show's creator, Jason Katims, has a son on the autism spectrum.
Source:
http://www.disabilityscoop.com/2010/11/09/parenthood/11084/print/

- *The Horse Boy* is an autobiographical book/documentary feature film that follows the quest of Ruper Isaacson and his wife to find healing for their autistic son, whose condition appeared to improve by contact with horses and other animals.
(Source: Liz Sterling, Happy Herald-Palm Beach (South), June 2012 Vol. 18, No. 02, pg. 24-25)

- *Temple Grandin* is an award-winning 2010 biographical movie about "a woman with autism who revolutionized practices for the humane handling of livestock on cattle ranches and slaughterhouses."
Source: http://en.wikipedia.org/wiki/Temple_Grandin_(film)/

- *The Curious Incident of the Dog in the Night-Time* is based on Mark Haddon's book (Simon Stephens adapted the original book for the stage) that tells the story of a teenage boy—who has a form of autism—as he investigates the death of a neighborhood canine. The play won five Tony Awards—including Best Play—in June 2015.

Source: http://www.disabilityscoop.com
http://www.disabilityscoop.com/2015/06/08/play-autismtonys/20363/

SPOTLIGHT ON CELEBRITIES

KNOWN/SPECULATED TO HAVE...

ASPERGER SYNDROME / HIGH-FUNCTIONING AUTISM:

Dan Aykroyd..................actor and comedian

Susan Boyle....................British singer and *Britain's Got Talent* finalist

James Durbin.................finalist on the tenth season of *American Idol*

Thomas Edison...............U.S. inventor

Albert Einstein................German/American theoretical physicist

Bobby Fischer.................World Chess Champion

Bill Gates........................entrepreneur, philanthropist, key player in

                  the personal computer revolution

Temple Grandin..............animal handling systems designer, author,

                  speaker

Daryl Hannah.................actress

Dan Harmon...................screenwriter and creator of *Community* and

                  Rick and Morty

Jim Henson....................creator of the Muppets, U.S. puppeteer,

                  producer, director, composer

Alfred Hitchcock........................English/American film director

Heather Kuzmich.......................fashion model/*America's Next Top Model* contestant

Wolfgang Amadeus Mozart.......Austrian composer

Satoshi Tajiri............................game designer, creator of the *Pokémon* series

Andy Warhol............................U.S. artist

Robin Williams..........................actor and comedian

(Sources: http://en.wikipedia.org/wiki/List_of_people_with_autism_spectrum_disorders

http://www.disabled-world.com/artman/publish/article_2086.shtml)

...CHILD WITH AUTISM SPECTRUM DISORDER (ASD)

Ed Asner (actor)...son and grandson

ToniBraxton (singer)..son

Will Clark (Major League Baseball player)..son

Ernie Els (professional golfer)..son

Doug Flutie (former New England Patriots quarterback).................son

Christopher Gorham (actor)...son

Tommy Hilfiger (renowned fashion designer).........................daughter

D.L. Hughley (actor and comedian)...son

Joe Mantegna (actor)..daughter

Dan Marino (former Miami Dolphins quarterback)............................son

Jenny McCarthy (TV personality)..son

Rodney Peete (former Carolina Panthers quarterback)

    and Holly Robinson Peete (actress)...son

Aiden Quinn (actor)..daughter

John Schneider (actor)..son

Sylvester Stallone (actor)..son

(Sources:

http://stars.topix.com/slideshow/15364Celebrity Parents of Kids with Special Needs

http://parade.com/49515/parade/100613-ive-got-a-boy-with-autism/)

Family
Follow-up

CHAPTER THIRTY-NINE

BLAKE

"Our goal is not to make individuals with autism find meaning in

our lives, but for us to help them find meaning in their own."

~ Dr. Temple Grandin

Beside my battles with the Family Court system during the ten years after our divorce, I also faced the unique trials and tribulations of raising our two young sons with "special needs"/Asperger Syndrome. As their Mom, I soon realized how hard it was for them to both fit into mainstream education and to conform to society. The endless meetings, disapproving looks from others, and the constant need to "explain" wore me down emotionally. Rather than just dismiss the negative aspects of my new reality, I would try to understand them and bring them to a positive place. From my sons' therapists, I learned that anything my sons might really focus on could potentially create an inner "spark." Despite how tough other aspects of life were for them, I vowed to support any "spark" that would ignite—whatever it might be.

Throughout the years (as they had been growing up) my boys and I would regularly have what we called "movie night" on Friday and/or Saturday nights. It was our designated end of the week "family time" when the three of us would watch a movie—usually Disney—and share popcorn. I soon noticed that Blake would frequently "script" lines—perhaps even dance—as he imitated the characters on the TV screen. As Blake grew older, he signed up—without hesitation—for grade school talent shows, and he often performed in the role of a Disney character. He displayed no inhibition as he performed animatedly before the audience.

Sadly, during his elementary school years, Blake was ridiculed by many of the boys in his class because he was "different" due to his interest in performing. I began to wonder if this interest in the theatrical might be connected to his Aspergers. He similarly signed up for talent shows while in middle school, and he also played percussion in the band—Blake had shown a real sense of musicality. As he later told me, "I stood my ground and continued to pursue opportunities in the performing arts despite what they (the bullies) thought—I am who I am."

To my surprise, I discovered that Blake's acting ability had another dimension. I'd taken him and his younger brother to our city's art festival one year, and as we walked from where our car was parked toward the festival area, Blake asked if we could go inside the movie theatre we had just passed. He told me that he knew of the group (shown on the theatre's marquee) that was performing there. I told him that on the way back from the festival area, we would stop in—and so we did.

As soon as the three of us went inside and took our seats, three people on stage requested "audience participation." Blake immediately raised his hand, and was promptly called up to the stage. I wondered what he had just done, and worried that he had impulsively put himself into an awkward situation. But there was nothing I could do because he was already on stage, so I sat in a seat next to Daniel and began to watch.

A group of improvisational actors then brought Blake onstage to participate in their comical sketch, and he made it through—he actually did rather well. As soon as he returned and sat down next to me in the audience, I asked him if he'd felt scared, had he known what he was going to do, etc. With a fair amount of confidence, Blake told me that he'd seen this group perform at his school, so he knew what to do. As much as I thought I was introducing my sons to the art world, Blake had actually introduced me to his natural ability for "improv!"

During the summer, Blake attended theatre camps, and then he extended his performing interest while in high school. His booming bass/baritone voice helped him become a member of the high school's Show Choir each year. During his sophomore year—just two weeks before the opening night of his high school's musical *Bye, Bye Birdie*—he was dismissed from his supporting male role as "Mayor" and given (instead) the part of "Conrad Birdie." It was the lead male role and—serendipitously—the senior class student (who'd originally been cast for the part) was forced to drop out because of other conflicts. Blake only had two weeks to "nail down his part," but when the show opened, the audience gave him a standing ovation. (Blake actually performed two roles in this musical—he was also the announcing voice of "Ed Sullivan," which I thought really showed versatility.) Thanks to his singing/acting ability and his unique announcing-type voice, he landed such other leading male roles in the high school musicals during both his junior and senior years. They included the role of Tom in *Suburbs,* and the voice of Audrey II in *Little Shop of Horrors,* respectively.

At the suggestion of friends and perhaps out of desire to want to fit in, as a junior in high school Blake went out for football. Physically, he had the build of a football linebacker. But because of his motor skill developmental history, he was somewhat awkward and not very athletic. A few days after he'd signed up, I was called one afternoon to pick him up from football practice because he'd injured his ankle. So due to his weak ankles came the early (if fateful) end to his football endeavor.

~ ~ ~ ~ ~ ~ ~ ~ ~ ~ ~ ~

One day when Blake told me that some talent scouts would be in town and that he wanted to pursue meeting them, my first thought was of disbelief—why would notable talent scouts come to Green Bay? I even asked him to call the phone number to make sure that this was not a scam of some sort. Blake made the call, told me that it was for real— and then announced that seeing them wouldn't cost anything.

That evening, Daniel and I tagged along as I drove Blake to the hotel where these talent scouts were scheduled to evaluate local talent. The three of us walked into a large conference room with lots of chairs set up theatre-style, and there was what looked like a head-table up in front. The talent scouts (one female and two male) introduced themselves to us—we were part of a large group (over 100 people) who had attended this event. The scouts explained who they were and why they were there. Then they asked anyone who was interested in a mini-audition to come forward, and speak to one of them—but for only 20 seconds. This was the amount of time each person was given to make an impression in order to receive a "call-back" from one of the talent scouts.

People between the approximate age of 5 and 55—which included Blake—lined up. Daniel and I stayed seated and watched while Blake took his turn in line, and finally spoke to the female talent scout. After everyone in line took their turn, we were informed that they would announce the names of the people they wanted to see again. Consequently, the three of us waited...and waited...and waited...along with everyone else. Lots of names were called (which took us late into the night), so Daniel fell asleep in his metal folding chair with his head in my lap. *Had Blake's name just been called?* Yes! The next step was for him to schedule a time to come back and talk one-on-one with a talent scout. Blake was scheduled the next day—over the lunch hour so he could be excused from school without missing any classes.

When Blake and I arrived back at the hotel the next day, the female talent scout walked by us in the lobby, and as she pointed at him we thought we heard her say, "You've got something." As she continued past us, Blake and I looked at each other and wondered what she'd meant. When it came time for Blake's appointment, the female talent scout met with us. She explained that she represented a nationally-known model/talent agency that had a local agency office in Milwaukee, WI, and they would be interested in providing Blake with acting training. It would entail Blake showing up for the next ten Saturdays for a few hours of acting training (which meant that I would have to drive him two hours each way there and back each time). She then explained that once he'd received his training certificate (from their Milwaukee agency), he could—potentially—have the opportunity to attend an international model and talent expo event scheduled just weeks later in Dallas, Texas. This, she told us, was an invitation-only opportunity. Needless to say, with Blake's established passion for performance, and this once-in-a-lifetime invitation/opportunity to broaden his acting experience to another horizon, I agreed to schedule Blake for the next scheduled acting training.

We made the most out of our "captive" two hour ride to and from Milwaukee on those consecutive Saturday mornings—whether it was to catch up with one another or just sing along with the CD music we played in the car. For the first trip or two while he was in acting training, I spent those few hours shopping, but I couldn't afford to do that every time we went down there. How else would I spend my time?? I decided to spend this time—sometimes at Barnes & Noble or even in my car, weather permitting—to start writing my (this) book. Others had encouraged me to start sharing my story, and it seemed like the perfect time. There were no outside distractions (since I was away from home), and a few hours was the perfect chunk of time for me to get focused, and get my thoughts down on paper. As Blake worked toward receiving his acting certificate, I worked on the beginning of my book.

~ ~ ~ ~ ~ ~ ~ ~ ~ ~ ~ ~

Once Blake had completed the training and gained his certificate as a John Casablanca Career Center graduate, he received an exclusive invitation to attend the Michael Beaty—Model & Talent EXPO, which was scheduled (the following month) on October 24-28, 2007, in Dallas, Texas. He would attend as a participant from the Milwaukee agency of MTM-Model & Talent Management (referred to as the "mother agency" at the EXPO)—where he'd been trained. Blake had a headshot and his acting resume ready for the times when he would sit down for a personal interview. He would have a chance—all in one setting—to meet with agencies and talent managers from major talent/modeling organizations both in the U.S. (i.e., Atlanta, Chicago, Los Angeles, Miami, New York, etc.) and throughout the world (i.e., Hong Kong, Milan, Paris, Tokyo, etc.).

Blake and I arrived in Dallas at the EXPO host hotel on Wednesday afternoon, and attended the scheduled events that ran through Sunday. He participated in the headshot competition, monologue, singer, and the two-person scene auditions, as well as many informational workshops by experts from various fields of the entertainment industry. Among other topics, they taught about auditioning skills, camera techniques, how to break into Broadway shows, runway techniques, and ways to deal with casting directors. I managed to see each of Blake's auditions—except the "cold read," which he'd performed well (so I was told by others in attendance), within (only) minutes after receiving the script for a "Gorilla glue" commercial.

Throughout the events of the EXPO, both Blake and I made several friends. The Showcase—where the talent agents/scouts (who acted as judges throughout the multiple talent auditions) had narrowed down fifteen dancers, singers, or songwriters to perform in random order for all the attendees—was held on Friday night. One of Blake's new EXPO friends had been selected to perform her song selection "Think of Me" from *Phantom of the Opera.* At the end of a workshop—which preceded the EXPO's Showcase—Blake told me that he needed to go on ahead of me because he needed to help his friend.

Once we had all taken our seats, it was announced that Blake's friend would be the first to perform. She began to sing "Think of Me," which is not an easy song to sing, but she showed great ability and had a beautiful voice. There was an interlude when the music played while she stood silently onstage. Then, as she continued the song, the audience heard an offstage male voice sing with her; all of us in the audience looked around, but he could not be seen. While the "unseen" voice continued, I thought—*I know that voice—that's Blake!* When the song ended, the audience loudly applauded this young female singer (who was near Blake's age).

The Showcase's emcee then came out on stage, and (after he'd asked Blake to come out from behind stage) made an announcement. He reminded us of what he had said on the first day of the EXPO during introductions, "All contestants here are 'contemporaries'—that's when helping improve someone's performance makes that person (as well as all of us) better artists." The emcee explained that this girl had wanted to perform the full musical piece—just as it was done in *Phantom of the Opera*—but she needed a male accompaniment. Blake—who represented a different agency than hers—stepped up, and offered to help her out. With this announcement, she and Blake received another enthusiastic round of applause. As Blake and this girl walked offstage, the emcee said, "Remember, the more you give in life, the more you will get back." When Blake came off the stage to come sit with me in the audience, I stood up, hugged him, and told him how proud I was of him. No matter how he would come home from this EXPO, I wanted Blake to know that I loved him, and was so proud that he'd been willing to help someone else (with no expectations of receiving anything himself).

The Model & Talent EXPO weekend came to its close with an Awards Banquet and Ceremony on Sunday. The backdrop to the stage was an impressive "wall" of award trophies of all sizes for participants in various categories. Blake's friend received an award (as did many others), and in his eyes I could see how hopeful he was as he watched others get called onstage for their award.

Near the end of the ceremony, I told Blake that while it's nice to receive an award, what's more important is the experience itself, and what you gain from it. And then—we heard Blake's name announced! When he went up to receive the award, he was handed a nearly two-foot tall trophy for *Male Actor of the Year 2007*! I'll never—ever—forget the happy smile on his face at that moment.

As Blake walked offstage, the female talent scout (who had "discovered" him in Green Bay) hugged him, and as he walked back down the aisle to his seat, others "high-fived" him with their congratulations. I gave Blake a huge hug—he had come so far! Who would have thought that he'd once been a boy who'd needed a speech therapist to help him learn how to even speak?! (MTM was awarded "Agency of the Year with 50 or More" (model/talent in attendance at this EXPO.)

Before we left the EXPO, a casting director spoke to Blake about a part that he thought would fit him well, but I—and others—felt he needed to finish high school before taking on an acting role. In the weeks that followed, Blake was told by the female talent scout (the one who had "discovered" him in Green Bay) that he would be considered for a scholarship at the New York Film Academy. It was his senior year of high school, so we made arrangements for Blake to meet and audition for her contact there.

~ ~ ~ ~ ~ ~ ~ ~ ~ ~ ~

While in NYC, Blake told me about another school—The American Musical & Dramatic Academy (AMDA)—that he wanted to consider. I told him that since it was nearby, we might as well check it out. After our tours of those schools in NYC, Blake decided that, although the New York Film Academy had offered him a scholarship, he felt more secure and "in touch" when he performed on stage before a live audience. Working before a film crew, and only seeing his performance later on a screen, just didn't seem nearly as rewarding.

Blake was accepted and consequently attended AMDA for its Musical Theatre program. But during his first year, he realized that the dance requirements were simply too challenging—and his weak ankles didn't help—so he then transferred into AMDA's Studio program. It proved a better fit for him—particularly stage combat (a combination of his boyhood passion for the Power Rangers and martial arts), comedic acting, and improvisation. In Blake's application to AMDA, he'd stated that he admired Robin Williams as a versatile performer (his comedic character roles as well as serious dramatic ones), whose performances were enjoyable, and meaningful. Blake knew that Robin had attended Julliard with Christopher Reeve, and they had been close friends throughout most of Reeve's life.

Blake had also written in his AMDA application, "Situations where I've experienced challenges, I learned to step up and face them, believing in myself, moving forward to do what is meaningful, which is pursuing my passion for the performing arts." The Broadway (but not the movie) version of *Aladdin* included a song titled "Proud of Your Boy," and—in real life—Blake had been providing that feeling for me. He had really come a long way from his challenging days as a toddler. Perhaps the phrase, "I think I can, I think I can..." from the book *The Little Engine That Could* (which we'd read so many years before) had left a lasting impression on him. And the animated "Genie" (voiced by Robin Williams) whom Blake had imitated as he'd watched *Aladdin* on our family room's TV/VCR also inspired him. Who would have thought back then that Blake would be headed to Broadway where he would receive professional acting instruction during his college years?!

252

CHAPTER FORTY

Fate of My Father—and My Sons' Father

One morning, I received a call and was told that my 84-year-old father had been taken to the hospital. I was asked to meet him there since my other sisters weren't immediately available. When I saw Dad sitting on the hospital gurney in the emergency room, it brought back memories of how I'd first seen Mom when she had been taken to the same hospital by ambulance. He looked alright and was conscious of where he was—just as she had been. One of his doctors requested that I step out into the hallway so he could show me (on a screen at the nurse's station) the spot on one of his lungs. It wasn't a great surprise, since he "always" smoked cigarettes—at one time, a pack a day—although in recent years he'd given up smoking for health reasons. Of course, this news was of concern. He was released from the hospital—and ultimately he moved from the non-assisted living community where he'd been living (in recent years) to an assisted-living residence. When my boys and I visited him there, he liked to tell us how this newly constructed building was located in the neighborhood not too far from where he'd grown up, and that he'd mowed the lawn across the street as a boy.

Over the years, his health had slowly declined—primarily due to his chronic obstructive pulmonary disease (COPD) diagnosis—to the point where he now needed services at a nursing home. He'd only been there for a matter of days, when on Labor Day weekend, 2008, I'd gone to visit him that Saturday afternoon. (It was a gorgeous weekend that year—in fact, I'd tried to make reservations for the boys and me up at the resort where we would usually stay, but had had no luck since everyone else wanted to enjoy this last summer holiday weekend before their children started the new school year.)

I noticed—as I walked toward the door to his room—that I could hear heavy, labored breathing. When I walked inside the room, he was lying in bed with an oxygen mask that covered nearly his whole face. Dad had always been very coherent and talkative in the past, but today I could see how difficult it had become for him to breathe. He tried to talk in an upbeat manner, but I could tell from his face that he was uncomfortable—and perhaps even scared? The large oxygen mask kept falling down off his face, so I buzzed the nurse—on his handheld call button—to come in and adjust it.

Dad liked to watch Fox News—which played on the television in the background—and he tried to make small talk as he expressed his concerns about the upcoming presidential election. When he asked me about the boys, I told him that Blake looked forward to his senior year in high school, but that Daniel—unfortunately—continued to be bullied at the public middle school he attended. (Dad was always concerned and interested in how my boys were doing—especially when it involved their diagnoses, and how they were treated by their own father since the divorce. He'd often told them—even in my presence—how he'd hoped that they could one day have the type of father-son relationship with their Dad like he'd had with his. He couldn't understand how "unlike" a loving father their Dad had been to them.)

During our visit that afternoon, Dad told me that his "angel" had come by earlier that day. I wasn't quite sure what he'd meant, but since his breathing seemed to become more difficult, I told him that I would soon leave to let him rest. Unlike Mom, who hadn't wanted her grandsons to remember her as she looked in her last cancer-ridden days, he asked me to bring the boys for a visit. Dad mentioned that the next day he would have his Sunday visit from his "lady friend" (as she was known); she had been "seeing Dad" in recent years. I told him that the boys and I would visit on Monday (since it would be Labor Day, and they would not have school), so that he and she could enjoy their time together on Sunday. It was after 2 p.m., and before I left his room I kissed him on his forehead—on the only spot that wasn't covered by the over-sized oxygen mask on his face—and told him that I loved him as I said "good-bye."

~ ~ ~ ~ ~ ~ ~ ~ ~ ~ ~

After I left the nursing home, I drove the long way home—it was a wonderfully warm day—one that might be the last of our nice weather in Wisconsin before we headed into the season of fall. When I arrived back home, I told the boys that we would all go visit their Grandpa on Monday, since he requested to see them. I then went into the kitchen, and started to make dinner for the boys and me. It was shortly after 6 p.m. when I received a call to tell me that Dad had just passed away, and that we (his family members) could come to the nursing home—for the last time. When I hung up the phone, I was in shock. I'd only seen him within the last four hours, and we had planned for the boys to come visit on the day after tomorrow! I quickly put the boys' dinner on the table, and then told them that I had to leave immediately to go see my father.

Unlike my drive in the snowstorm to the hospital to see Mom—only to learn that she had already passed on—this final drive to go see Dad was made in sunny, warm weather. When I arrived and walked in the room, I saw my oldest sister standing on the other side of the bed where Dad's body now lay lifeless. I was told that I'd been the last person he'd seen—beside his doctor—before he had died. It all seemed surreal—I told her about my earlier visit with him, the plans we'd made for him to see my boys on Monday, and how he was looking forward to his "lady friend's" visit. When she stepped out of the room, my second-oldest sister arrived. Soon we all were in tears, and each of us took time for a last "visit" with Dad before it was time for us to leave.

When I returned home, I shared the sad news about Grandpa with my boys. Since they both had been very young when their Gommy died, they had become very close to my Dad. They both expressed their sorrow and added that they felt bad because—on their last visit with him—they had hurried their stay because of plans they'd already made. I comforted them and told them that Grandpa had totally understood because he'd once been a boy their age. I hugged them, and then I told them that they both—along with their male cousins, all of whom were older than my two sons and ranged in age between 26 to 32—would be asked to be pallbearers for Grandpa's funeral. It was scheduled to take place only a couple of days later.

The day of Dad's funeral arrived, and the service was held at the parish church where my parents and my siblings—when we'd grown up—had been parishioners. Visitation was scheduled before the mass in the church's chapel where Dad was laid out in his casket. He was dressed in a dark suit, white shirt with tie—we'd often seen him dressed that way every day when he'd worked as an IBM salesman until his retirement. My sons—aged 17 and 14—lined up with their male cousins to walk beside their Grandpa's casket. After they'd walked inside the church, my siblings and I—by chronological age—then followed down the aisle. Since all my siblings were paired up and I was not, one of my cousins—whose mother was Dad's only surviving sibling—jumped in to walk beside me (which I really appreciated). After the funeral mass, a brother of the cousin (who had walked in with me) took my arm so I wouldn't have to walk alone in the procession behind my siblings and their families.

Outside the church, a final military salute was provided by an Honor Guard team—Dad had served in the Army during WWII—and then we all released balloons to symbolically sail off to heaven with Dad's spirit. After that, we drove to the cemetery for a graveside memorial service—it was raining that day so we all crowded under the tent that had been provided to cover Dad's burial site, which was next to the gravesites of his mother and father. After the service, Dad's only surviving sibling approached me, took my hands in hers, and said, "Your father had often expressed how he'd been so proud of you raising your two sons as you have." I thanked her for her compliment and responded, "They're my sons…I love them both…so much…"

The boys went to school the next day since the new school year had begun—and they'd been taken out of school for the day of Dad's funeral. Daniel was doing well academically, but struggled emotionally because he'd been bullied by others at his public middle school—sometimes he was even afraid to go to school. Meanwhile, Blake was busy with all the events of his high school senior year. He, again, was cast in the high school musical, so he regularly attended play practices. In the spring—as in previous years—Blake performed at "Solo Ensemble" among other area public high school students. As a fourth year member of his high school's Show Choir, he and the other members had even been invited to perform at Disney World in Orlando, Florida, over the spring break.

While Blake took this wonderful opportunity, I made arrangements for Daniel and me to spend time over Spring Break in Florida as well. The two of us would be a three-hour drive southeast of Orlando, where we would meet with the admissions counselor and founder of a high school in West Palm Beach that integrated film production into its high school academic curriculum. (During a long weekend trip I'd taken the previous year—to visit where my mother and grandmother had stayed as "snowbirds" in southeastern Florida each year—I'd learned while chatting with the locals, about this unusual local high school.)

~ ~ ~ ~ ~ ~ ~ ~ ~ ~ ~ ~

On Thursday—before the Saturday when Blake would board a bus to ride with fellow choir members to Orlando, and Daniel and I would fly down to West Palm Beach—I'd put in a call to my neighbor to ask her if she could please take in our mail/newspaper while we would be away. Since I'd reached her answering machine, I left her a voicemail to call me back. When she returned my call—before I could even explain about my request—she asked me if I was calling about Jay.

I was confused by her question, but went on to say that I'd called to ask if she could possibly pick up our mail/newspaper while we would be in Florida. She told me that she would, but then asked me again if I'd heard about Jay. I replied that I didn't know what she was talking about. She then said that she'd heard Jay was in the hospital—he'd suffered a stroke! I couldn't believe what I'd just heard, so I asked if—perhaps—it was Jay's father who'd had the stroke. She said that other neighbors had told her that it was Jay—they'd mentioned his age—and his father was, of course, much older. At first, I was in shock after hearing this news, but then I thought how typical it was that Jay's own sons and I would be the last to know. It was ironic that we would have to learn what had happened to him from others.

At the suggestion of a friend, I contacted the hospital across town where he'd been brought, and asked the floor nurse about Jay's post-stroke health status. She explained that it was a pretty bad stroke, but because the ambulance was able to get there quickly and administer help in a timely manner, he was fortunate. His relatively young age was also

257

in his favor. Essentially, the stroke had affected the right side of his body, and he wasn't able to speak. I explained to her that his sons (and I) were scheduled to leave for Florida the day after tomorrow (which Jay had known), but now wondered—due to his condition—*should we still go? Could the boys visit him? If so, how soon?* She told me that she would share this information with Jay, and ask him to let her know—by the blink of his eyes—if he wanted to see his sons. She later called back to say that he'd responded, and that I could bring the boys up to the hospital the next day during visiting hours.

Now that I'd been able to make this step, I needed to take the next—much greater—one. How would I break the news to Blake and Daniel that their father was in the hospital due to a stroke?! What's more, would they understand—especially in light of their Asperger Syndrome—and how would they react? With this in mind, I started to become increasingly anxious myself!

After I'd asked the boys to sit down with me, I calmly explained what had happened to their father—in simple terms as best I could—and that he wanted to see them. I tried to describe how they might see their father—unlike the way they'd seen him before—lying in a hospital bed and unable to move the right side of his body, and unable to speak.

The next day, when the three of us arrived at the hospital and stepped off the elevator, Jay's Mom and a childhood friend of his could be seen down the hall from the nurse's station. The friend came up to us and said that I should leave—they didn't want me there. I told her that I would stay—not for Jay—but for my sons. Just as Jay had his parents present at this difficult time for their son, so I would be there—as Blake and Daniel's Mom—to provide them comfort and support needed. I told her that I would sit on the bench by the elevator while she and Jay's Mom (who could be seen in the hallway) took the boys to see their father in his hospital room.

Within only minutes, Blake—in tears—hurried down the hall toward me. I hugged him, and told him that it was alright, as he tried to say (through his tears) that Jay's stroke "was all my (his) fault." As with past situations with his father, Blake had been made to be responsible— they had used blame and/or shame to hurt him. I assured Blake that it

258

was not his fault—nobody knew why his father had suffered a stroke. Jay's childhood friend and her husband then came up to us and also assured Blake that it was not his fault. When he calmed down, they took Blake back to Jay's hospital room.

While I waited for the boys, I walked up to the nurse's station to find out—as his sons' mother—more about Jay's condition, and was told that Jay would have therapy sessions in the upcoming days. When the boys came out of Jay's hospital room, the three of us discussed whether or not their scheduled trips to depart tomorrow for Florida should be cancelled.

Since there really wasn't anything more that the boys could do for their father by cancelling their trips, the decision was to go ahead with the trips. Jay would need to rest and take the needed therapy sessions scheduled each day. So Blake went to Orlando with the Show Choir members, while Daniel and I toured the high school in West Palm Beach that he seriously hoped to attend later that year. Once the decision to travel to Florida was made, Jay was informed that each of the boys would call him (to check in and find out how their father was doing) while they were gone.

~ ~ ~ ~ ~ ~ ~ ~ ~ ~ ~ ~

NOTE: As I write this book, it has been over six years since Jay had his stroke. Subsequently, communication with Jay since our divorce had been—and continues to be—practically impossible (aside from his stroke). In fact, my Counselor had told me frankly that I could (in theory) tell Jay that he "won the lottery!" and he would still tell me to go to hell! Sad, but true. Consequently, it's my understanding—through hearsay—that he has since (through therapy) regained his speech as well as some limited motion on the right side of his body (his car has consequently been modified so that he is able to drive), and returned to work (at least, part-time).

CHAPTER FORTY-ONE

DANIEL

"The EMPHASIS needs to be on what individuals with autism

CAN do" ~ Dr. Temple Grandin

Like his older brother, Blake, Daniel had attended our parish school up through the fifth grade. Each week, through the public school system, he received both occupational and speech therapists, which meant that I would chauffeur him between the schools. His sessions were usually scheduled after school or sometimes during lunchtime, so he wouldn't miss any classes. As we had done with Blake, we enrolled Daniel in the public middle school (as advised), because the academic class schedule would become more rigorous at this developmental age. Also, the occupational and speech therapists would be conveniently located onsite at the public school to provide services as stated in his IEP—Individualized Education Program.

When he entered public middle school as a sixth-grader, I was given a "Positive Student Profile" form to complete. The idea was to provide a "snapshot" of Daniel that would help the school staff get to know him. So far, Daniel had made tremendous progress through his developmental years due to the early intervention services of physical and occupational therapy. He still had speech therapy to help him gain a better understanding of "pragmatic language"—Daniel tended to take things literally. Fortunately, he had been able to succeed in the mainstream educational classroom through his elementary grade school years. His strengths included art, computer skills, and any academics that involved memorizing, (i.e., spelling), while his difficulties included learning introspectively.

The greatest challenges for Daniel were situations where multiple steps or tasks needed to be taken in order to arrive at a desired outcome, i.e., multiple-step math formulas and/or follow through on tasks or assignments that involved multiple tasks to complete sequentially. I

260

learned how to break down the larger task into smaller steps or tasks, and help him step-by-step—each small step confirmed that he understood the process (to that point)—so he would ultimately gain the desired result needed for completion. Visuals often helped with this process, because they helped Daniel rise above his frustration, and feel a sense of accomplishment. Naturally, this positively influenced his behavior toward a situation. Similarly, he benefitted when—with an exercise that he was expected to perform in a group setting—a few others went before him. That way, he could visually watch what was expected of students who performed the exercise, and he would then be more likely to succeed when it was his turn.

Daniel could, of course, easily become frustrated at times, so calming activities for him included swinging, bouncing a ball, or pounding rhythmically, i.e., playing the drums. He also liked to play videogames, watch and script shows on TV (Disney, Nickelodeon, etc), work on the computer, draw/illustrate and write his version of sci-fi-stories/cartoons, and (like his brother Blake) play the drums/percussion. His dislikes included reading as well as being outside—particularly when it was quite warm or if bees/flies buzzed near him. He had a tendency to pace back and forth when required to wait. Daniel had difficulty with organizational skills, and was "forgetful," which could negatively affect his grades and consequently, not be representative of either his ability or knowledge.

In social situations, Daniel tended to be more comfortable on the perimeter of the activity rather than "in the center of attention"—he was wary of feeling embarrassed or making a mistake. When he became interested in either the subject matter or the environment at hand (i.e., a strong area of interest), he would want to open up more and share information with others, and participate. But he would still be somewhat shy. Overall, Daniel was easy-going, approachable, liked to be included, and enjoyed being a part of whatever his friends were involved in. Unfortunately, in light of his Asperger Syndrome, he didn't know how to make friends easily—he found it hard to understand the rules of friendships and other social activities.

~ ~ ~ ~ ~ ~ ~ ~ ~ ~ ~

Ever since kindergarten at his parish elementary school Daniel, had one close friend; but it was now time to move from the "little pond" of peers. Instead of a *grade* that consisted of 20-30 classmates, he would be in a "big pond," where *classes* of 20-30 students would make up each of the grades at the public middle school. During his second year in middle school Daniel told me that he had been called "idiot" by some of his classmates. This form of bullying continued to be a concern for Daniel, and he told me how much he missed his former classmates at his parish elementary school (who he said had accepted him for who he was). In February of that year, Daniel told me about times when he'd had lunch with another "special ed." classmate and friends, and another student—he mentioned the boy's name—had thrown food at him.

As an advocate for my son, I contacted his assigned Special Education teacher at the public middle school, and informed her (as well as Daniel's other teachers) about what he'd told me. He, naturally, had difficulty standing up for himself due to his Asperger Syndrome, and I explained to the teachers that I'd suggested to Daniel that he "branch out" and look for some other/new friends. I also told them that I was concerned how both his self-esteem and self-concept—personally as well as socially—could be negatively affected by some of these peers' unkind actions toward him. They suggested that his speech therapist would engage in one-on-one role-playing with him to help Daniel become more aware, and better able to handle these social situations at school.

Not long afterwards, Daniel told me about an incident during his P.E. (Phy. Ed.) class. He explained that before the class warm-up exercises (while the instructors weren't looking or present to see the behavior), a couple of boys kicked him "in the balls." He then ran around in an attempt to get away from them, but (as he told me), "To have to run around to avoid these boys, and then do the class warm-up exercises, made me very tired by the time we had to do push-ups." I told his P.E. Instructor (as well as his Special Education teacher), about what had happened, and asked that he and the other P.E. instructors help insure that Daniel would no longer be bullied by his peers.

I'd received an email from his P. E. instructor, who explained that the P.E. teachers are "sometimes split between dealing with locker

262

room situations (missing clothes, locks, etc.) and what's going on in the gym." He continued, "First of all, Daniel hasn't approached me with any problems regarding other students in class. He needs to do that. If that occurs again, he needs to find me right away so I can deal with the situation. I understand that Daniel needs an adjusted approach in some situations, and normally I would say that I have no difficulties with his attitude or effort in P.E. However, when everybody else was ready, Daniel had not responded. We were waiting for him….Please be assured that I will talk with Daniel about the situation, and will deal with the students that are chasing him, etc., should that occur again…"

In my "Battle-Maiden Mom" mode, I responded to his email message: *"…Daniel said that he was waiting in his space for class when he was then chased by the boys who kneed him in the balls. Any boy, much less a child with Asperger Syndrome, would have been triggered to be hesitant to join in with the class in light of the bullying behavior of other boys in the class. I appreciate that (as you said), you do not expect perfection but rather expect their individual best. Daniel is not always able to be expected to report a situation (due to his neurological weakness to respond to social situations) as would be expected of another child his age, who does not have Asperger Syndrome. This is not said to excuse Daniel, but rather to help you gain a better understanding of him as a student with Asperger Syndrome, and consequently, one who has an IEP.*

In some of his other classes there have been unseemly social situations, and I have also contacted those teachers as well. My intent is to advocate for Daniel since he has difficulty advocating for himself— especially in social situations. It is hoped that Daniel be assisted in the school environment—with the help of his speech therapist through role-playing—to learn/gain better understanding of social situations, and acquire effective skills so that he can learn how to respond when posed with a difficult social situation at school. I'm excited to hear that he is eligible to enroll in "Navigating Social Dynamics" as an elective class next year (8th grade)—a new class offering that could really help children like Daniel who have Asperger Syndrome/high-functioning autism. Thank you for taking the time to respond to the concerns regarding Daniel. Please feel free to contact me at any time as I believe that an open line of communication between parents and teachers can only stand to benefit the student! Thank you!"

~ ~ ~ ~ ~ ~ ~ ~ ~ ~ ~ ~

Less than a week later, I (once again morphed into my "Battle-Maiden Mom" mode) sent the following email message to Daniel's public school Special Ed. teacher: *"I don't mean to sound like a broken record, but I AM concerned about the bullying that Daniel is experiencing at school from some of the students on an almost daily basis. He mentioned that yesterday, as he waited in his place for the P.E. class to begin, some boys in the class took their hands to wipe themselves (their balls) and then touch Daniel with their hands (he said that he reported this to one of the teachers)...this is disgusting behavior, and a health issue that goes beyond the bullying aspect. He also said that food was thrown at him again in the downstairs lunchroom while he was having lunch. I have left a voicemail message at the office, and would truly appreciate it if you would call me at your earliest convenience today! Thank you!"*

Daniel's Special Ed. teacher contacted his Speech Therapist, who offered to work with him on a "strategy" or "social story" for dealing with some of the issues that had occurred. Together, she and Daniel wrote up the "plan" that was put in his agenda so he could refer to it during the day at school. She was not really sure, however, how to address the bully issue in gym class. With suggestion, I contacted the school's Assistant Principal (who handled student discipline) to inform him, and get him involved in addressing the bullying/harassment behaviors by some particular students toward Daniel. With all that had happened recently at school, Daniel was more distracted and unable to process information—he was literally afraid to go to school. My hope (as well as Daniel's) was to—with the Administration's assistance—provide him with a safe educational environment where he would be less anxious, and have a better chance to focus on his school day activities, which would ultimately enable him to learn.

I was later informed that the Assistant Principal had spoken with the boys who had been involved in bullying/harassing Daniel, and that Daniel's Counselor would contact them as well. She told me that she

264

had met with these boys, and explained to them that Daniel had Asperger Syndrome. Perhaps she thought that they would be more understanding of Daniel in light of his disability, but it backfired in more ways than one. Daniel's diagnosis (like others with disabilities) was supposed to be held as confidential information, and when I picked him up after school that day, he was "beside himself." He told me about the repercussions (from her meeting with those boys that morning), which lasted for the rest of that school day. He said that because we'd reported the incidents he experienced, everything was worse—and now he'd been called a tattle-tale by his "friend." As a parent whose son had these ugly situations happen to him nearly daily by these boys, I was—naturally— concerned about Daniel's health, self-concept, and well-being. He was already self-conscious, did not want attention drawn to himself, and self-aware enough to want—like every other child—to fit in with friends at school.

I'd engaged (as "Battle-Maiden Mom") on five "fronts" in a matter of only a couple weeks by the time I ultimately approached the Principal to address the harassing behavior my son had repeatedly been subjected to by peers. She followed up to tell me that (1) all four boys had been interviewed, (2) each of Daniel's teachers had been notified to "keep an eye" on these boys' interactions with him, (3) one of the boys had been suspended for the rest of that day—the next incident would mean one to three schooldays suspension, and after a third time the boy would be expelled from school altogether, (4) three of the four boys' parents had been called—and seemed supportive regarding their son's behavior at home as well, (5) if any additional incidents happened, Daniel and/or I were to report them immediately.

Fortunately, Daniel was scheduled for his annual IEP Team Meeting the following week. We could gather—at that time—to discuss and address Daniel's educational as well as social concerns in light of the recent (and more frequent) harassment he'd been subjected to by some classmates. Proactive strategies included: (1) the public school district's program support teacher for students with Autism Spectrum Disorders would (a) talk to Daniel's classmates about the "Social Sense" to open up their thoughts, and create awareness of ASD, and (b) meet with Daniel's teachers for an hour on one of the teacher workdays in August of the upcoming school year, and present a brief introduction to "Autism and Social Thinking" session—with the purpose of helping staff who worked with Daniel better understand how he's affected by his disability, and how to better support him, (2) Daniel would be able to physically walk through his schedule prior to the start of the school year, (3) he would have his locker near the P.E. teachers' offices, (4) the teachers were directed to provide additional monitoring in the locker room and gym prior to the start of class, (5) Daniel would use either (a) the buddy system when walking between classes, or (b) delayed/early passing between classes.

NOTE: "Bullying not only threatens a student's physical and emotional safety at school, but fosters a climate of fear and disrespect, creating conditions that negatively impact learning—undermining students' ability to achieve their full potential. Unfortunately we know that children with disabilities are disproportionately affected by bullying. More troubling—students living with autism spectrum disorder are 63 percent more likely to be recipients of bullying behavior than typically developing peers," stated Autism Society President/CEO Scott Badesch in October (2014), which has become the month for Bullying Prevention/Awareness.

~ ~ ~ ~ ~ ~ ~ ~ ~ ~ ~ ~

I later received a nice note from one of this meeting's attendees that read: "...make sure to take some time for yourself...I know all too well that—as Moms—our needs are often the last ones to be met when our heartfelt devotion is given to the needs of our children." Following her suggestion—and knowing that the court orders gave Jay the boys over spring break that year—I decided to take a long weekend get-away. But where would I go? Every winter Mom would go along to care for her mother at her condo that was located in a "hot spot," which provided warm weather they enjoyed and time spent together as "snowbirds."

I chose to visit their refuge from Wisconsin winter weather in southeastern Florida for my five-day respite. Although several of my friends questioned my decision to "fly solo" on this trip, I told them that I looked forward to not being on (anyone's) schedule except mine. For the first time in years, I could stay up as late—or sleep in as long—as I wanted to!

Once I arrived at the hotel that overlooked the Atlantic Ocean (and was just a few blocks from the condo where Mom and Grandma had stayed), I took off my wrist watch and decided to spend the next five days on "beach time." One day, I took a walk down "memory lane" to Grandma's condo, and reminisced about my time spent with her and Mom over the years. I then walked down the Avenue to browse through the boutiques—just as I had done with them in the past. I stopped in a shop to pick up some art supplies for Daniel, who had a passion for drawing. While conversing with the shop clerk, I learned that there was a local charter school in West Palm Beach that integrated film production into its academic high school curriculum. One of her relatives had attended that school.

Ever since Daniel had been a young boy, he'd had a passion for film production—when he'd attended my nephew's wedding reception, he followed the photographer as a shy but focused observer throughout the entire evening. Could this unexpected find in Florida be the solution for Daniel to avoid being bullied by school classmates? Could it offer him a whole new beginning? As I lay in the sun on Delray Beach, I remembered Mom's speech to a graduating class of high school students where she'd taught years earlier: "When One Door Closes, Another Opens." So, I wrapped up my five-day respite in Florida, flew back to Green Bay, I researched this WPB high school, and then contacted Daniel's middle school support staff—who responded with support for this venture.

After I met with them, I encouraged Daniel to apply to the charter high school where the student population was comparably smaller than his current school, and the students had common interests in the arts that included acting as well as film production. I helped Daniel through the application process, and then we were invited to tour the campus and meet with both the admissions department as well as the founder of this school. Since we lived not just out of town—but five states away—I'd arranged for us to visit over his spring break. (Ironically, at that same time, Blake would be in Florida performing with his high school show choir in Orlando.)

Seated next to Daniel during our flight to WPB, I watched as he drew in his sketchbook—he liked to draw characters from cartoons or videogames. Interestingly, he started to create a portion of a character in detail and then he added the rest of the subject's image in a similar fashion. He worked that way rather than making an outline of the character, and then filling in the detail. This particular drawing on our flight was of Sly Cooper—a videogame character that looked somewhat like a raccoon. A few weeks after we had returned from the high school visit in Florida, I'd cleaned out his school backpack and found this drawing—or so I thought. Daniel then explained that he'd had time in study hall to draw—so he'd drawn Sly Cooper once again. When I asked him to get the sketchbook drawing that he'd previously created on the plane, we held the two drawings side-by-side—they almost looked like carbon copies. But Daniel had drawn each at different times! Once we learned that Daniel had been accepted at the charter high school in Florida that integrated film production as well as animation, it only confirmed Rick Warren's statement that: "God put you where you are for a PURPOSE...He will let you know if He wants you somewhere else."

The next hurdle I faced was to receive a legal agreement from Jay to allow Daniel (and me) to move to Florida to attend high school. I asked the Family Court Commissioner's office personnel about how to notify my ex regarding our change of residence so that Daniel could move out of state. I was directed to visit the Court's website, and to complete—following the online instructions—the "Stipulation and Order to Change" form.

I first had to "make the case" and present the facts explaining the substantial change in circumstances to "Modify Legal Custody and/or Physical Placement Order(s)." I'd learned from Daniel that he and his father—on various occasions throughout the year—had conversations about attending this high school out of state. Jay had told him that "he would not stand in the way," which was a relief to hear—especially since Jay's mom had given me a guilt trip regarding why I would "take Daniel away." I'd responded straight-forwardly, and told her that this move was

268

not about Jay, and not about me. It was about Daniel, but she didn't realize just how badly Daniel had been bullied by some of his classmates at the public middle school. Jay signed the necessary paperwork in July 2009.

One month later, Daniel and I finished packing the last of what belongings we could put in my car before we—and our dog—left the house, and started on our roadtrip to West Palm Beach, Florida. We'd sent other items ahead by UPS to where we would initially stay at a (WPB) Marriott Residence Inn—as their advertisement states, it's "not a roof but a residence." Within three days, we drove 1500 miles from Green Bay, and arrived just in time so that we could attend Daniel's high school orientation meeting. As he began attending classes, I searched for our next real "home" with the assistance of a realtor I'd met at the school's orientation. After only three weeks, Daniel, our dog, and I moved into our new home away from home in Florida. (Just a few months earlier we'd taken Blake to New York City to attend the acting school where he'd been accepted.)

In spite of Daniel's IEP, he thrived throughout his high school years—both academically and socially. He made the Dean's List as well as graduated in 2013. (Jay, his wife, and his parents flew down to Florida for Daniel's graduation.) Daniel was accepted, and currently pursues a BFA degree in Computer Animation, at a nearby college in Boca Raton, Florida.

Sometimes life takes us places

We never expected to go

And in those places

God writes a story

We never thought would be ours.

~ Renee Swope

EPILOGUE

Only GOD

can turn a MESS into a Message…

A TEST into a TESTIMONY…

A TRIAL into a TRIUMPH

A VICTIM into a VICTOR!!

~ Unknown

After I'd been "bombarded on all four fronts"—abuse, autism, deaths (of loved ones), and divorce—I realized that my faith had sustained me and provided the fortitude I'd needed to endure and overcome these overwhelming challenges. At first, I felt at a loss because all these "battles" had come my way within a significantly short period of time. Just one of these issues could make a person feel devastated, but facing such an overwhelming onslaught stretched me to the limit. I tried with all my might to manage—or "juggle the spinning plates"—all that had been simultaneously placed in front of me.

Perhaps a different type of woman might have responded to such an unsavory surprise in a wiser (or worse) way. I know that my various options included seeking revenge, becoming vindictive, or—worse, yet—simply giving up and embracing "poor me" or "victim" status. But these options were neither acceptable nor available to the resourceful Midwestern girl I'd been raised to be, especially in light of the faith, integrity, and values that my parents had given me. So, I chose to embrace endurance rather than indifference. Those four challenging life circumstances had certainly put me in a "no comfort zone," but complacency, self-pity and excuses would—I instinctively knew—have been counterproductive. During that painful period of time, I often turned to Rick Warren's book *The Purpose Driven Life*, and reaffirmed my faith. His words helped me understand why we are alive, and what God's plan is for us—here in the present as well as for all eternity.

In those pages, I learned that "God has a purpose behind every problem." And in light of my life's circumstances at the time, it became crystal clear that I was being called upon to live up to my name—literally as well as figuratively—and embrace the mode of "Battle Maiden." I learned how to protect my sons and (Ephesians 6:13-18) "Put on the full armor of God, so (to) be able to stand your ground...stand firm then, with the belt of *truth* buckled around your waist, with the breastplate of *righteousness* in place, and with your feet fitted with the readiness that comes from the gospel of *peace.* In addition to all this, take up the shield of *faith,* with which you can extinguish all the flaming arrows of the evil one. Take the helmet of *salvation* and the sword of the *Spirit,* which is the word of God. And pray in the Spirit on all occasions..."

During those difficult times I felt (at first) as if God was farthest away from me exactly when I needed him the most. But in time, I came to realize that He had actually been carrying me all along! My prayers for His guidance, protection and strength (G.P.S.)—as well as much-needed wisdom—helped show me a workable way to overcome the incredible adversity I was facing. I soon regained hope, and also received the love and support of friends—and it's no secret that the toughest battles call for the best of friends! Undoubtedly, these wonderful gifts in my life—as well as my amazing sons—had all come from God. In the words of Psalm 46:1-2, "God is our refuge and strength, an ever-present help in trouble. Therefore, we will not fear, though the earth give way and the mountains fall into the heart of the sea."

My goal, through everything I have been forced to endure, has been to accept the journey, face the challenges of my new reality, and simply pursue the promise of a brighter future. That's how I withstood the overwhelming onset of abuse, autism, deaths of loved ones, and divorce. The lyrics "What doesn't kill you makes you stronger"—from Kelly Clarkson's song *Stronger* (originally penned by the German philosopher Nietzsche)—expresses a resilient and determined attitude. I hope—and plan—to ultimately reach the goal of creating a positive

271

reality for my sons and me. "I've fought the good fight...I have kept the faith." (2 Timothy 4:7), hence, the moniker "Benevolent Battle Maiden"! (I prefer to be a peacemaker—it's only my passion for my children when their best interests and well-being are "at stake" that morphs me into "battle-maiden" mode.)

This whole journey has (admittedly) been a "rollercoaster ride"—with an overload of "ups and downs" as well as "twists and turns." The good side is that it's been like "jet fuel," which has motivated me to change my life and its direction—I took my life's unwelcome "ingredients" and tried to create something much better. For the past two years, I have been trying to make sense of the last two decades as I sat in my living room—surrounded by several boxes filled to the brim with countless files (legal, medical, school reports/records, etc.) that document the journey that my sons and I shared together. With encouragement and inspiration, I pressed forward to complete my memoir—the process has not only been painful, but also tedious as I recounted details of abuse, autism, divorce, as well as my Mom's concurrent death, and those of other loved ones. Writing this book was like reopening scars to the incompletely healed wounds.

I discovered that (over the last two decades) every time I'd been asked (in conversation) about my life, it was difficult to condense my story—without feeling twinges of pain. Consequently, it is now all on paper—and my story has been told with messages for its readers. I truly hope that any person reading this book can (1) take away at least one lesson that they can apply to their life, and that will help them in situations similar to ones I experienced, (2) not feel alone or isolated in the midst of multiple life crises, and (3) know that there are available resources for them so they don't have to struggle as I did. If my story helps one person have an easier time finding what he or she needs for a critical situation, then I will feel that I've accomplished my goal for writing this book. I hope that my memoir shows that my life (like everyone's) has not been in vain. Instead, it was written to connect with, help, and share with others.

Instead of "tenderness under the scar," I've learned to feel proud of the woman I've become, and the challenges that I've managed to accomplish. Now when I look back it doesn't hurt (as much). *"It's been said, 'time heals all wounds.' I do not agree. The wounds remain. In time, the mind, protecting its sanity, covers them with scar tissue and the pain lessens. But it is never gone."* ~ Rose Kennedy

It never occurred to me that I would evolve into the woman I am today—instead of being a heroine, I've become a survivor. After I'd "been burned" by these challenging life experiences, I worked hard to "rise like the phoenix" from "the ashes." And with a lot of effort, I managed to come out the other side—it simply wasn't in my nature to give up on my sons—or on me. I can now see that, thanks to the challenges of my sons' Autism/Asperger Syndrome, I've (unexpectedly) been given everything I wanted, including:

1) increased levels of empathy and understanding—particularly, my ability to validate the feelings of children with ASD/Asperger Syndrome as well as their parents and others. Those diagnosed with Asperger Syndrome are NOT to be understood as "mentally retarded"—rather their brains are *neurologically wired differently*, which can actually be advantageous when channeled appropriately. The phrase "Don't judge a book by its cover" can very much apply to those with Asperger Syndrome/high-functioning ASD, since outwardly they look fine—so they can often be mistakenly judged by others. This becomes a challenge in itself for them (and their parents who feel the constant need to explain)—beyond the challenges that their *neurological* condition present—because it is not easily understood by *neurotypical* others.

2) I gave every ounce of blood, sweat, and tears that I could in order to ensure that the three of us led fulfilled lives. And as I've raised my two boys, who continue to learn how to cope with their disability—its cure still (unfortunately) remains to be found. Today, they are transitioning into adulthood as they each strive to reach their own potential and purpose—no matter a child's age, a Mom's love never gives up!

3) I developed unforeseen skills, including:

273

- how to research the condition of Autism/Asperger Syndrome and obtain support services for my two sons. It took countless hours and concentrated effort to seek out resources that both my sons needed in their individual development—while I also filled the role of Mom, who cared for their other needs as a child (like moms provide to their neurotypical children). It has been a "double-duty" lifestyle for me (as a Case Manager as well as a Mom), and continues that way—in some aspects—even today.

- how to write and speak up passionately for my children and their well- being to the public. I raised my voice to be heard, and this has opened up new doors for me as well as for my boys, "Do not be afraid. Go on speaking, and do not be silent. For I am with you, and no one is going to attack and harm you..." (Acts 18:9-10) "Going public" turned into a blessing in disguise!

"If God brings you to it, He will bring you through it" is a saying many of us have heard—I can also appreciate the since-added line "...I just wish He didn't trust me so much!" Well, He entrusted me with two sons whom I love with all of my heart, and I'm so proud of them as they've withstood these years faced with Asperger Syndrome related challenges—unlike neurotypical children.

My sons and I watched the animated Disney movie *Tarzan* when it was first released in 1999. The song "You'll Be In My Heart" (music and lyrics by Phil Collins from the movie's Original Soundtrack) has remained "our" song through these challenging years because the lyrics so perfectly capture our shared experience.

Heaven knows where Blake and Daniel will be five years (or more) from now. What I do know is that I look forward to where they will lead me—and hopefully you feel the same way. Stay tuned...

Each of us has a unique and worthy story. We all have lives that take us on a journey. What you learn in the process—and what you can share with others to help them along the way on their life's journey—is what our lives should be all about! It's not as much about where we come from but more about becoming empowered to see what we can be—that is the missing piece of the puzzle. (The Autism symbol—represented by *puzzle piece(s)*—speaks for those affected, as well as to the need for effective responsive community supports.) For anyone who has weathered a difficult time or faced a challenge in life, the following words from Ralph Waldo Emerson will have extra meaning: "What lies behind us and what lies before us are tiny matters compared to what lies within us."

As in this book's Introduction, so in the Epilogue, I close with statements from Oprah Winfrey: "Do you hear me, see me? Everyone has a calling (validation)...honor that!" and "You become what you believe."

APPENDIX A

(CHAPTER SEVENTEEN)

It Matters to This One

As I walked along the seashore

This young boy greeted me.

He was tossing a stranded starfish

Back into the deep blue sea.

I said, "Tell me why you bother.

Why you waste your time this way?

There's a million stranded starfish.

Does it matter anyway?"

And he said, "It matters to this one.

It deserves a chance to grow.

It matters to this one.

I can't save them all, I know.

But it matters to this one,

I'll return it to the sea.

It matters to this one,

And it matters a lot to me."

As I walked into a classroom

The teacher greeted me.

She was helping Johnny study.

He was struggling – I could see.

I said, "Tell me why you bother.

Why you waste your time this way?

Johnny's only one of millions.

Does it matter anyway?"

And she said, "It matters to this one.

He deserves a chance to grow.

It matters to this one.

I can't save them all, I know.

But it matters to this one,

I'll help him be what he can be.

It matters to this one,

And it matters a lot to me."

~ Author Unknown

APPENDIX B

(CHAPTER THIRTY-FOUR)

New Stipulation and Order from Family Court Commissioner

(June 21, 2004)

The Parties Hereby Agree...

1) *The parties will work on a one (1) week on/one (1) week off placement of the minor children...such schedule to begin with the Respondent/Father receiving the first week beginning Friday, July 23, 2004.*

2) *The placement schedule will continue on a Friday to Friday basis. During the summer, whoever is beginning placement on Friday will pick up the children from the other parent's residence at 3:30 pm. During the school year, placement will begin at the end of the school day on Friday, 3:30 pm if no school.*

3) *There will be no court-ordered Wednesday placement with the other parent.*

4) *There will be a limited right of first refusal whereby if either parent is gone for a period of three (3) days (a consecutive 72 hours period of time) or more, the other parent will be given the first opportunity to care for the children prior to the children being left with some other care provider.*

5) *Two (2) times per year, each parent shall have the opportunity to move the weekly placement rotation schedule up from Friday to Thursday at 3:30 pm (rather than Friday). Such request needs to be made to the other parent, giving the other parent at least 30 day advanced notice.*

6) - 7) Each parent is to attend counseling with his or her specified counselor

8) The children are to continue counseling with (their Clinical Psychologist), the parents are to attend co-counseling with the children per (the children's Clinical Psychologist's) request.

9) All above referenced shall be commenced within 30 days of the execution of this Order.

10) It being understood that as to any and all counseling listed above, within six (6) months to one (1) year, the Guardian ad Litem will meet with (or call) all counselors for an update as to the current treatment and verify that the folks are following through with the court-ordered counseling. All parties will need to continue with counseling until dismissed by their given therapist.

11) Beginning July 23, 2004, the Respondent/Father shall pay to the Petitioner/Mother the amount of $1,200.00 per month as and for child support. Such support is based upon the Respondent/Father's annual earnings, and the Petitioner/Mother's estimated annual earning ability. It is also understood that the Respondent/Father shall continue to provide any and all health insurance coverage for the minor children. 12)... 16)...

17) As to the holiday placement, the holidays will be split as has been done in the past, with the following exception:

A. The parties agree that with the Winter school vacation and the Spring school vacations, these vacations will be split equally along the following lines:

1) As to the Christmas break, one party will be awarded Christmas Eve and the other party will be awarded Christmas Day. Whoever has Christmas Day

279

placement will have their half of the winter vacation immediately following Christmas Day, to allow that parent a specific block of time to travel with the children should he/she choose.

2) *As to Spring break, which ever parent has placement on the Easter Sunday holiday, will also be awarded the entire spring vacation, allowing this parent the opportunity to travel with the children should he/she choose. The schedule will alternate on a yearly basis allowing both parents the opportunity to spend the Easter holiday with the children and travel with the children on their given year.*

18) This Stipulation and Order modifies all previous Court Orders relating to custody and physical placement of the parties' minor children. Further, this Stipulation and Order addresses ongoing child support obligations by and between the parties.

ACKNOWLEDGMENTS

Just as pieces of a puzzle form a picture in its entirety, we have been connected to enable this book reach its completion. I'm a firm believer that people "cross our paths" in life not necessarily by accident, but— instead—for a particular purpose in order to fulfill God's plan for us during our lifetime. Matthew 18:20 states "For where two or three (or more) gather in my name, there am I with them." With reference to the poem "People Come into Your Life for a Reason, a Season, or a Lifetime" (written by an unknown author), I am grateful for the blessings, benefits, and even the lessons learned that I (as well as my two sons) have gained through the seen—as well as the unseen—presence of others listed as follows:

- The memory of my Mom, who has been on my shoulder; and God, who has kept us connected in spirit and provided guidance as well as the strength needed through these years as a single Mom raising two "special needs" sons since their childhood.

- My two wonderful sons, who have unwittingly taught me—as their mother—much more than I would have ever dreamed. My sons have battled—far more than I—to be where they are today after their struggles to overcome obstacles presented by Asperger Syndrome/ASD. I'm so very proud of you both! You've developed to show everyone that ASD (Autism Spectrum Disorder) can be seen—instead—as Autism Spectrum "Difference!" Whether together or forced apart, we three have "weathered the storms" over many difficult years, but we've "made it through to see the rainbow." I love you "the purplest," and I "love you forever!"

- Teachers who, with open minds and open arms, accepted each of my two sons—among your other students—and willingly helped them both to succeed in learning despite their "special needs."

- The talented occupational/physical/speech and language therapists, who are too numerous to list. Each and every one of you who worked with my two sons so that they could make great strides developmentally, are held close in my heart and will never be forgotten!

- Counselors and Advocates who helped to keep me (and my sons) strong through their encouragement, guidance, and support as we faced traumatic—and nearly life-threatening—times in light of the behaviors of both my ex and the legal system.

- Delilah, songs and their artists who "kept the music playing" that I needed to hear to keep "my head up" in times that felt "like hell." You helped me look forward to tomorrow with the hope that each program would make a difference for the better. The song "Smile" (composed by Charlie Chaplin/lyrics and title later added in 1954 by John Turner and Geoffrey Parsons) tells listeners to cheer up, that there's a bright tomorrow—just as long they smile. Many have commented on my smile through the years—little did they know how sad I felt inside due to the draining circumstances that my sons and I endured.

- All my dear friends, mentors, neighbors (you know who you are)—and even acquaintances I've encountered in conversation—who have (through the years) encouraged me to "tell my story" and write this book. Ecclesiastes 4:12 states: "Though one may be overpowered, two can defend themselves. A cord of three strands is not easily broken." Thanks for being my cheerleaders and "go to girls" whenever I needed you. You were not merely bystanders—instead you stood up and stepped in to help me (and my boys).

- Lisa Murphy, who inspirationally spoke (at the parish church I attend) about her first book, which she'd written and published about her life's journey with her husband to China. She shared the process of their adoption of a son, a toddler who'd had serious health issues since birth. During her book signing, I shared that I'd been working on a tentative book, and she generously referred me to a local published author who'd helped her "build" her book.

- Marilyn Murray Willison, who invited me into both her life and her home as one of her writing students. We found out that we share much in common—our November birthdays, single (by divorce) mothers of two young sons, owners of tri-colored shelties, and her red pens (she

282

corrected my prose to sculpt poetry) with the exact same style that my English teacher Mom had used when she'd corrected papers handed in by her high school Junior students. For nearly two years, my "Wednesdays with Ms. Willison"—who is a truly amazing woman, notable journalist, and published author—gave me the blessing and breakthrough I needed to become empowered to write my first book. I offer my deepest appreciation to Marilyn—personally as well as professionally—for the platform she provided that made it possible for me to fulfill this purpose in my life.

- Anyone I may have overlooked…surely know that I appreciate you. *When someone is going through a storm, your silent presence is more powerful than a million empty words. ~ Thema Davis*

RESOURCES

Autism Society

4340 East-West Hwy., Suite 350

Bethesda, Maryland 20814

Phone: (301) 657-0881 or (800) 3AUTISM / (800) 328-8476

Email: info@autism-society.org

Website: www.autism-society.org

Autism Speaks

Phone: (888) 288-4762

Website: www.autismspeaks.org

Division of Birth Defects, National Center on Birth Defects and Developmental Disabilities, Centers for Disease Control and Prevention

Website: www.cdc.gov/ncbddd/actearly

The Arc of the United States

1825 K Street NW, Suite 1200

Washington, DC 20006

Phone: (202) 534-3700 / (800) 433-5255

Website: www.thearc.org

~ ASPERGER SYNDROME RESOURCES ~

ASPEN (Asperger Autism Spectrum Education Network)

9 Aspen Circle

Edison, NJ 08820

Phone: (731) 321-0880

Website: www.aspennj.org

Asperger Syndrome and High-Functioning Autism Association

P.O. Box 916

Bethpage, NY 11714

Phone: (888) 918-9198

Website: www.ahany.org

Online Asperger Syndrome Information and Support (OASIS) center/MAAP Services for Autism and Asperger Syndrome

P.O. Box 524

Crown Point, IN 46308

Website: www.maapservices.org

SUGGESTED READING

Attwood, Tony (1998) *Asperger's Syndrome: A Guide for Parents and Professionals*. London and Philadelphia: Jessica Kingsley Publishers.

Burrows, Emily L., Ed. S., and Wagner, Sheila J., M. Ed. (2004) *Understanding Asperger's Syndrome: Fast Facts: A Guide for Teachers and Educators to Address the Needs of the Student.* Arlington: Future Horizons.

Dunn, Winnie (2009) *Living Sensationally: Understanding Your Senses.* London and Philadelphia: Jessica Kingsley Publishers.

Faherty, Catherine (2000) *Asperger's...What Does It Mean to Me?: A Workbook Explaining Self Awareness and Life Lesson to the Child or Youth with High-functioning Autism or Asperger's.* Arlington: Future Horizons, Inc.

Grandin, Temple (1996) *Thinking in Pictures: And Other Reports From My Life With Autism.* New York: Vintage Books, a division of Random House, Inc.

Kaufman, Nancy J., PhD, and Larson, Vicki Lord, PhD (2005) *Asperger Syndrome: Strategies for Solving the Social Puzzle.* Eau Claire: Thinking Publications, A Division of McKinley Companies, Inc.

Kranowitz, Carol Stock, M. A. (1998) *The Out-of-Sync Child: Recognizing and Coping with Sensory Integration Dysfunction.* New York: Skylight Press, A Perigree Book published by The Berkley Publishing Group, division of Penguin Putnam, Inc.

Suskind, Ron (2014) *Life, Animated: A Story of Sidekicks, Heroes, and Autism.* New York, Los Angeles: Kingswell.

Winner, Michelle Garcia, MA CCC, SLP (2007) *Social Behavior Mapping: Connecting Behavior, Emotions and Consequences Across the Day.* San Jose: Think Social Publishing, Inc.

Made in the USA
Columbia, SC
10 August 2017